Learning Futures

Educators around the world are being told that they need to transform education systems to adapt young people for a future global knowledge economy. But is this future vision robust, achievable or even desirable? What other futures might be emerging from the convergence of social and technological change? What might these other futures mean for education?

Drawing on over 10 years of research into digital technologies, social change and education, and on a major long-term futures project conducted for the UK government while Research Director at Futurelab, Keri Facer makes a compelling argument for thinking differently about the futures for which education might need to prepare. Arguing that we have been working with too narrow a vision of the future, Facer makes a case for recognizing a set of serious emerging developments, including:

- the growth of new relationships between humans and technology
- the emergence of new intergenerational relationships
- struggles over new forms of knowledge and democracy
- the intensification of radical economic and social inequalities.

This book explores the implications of these social and technological developments for critical aspects of education, from human relationships, to curriculum, to the role of schools in their communities and in relation to the market.

Packed with examples from around the world the book helps to bring into focus the risks and opportunities for societies and for schooling over the coming two decades. It makes a powerful case for reimagining the role of education in responding to social and technological changes, and presents a set of key strategies for creating schools able to equip all students and communities to build better futures.

An important contribution to the debates surrounding educational futures, this book is compelling reading for the educators, policy-makers and parents who are asking the question 'what sort of education do we need to enable all children and communities to flourish throughout the twenty-first century?'

Keri Facer is Professor of Education at the Education and Social Research Institute, Manchester Metropolitan University, where she works in the fields of digital cultures, educational change and social justice.

Learning Futures

Education, technology and social change

Keri Facer

Routledge
Taylor & Francis Group

LONDON AND NEW YORK

First edition published 2011
by Routledge
2 Park Square, Milton Park, Abingdon, Oxon, OX14 4RN

Simultaneously published in the USA and Canada
by Routledge
711 Third Avenue, New York, NY 10017

*Routledge is an imprint of the Taylor & Francis Group, an informa
business*

© 2011 Keri Facer

The right of Keri Facer to be identified as author of this work has
been asserted by her in accordance with sections 77 and 78 of
the Copyright, Designs and Patents Act 1988.

Typeset in Galliard by
Saxon Graphics Ltd, Derby

British Library Cataloguing in Publication Data
A catalogue record for this book is available from the British
Library

Library of Congress Cataloging-in-Publication Data
A catalog record has been requested for this book

ISBN13: 978-0-415-58142-4 (hbk)
ISBN13: 978-0-415-58143-1 (pbk)
ISBN13: 978-0-203-81730-8 (ebk)

Table of Contents

Acknowledgements

This book grows out of the Beyond Current Horizons project that we ran at Futurelab between 2007 and 2009. While the book has now taken on a life and a set of arguments of its own, I am hugely indebted to the team involved in that project. In particular, I would like to thank Steve Sayers for making Futurelab work, for being a wise friend and a cool head in a crisis, and for offering good advice on an early version of this book. Thanks also to Richard Sandford, whose expertise and imagination strengthened the project and improved my arguments. To the leaders of the four research challenges who marshalled evidence and ideas from myriad sources in an unfeasibly short period of time, Carey Jewitt, Rob Wilson, Sarah Harper and Helen Haste. Thanks also to Dave Cliff who provided a strong backbone of technical expertise and moral support, to the members of the Expert Advisory Group and to the Department for Children, Schools and Families, in particular Doug Brown and Dominic Flitcroft, for funding and nurturing the project.

Particular love and thanks must go to the Futurelab team from 2002 to 2008, who made Beyond Current Horizons and many other fantastic projects happen.

Thanks also to my colleagues at the Education and Social Research Institute at MMU, who have reminded me of the often overlooked rich history of radical education change and the value of critique. Thanks to friends Michael Fielding, Richard Hall, Neil Selwyn, Adam Nieman and John Schostak who have tried to point me in the right direction and to my co-conspirators on the ESRC Seminar series on Educational Futures, Anna Craft, Mike Sharples, Simon Mauger, Richard and Carey. Thanks also to the Create Research Group at MMU, in particular Cathy Lewin for helpful comments on early drafts and Nicola Whitton for moral support. Finally, Philip Mudd at Routledge offered much needed encouragement that this book might be a good idea and ensured that it actually came to fruition, while Marie Lister and Rob Brown brought a precise eye for detail to the text itself. Many thanks to them all. The book would not have been possible without all of these people; any errors, omissions or idiosyncratic interpretations are, of course, my own.

Most of all though, thanks to Craig, for only he knows how much, and for being prepared to imagine that good futures are possible even when original plans don't work out.

Preface

What hope offers is the belief, simply, that different futures are possible.
(Henry Giroux, 2004)

The educational imagination of the last two decades has been dominated by one particular vision of the future, a vision of a global knowledge economy fuelled by international competition and sustained by digital networks. This vision has driven investment in new technologies, new approaches to teaching and learning, new education industries and massive school rebuilding programmes around the world. This vision has promised students and nations that with enough education, creativity and new technology, their futures will be secure.

This vision of the future, however, can no longer be considered either robust or desirable enough to act as a reliable guide for education.

This book is about the much more diverse, more dangerous and possibly more desirable futures that education might need to address. It is about some of the developments in knowledge, identity, human relationships and social justice that are emerging at the intersection of social and technological change. And it is about the opportunity that schools have to act as democratic resources for building secure and desirable futures for all of their students.

When we look at some of the possible futures we may confront over the next two decades, the need for a new vision for education is clear. We need to start thinking now about how schools can act as resources for intergenerational solidarity as populations are ageing, generations are being brought into competition for resources, and rapid technological development changes traditional patterns of expertise. We need to start thinking now about how schools can act as resources for fairness if children bring highly diverse digital, social and pharmacological resources into the classroom. We need to start thinking now about how schools can equip students for democracy when technologies of surveillance are expanding and new networked public spaces are emerging. And we need to start thinking now about how schools can act as resources for building sustainable economic futures when networked globalization promises increased polarization, radical inequality and environmental degradation.

As access to educational resources outside the school walls increases, as new tools for informal learning emerge, there are calls for the school to fragment itself into millions of personalized learning environments, to become an integral part of the homes, workplaces and streets of a learning city. The future for the school, in some visions of the next two decades, is that it should disappear.

I want to make a different argument in this book. I want to argue that the potential for socio-technical changes to massively amplify social and economic inequalities in the coming decades is significant. This means that, more than ever, we will need schools that are physical, locally accountable organizations, committed to building viable and sustainable futures for *everyone* in their communities.

The stories we tell about the future are powerful resources for shaping our sense of possibility and our readiness to fight for change. This book argues that we need to rethink the stories we tell about socio-technical change and the future of education. We need to reclaim the right of educators, students and communities to challenge the orthodox future we are being sold, and to imagine and build viable alternatives. Only by rewriting the stories we tell ourselves about the relationship between education, technology and social change can we ensure that schools are really equipped to prepare all of their students for the future.

Education, technology and the future

Education is a site in which visions of the future proliferate. Visions of a future world – its demands, its threats, its opportunities – are constantly mobilized as warrants for rethinking education.[1] Take, for example, President Obama's call for new investment in science, technology and mathematics education:

> So make no mistake. Our future is on the line. The nation that out-educates us today is going to out-compete us tomorrow. To continue to cede our leadership in education is to cede our position in the world. That's not acceptable to me and I know it's not acceptable to any of you. And that's why my administration has set a clear goal: to move from the middle to the top of the pack in science and math education over the next decade.[2]

Or Bill Gates' argument in favour of creating radically new schools:

> America's high schools are obsolete. By obsolete, I don't just mean that our high schools are broken, flawed, and under-funded – though a case could be made for every one of those points. By obsolete, I mean that our high schools – even when they're working exactly as designed – cannot teach our kids what they need to know today. Training the workforce of tomorrow with the high schools of today is like trying to teach kids about today's computers on a 50-year-old mainframe. It's the wrong tool for the times. Until we design them to meet the needs of the 21st century, we will keep limiting – even ruining – the lives of millions of Americans every year.[3]

The relationship between education and the future is also played out in the everyday interactions between educators and students in schools. It is implicit in the classroom tussles between teachers and students about relevance: 'but what's the point of this?' 'how's that going to help you in the long run?' On a day-to-day level, we constantly ask children to project themselves into 'the realm of the not yet',[4] asking them to imagine who they might be, what they might want to do, how they might get there. And young people themselves are often conscious of the fact that education is a process that comprises a cost now (in freedom, in time, in effort) to be paid against a future promise that is not always, or for all children, fulfilled.[5]

Ideas of the future therefore matter to education, to its institutions, its people and its sense of purpose. They shape our sense of the personal and collective possibilities of education. They frame our expectations about the sorts of change that can be considered 'realistic' and the sorts of change that are seen as hopelessly utopian or overly pessimistic. At their heart, our ideas of the future frame our assumptions about the possibilities, the limits and the purposes of education.

For the last two decades, the ideas of the future that have dominated educational policy have been structured around two stories of the relationship between education and socio-technical change.

The first story concerns the relationship between society, technology and the economy. In this story, the combination of massive increases in computing power, the emergence of global digital networks, and the growing populations of China, Brazil and India are conflated with an account of the inevitability and importance of market economics to produce one all-pervasive orthodoxy: that social and technological change in the twenty-first century means that we have to adapt to a high-tech, globally competitive world or risk economic and social oblivion. In this story, education's role is to orientate itself and its learners, as rapidly as possible, to adapt to this future.[6]

The second story commonly told about education's relationship to socio-technical change is an account of educational inertia and failure to respond to changing technological times. This is best exemplified by the commonly repeated tale, first told by Seymour Papert[7] and recycled endlessly since, of the time-travelling surgeon and teacher. In this fable, a mid-nineteenth-century surgeon is magically transported through time to a modern operating theatre. Once there, he finds himself completely at a loss to know what to do or how to help. In contrast, a mid-nineteenth-century teacher is transported through the years to a modern classroom. Once there, he picks up seamlessly where his modern peer left off. The implication of the narrative is clear: unlike medicine, the education community has failed to appropriate the technological advances of the contemporary world.

These twin narratives circulate widely in the education community, linking together visions of inevitable technological and economic change with the failure of educators to respond and adapt. They have become familiar and banal parts of educational discourse, whether in the illustrious surroundings of world education forums populated by ministers of education and captains of industry, or in the school halls and community centres that host training days for teachers. The stories become elided, accepted, and an overarching myth about the relationship between socio-technical futures and education comes to be taken for granted. This myth goes as follows:

> Rapid technological change in the 21st century will lead to increased competition between individuals and nations; education's role is to equip individuals and nations for that competition by developing 'twenty-first

century skills' that will allow them to adapt and reconfigure themselves for this new market. But education and educators are ill-equipped to make those changes, as they have failed to adapt successfully to technological developments over the last 100 years. Educational change, therefore, needs to be directed from outside.

This is the myth that pervades much of the thinking about education and its relationship to socio-technical futures. It can be described as a myth not because it is wholly fictional – indeed, there are elements of this story for which there is some evidence and empirical support – but because it comes to act as an unquestioned cultural resource, to function as a dominating narrative that allows educators, policy-makers, parents and designers, without too much reflection, to make decisions and take action in the present. It has underpinned the educational 'modernization' agenda across the world for the last two decades.

There are a number of problems with this myth of the future and the way that it is used to justify decisions about education.

First, this highly partial view of the future is presented as an inevitability, as uncontestable, as unchangeable. The future, from this perspective, is not a world that can be shaped by individuals, organizations and social forces, but a predetermined landscape to which everyone must adapt.

Secondly, it offers a highly partial view of technological change. It assumes that the only significant implication of technological change in the twenty-first century is in the area of economic identity. Such an assumption overlooks a wide range of other significantly more profound changes to our sense of selves, community and society that may emerge as we appropriate different technologies over the coming decades.[8]

Thirdly, this myth assumes that the primary function of education is to prepare young people for the formal economy. While the desire to ensure that young people are able to generate a living income for themselves in future is perfectly reasonable, the idea that this is *all* that education should be concerned with, or even that preparation for the formal economy should be the pre-eminent function of education, is highly debatable.

Finally, this myth presents a profoundly anti-progressive account of education history, one which does little justice to the dynamism of educators, educational activists and their capacity to act as a force for change in the world. The argument that the last century has seen few changes in schools, after all, relies on a particularly partial view of what counts as change. It requires in western countries, for example, that we overlook the fact that women and people of colour are now assumed to have the same educational rights as men and white people, that those with learning difficulties and physical disabilities are accorded respect and education rather than being consigned to asylums, and that children and young people have a right to protection from physical harm and abuse, rather than benefiting from being 'taught a lesson'. While such rights are yet to translate into true equality, a perspective that nothing has changed in education might nonetheless be seen to be one that emerges from a particularly privileged position in which such rights are taken for granted. Such a 'no change' narrative serves to exclude progressive accounts of educational change, and to discourage an awareness of the gains that have already been made and consequently might be built upon in the future.

The myth of the future that dominates discussions of the relationship between education, technology and society today has serious implications for the capacity of educators to think clearly about the relationship between education and future socio-technical change. It provides no opportunity for parents, students and communities to debate whether alternative social and educational futures might be imagined and created. More importantly, it may blind us to some of the more substantial risks to democracy, equity and sustainability that might be presented over the next couple of decades by socio-technical developments already in train.

Other visions of the future are, however, both possible and desirable. What's more, educators, students and communities have an important role to play in imagining and building them. To play that role well, we need to explore the sorts of future that are latent in contemporary socio-technical change, to explore the risks and opportunities that are posed by major social and technological trends and to think through the range of future trajectories these might offer. We then need to understand where and how education and educators might play a role in nudging such developments towards more equitable, democratic and desirable futures. We need, in other words, to know what we might be up against, where the possibilities might lie and where we can best intervene.

To do so we need to rewrite the relationship between education, socio-technical change and the future. And that means addressing three important questions:

- How can we understand how the future gets made?
- How can we understand the relationship between social and technological change?
- How can we rewrite the relationship between education and the future?

Thinking about 'the future'

Thinking about the future is something that we all do whether as individuals or as educators, researchers or policy-makers. We plan what we might do later in the day, we imagine what might happen over the coming week and figure out how to deal with issues that may emerge, we dream about the holiday in a few months or the life we may be living in a few years. Anticipation and projection, planning and imagination are core to our day-to-day experiences of the world. As institutions and cultures we are also always anticipating futures and responsively shaping practices and social structures. The arts, architecture, political science, religion and philosophy have provided diverse visions of the future throughout history that have acted as warnings and beacons for human activity.[9]

Since the middle of the twentieth century, however, a research field dedicated to 'futures studies' has been formalized in a range of academic, commercial and governmental spheres. The purpose of futures (or foresight) studies is diverse and, at times, conflicting. Originating, arguably, in the military-industrial complex of the mid-twentieth century, the most publicly visible form of futures studies was indebted initially to the playing of war games, to the attempt to forecast potential alternatives in order to ensure success, whatever future might emerge. From these early activities came the application of such processes to industrial strategy, and from this has emerged a method for thinking about the future that has dominated the field, namely, the scenario method. In this approach, a set of different possible future scenarios is produced that encourages those involved in the process to consider plausible but challenging alternatives to the status quo, and to ask how far current strategy and thinking would be successful in these different contexts.

Such approaches are commonplace today in policy and industry fields. They can tend, however, to see 'the future' as something that is to be managed and planned for, rather than something to be actively shaped. The future, in these perspectives, is a problem to be solved rather than a world to be created. The purpose of such activities is often about equipping managers to get better at taking decisions, at responding to uncertainty and at building strategy.

In contrast, other branches of futures-oriented research have emerged in university sociology departments, in non-governmental organizations, and in loose coalitions of researchers operating across commercial, government and academic settings. These areas of inquiry see the production of images and ideas of the future as embedded in struggles for power over the shape of society and, indeed, the future survival of the planet. Rather than seeing the future as a problem to be solved and 'managed', these perspectives see the future as a lived consequence of decisions taken today and in the past, and as emerging from social and political struggles over how the world should be. The challenge in these perspectives is not simply to figure out how to survive whatever the future throws at us, but how to create a world that we want to live in. And a core strategy for this approach is to critique the visions of the future that are being presented to us, to challenge assumptions about what is possible when we think about the future, to explore what resources we have at hand to build alternative visions of the future towards which we can start working today.

When we seek to reclaim the right to think about the future in and for education, then, we need to recognize that its purpose is less to do with producing a set of predictions, and more to do with challenging assumptions and supporting action in the present; less to do with 'divining the future' and more to do with making visible the materials – ideas, aspirations, emerging developments and historical conditions – from which better futures might be built.[10]

If we want to challenge the orthodox future in education, we need to recognize that the future is a dynamic and emergent reality. It is produced out of the ideas and assumptions people have about the future, out of the contemporary and emergent resources at hand, and out of the structural inertia that works against change.[11] In other words, the future isn't an empty space that exists 'out there' for us to shape with no constraints; it is not virgin terrain, it is already being produced by the historical forces that are in train. Nor is the future predetermined; it can be shaped by our actions and our aspirations.[12]

The future, then, can be understood as a real site of responsibility and of consequence arising from the history of the world we live in already, from social, technological, demographic and economic developments that are emerging, and from our aspirations for and assumptions about the worlds that we believe ourselves able to build. *The future is not something that is done to us, but an ongoing process in which we can intervene.*

Relationships between social and technological change

Technological and scientific development is often presumed to have a privileged relationship with the future. Such and such a new invention, it is often argued in the popular media and in politics, 'will change the way we live'. New technologies will transform society. Well, yes ... and then again, no.

If anything has been learned from the last 30 years of social studies of science and technology – a field that has paid close and detailed attention to the ways in which scientific and technological communities generate new ideas and new technologies and to the ways in which new scientific concepts and technologies are taken up (or not) in social settings – it is that the relationship between technology and society is far more complex than the narratives of 'technology-led change' would have us believe.

First, studies of how technological developments are actually produced show that scientists, developers, engineers and others creating 'the technologies of the future' are, it turns out, human after all. Scientific communities are shaped by funding priorities (often set in the political or industrial fields). They are shaped by personal priorities that participants bring into the community and by expectations about 'what counts' as valuable knowledge and development in their field. They are shaped by the wider social resources that they are able to mobilize to generate support and development for their programmes. The development of new scientific knowledge and new technologies, therefore, can't be seen to be entirely independent from wider society. Instead, examples as diverse as the development of pasteurization or the invention of the telegraph show that scientific and technological breakthroughs are as much products of their historical period as they are challenges to it.[13]

Secondly, studies of the use and appropriation of technologies show that just because a technology was designed for one purpose, doesn't mean it won't be used for another. Once tools get out 'into the wild' they are appropriated in multiple and complex ways for purposes that are hard to foresee. Bicycles, for example, came to be appropriated in the struggle for women's emancipation in the early part of the twentieth century; record 'players' changed from being instruments for dictation to become a tool for capturing and sharing diverse musical cultures around the world and then were the basis of a massive globalizing and standardizing music industry.[14] More recently, text messaging, considered a useful but uninteresting tool for technicians, once combined with European phone tariffs, became the communication medium of choice for much of the European population and the basis for the development of new moral panics over 'declining literacy standards'.

When technologies are released, they are adopted and appropriated within existing social values, structures and expectations; they are shaped and reshaped by beta testers, early adopters and marketers; and they come to mean different things and be used for different purposes by different people. Different social, religious and cultural values, for example, pattern the uptake of medical technologies such as in-vitro fertilization, leading to very different reproductive practices and regimes in different countries. At a more local level, domestic technologies are appropriated into the existing values and cultures of families. Computers, for example, may be resisted by some, seen as children's technology by others, or come to form the hub of family life by others; similarly, washing machines or dishwashers can be used to liberate the family equally from domestic chores, or come to raise the standards expected of a female housekeeper. The 'impact' of technologies is neither predetermined by their designers nor universal.[15]

And yet, this does not mean that new inventions have no effect on the world or that they simply come inevitably to be co-opted within existing social formations. Instead, a useful way of considering how technologies 'shape' the world is to consider it as a process of 'co-production' between the potential capabilities of the technologies and the ways in which they are perceived and taken up in the social context. For example, the capacity for personal communication offered by a mobile phone might be appropriated in some settings as a way of managing and controlling the individual from a distance, a means of allowing that individual independence by giving them access to back-up and support when necessary, or a way of building personal relationships on a constant and ongoing basis through increased two-way communication. At the same time, the functionality built into the phone through its development and its marketing – whether it allows text or voice communication, whether it gets reception in some places rather than others – will also shape the ways in which it can be appropriated. Finally, different cultures of use may grow up in different settings – a particular company may expect certain mobile practices from its employees, a family or a peer group will develop its own distinctive conventions of use – and such conventions may lead to the demand for new products.

How we perceive the potential use of the technology in existing social settings, combined with the new capabilities it offers us, shapes what that technology comes to mean. This process of co-production is particularly visible when we look at consumer digital technologies, many of which are designed to be personalized, customized and to fit into our lives. In respect of other technologies, however, the latitude for co-production may be reduced. Prior design choices, for example, may be particularly important when technologies have certain intrinsic properties that make them hard to change further down the line. Technologies such as genetically modified organisms, pharmaceuticals or food additives, for example, may 'lock in' certain properties at the design stage that are hard to reverse once they are 'launched'. In these cases, the language of technology 'impact' may more properly be used.[16]

What does this mean for how we might think about social and technological futures? It requires that we attempt to think the social and the technological together. It requires that we explore not only scientific developments and technological trends, but the ways in which these are appropriated within existing socio-cultural contexts. This means that we need to explore what can be called 'socio-technical' formations: the conglomeration of businesses, commentators, users and policy-makers that come to shape how technological practices are brought into being. At the same time, it requires us to ask why some socio-technical futures might become a focus for intense social scrutiny and debate while others are relatively unexamined. Where some technologies – genetic modification, nanotech, nuclear – recruit significant debate and concern, others, such as the seemingly banal capturing of data from our mobile phones, or the introduction of surveillance cameras in schools, seem to escape significant comment.

This approach also requires us to recognize that the wider 'weight of history' will not simply be eradicated by technological development, but that it too will play its role in shaping how the new technologies and new science coming to fruition today will play out over the coming decades.

As a result of trying to think the social and technological together, I will use the slightly ungainly term 'socio-technical' throughout the rest of the book, to try to foreground the extent to which any developments and change I talk about are not the product of some magical power of 'technology alone' but are co-produced through social, material and epistemological practices.

How can we rewrite the relationship between education and the future?

Thinking about the future is always a case of thinking about it from somewhere and from a particular set of concerns. The defence industry might want to explore possible futures for weaponry, political stability or religious tolerance, for example. The Environment Agency might be concerned with questions of variables in sea level, attitudes to environmental change or the development of geo-engineering. A commercial company may be concerned with questions of competitor products, materials costs, consumer demand or new production processes. The questions that we ask of the future are acutely shaped by our perception of our sphere of activity, by our sense of what it is that we think we do.

Today's dominant myth of the future of education emerges out of an instrumental conception of education as primarily concerned with serving the formal economy. It asks: what sort of competition will our businesses be up against in future? What sorts of skill will our workers need for the workplace? How can we ensure competitive advantage for the nation in the context of socio-technical change?

A different conception of education, however, requires us to ask different questions of the implications of socio-technical change for education's futures.

For example, we can conceive of education's purpose as being broader than simply serving the formal economy. We can acknowledge education's role in creating citizens and social beings who will live in and act upon the world beyond the workplace as parents, as neighbours, as members of civil society. We can acknowledge education's role in nurturing and developing the individual, in supporting them to understand, know and become themselves. We can acknowledge education's role in caring for children and in acting as a foundation for the intergenerational contract. We can acknowledge education's role in apprenticing novices into the rich histories of knowledge, culture and craft that humanity has developed over centuries and that we seek to pass down the generations. We can also acknowledge education's role in building the economic and environmental sustainability of the communities it serves.[17]

Any educator thinking about how education might need to adapt to future change, therefore, can't simply see the future workplace as a proxy for 'the future'. Instead, they will need to ask whether socio-technical developments might offer new resources or contexts for us as citizens, as children, as workers, as parents and as learners over the coming years.

Above all, if we see education as having a role in mitigating inequalities and in contributing to the creation of fairer and democratic futures, we have a responsibility to ask whether socio-technical developments will contribute to or impede that role. We need to ask, 'who benefits?' in any of the visions of the future we are offered or that we are working towards. And we need to examine where educational institutions might productively play a role in helping to ensure that the least advantaged communities are equipped with a fair chance to shape socio-technical developments in ways that will not see them even further disadvantaged.

At this point, it is also worth noting that the relationship between education and the future can be turned on its head. We should also conceive of education as a primary motor for *shaping* social values, ideas, beliefs and capabilities rather than as a servant of society, laggardly following on behind wherever socio-technical change might lead. Indeed, as the researcher David Baker has recently argued:

> Schooling, as it has been practised over the past 150 years, is far more than a preparatory exercise for youth, merely following where the technological and social demands of society take it. Rather, the educational revolution has constructed, for better or worse, most of the dominant ideas, beliefs, and human capabilities that underpin human society as we know it at the beginning of the twenty-first century. This is how best to think about formal education and its possible future impact on society.[18]

With such a recognition of agency comes responsibility, an acknowledgement that the futures we come to inhabit will be ones that educators, along with others, create. With such a recognition comes the question – who benefits from the futures we are imagining and building in education?

Our concern as educators when we inquire into the future, then, should not simply be one of preparing ourselves for an inevitable future and attempting to 'future-proof' our systems. Instead, we should see the relationship between the future and education as a reciprocal dialogue of anticipation, adaptation and creation. We may need to adapt to change on a short timescale, but over the longer term education can also be a motor for radical transformation of social values, practices and ideas. This requires both agility and ambition, responsiveness and imagination.

We can rewrite the relationship between education and socio-technical change. We can reclaim the right of schools to act as resources for their communities to imagine and build the futures that they want rather than simply training them for the futures they have been given. To do so, we need to remember that the future is not set in stone, that technology is not some magical force driving us down one inevitable path, and that education is also a force to be reckoned with when it comes to shaping progressive futures.

Key assumptions

In 2007, a team at Futurelab (an independent research and development lab in the UK) and the UK Government's Department for Children, Schools and Families set up a major two-year educational futures programme.[19] This programme, called Beyond Current Horizons, brought together academics, policy-makers, educators, parents, students and a range of others to think about the implications for education of long-term socio-technical change.

Over the two years of the programme, we asked these groups what questions about possible future socio-technical changes they were most interested in and what they were working to bring about. We explored their ideas, aspirations and assumptions about the future. We talked with academics working across multiple disciplines and asked them to document what they saw as the current trends and critical uncertainties in these fields. In total, we commissioned evidence reviews from over 80 academics in fields as diverse as neuroscience, demography and economics, and had conversations about the future of education and socio-technical change with over 130 organizations working in education, and with several thousand educators, students and other interested individuals online and face-to-face. On the basis of these conversations and the researchers' evidence of contemporary change, we worked with policy-makers and academics to build a set of possible future scenarios for socio-technical change, and for different models of education in those futures. These scenarios were intended as prompts for thought, as possible alternative trajectories that education leaders might want to prepare for, and they are now widely available as resources for discussion.[20]

It is this programme that I draw upon as a basis for the assumptions I make about the underlying features of socio-technical change over the next two decades. These assumptions inform many of the opening arguments I make in this book, but with an important difference: The Beyond Current Horizons programme was set up to explore a range of possible futures, not to recommend movement towards one future for education or another. In many ways, its aim was essentially concerned with future-proofing educational systems and schools against socio-technical change. In the arguments that follow here I am trying to do something different. I am trying to foreground the features of socio-technical change over the next two decades that pose the most serious risks of amplifying educational and social inequalities, and to advocate a democratic, sustainable and fair response by educators and educational institutions to such developments.

The assumptions about socio-technical change over the next two decades that underpin my arguments are as follows:[21]

First, significantly increased computing power will be available at significantly reduced cost, available on demand.

Historic and contemporary trends strongly indicate that 'Moore's Law' will continue to hold good over the next quarter century; this holds that computing power doubles every two years, yielding an exponential growth curve in processing power. The short-term implications of this are that a device bought today for £1000 could be bought in 20 years for £1.[22] This implies that massive computing capacity is increasingly affordable. The cost of saving information, manipulating it, mining it, becomes massively decreased. So-called 'utility' or 'cloud' computing also emerges from this trend, as commercial companies begin to offer a service that allows individuals to tap into huge processing power on an 'on-demand' basis.[23] We need to be cautious about what this increasing power means, however. The implication that it will lead inevitably to a more democratic and level playing field, for example, is far from plausible unless relative economic inequality is also addressed.

Second, there will be a shift towards ubiquitous computing and the merging of digital and physical artefacts.

The once per decade disruptions of the last quarter century have included the shift from mainframe computers to personal computers, from personal computers to networked computing, and from networks to cloud computing.[24] Industry and academia are currently working towards and betting on ubiquitous and pervasive computing as the next big shift.[25] This change in computing practice would see hundreds of thousands of small computing devices embedded in objects, buildings, textiles and city streets and able to interact autonomously with one another. These devices extend the functionality of barcodes and radio frequency identification (RFID) tags that are already being used to give everyday objects a digital identity. Sensors embedded in everyday objects can be used to track movement, sound, smell, atmospheric pressure and pollution, among other things; the devices can communicate and learn from one another to create responsive environments which remember individual and group interactions. Pervasive computing also implies the capacity to draw down the massive computing power of the network on demand and in location.[26]

Third, rich audio-visual communications allowing easy communication at a distance will become taken for granted by the large majority of people.

A number of social, technological and environmental factors are converging to suggest that remote interactions are likely to become more normalized as part of day-to-day activities and for a wider range of activities.[27] Increasing energy costs, decreased communication costs, improved audio-visual tools, increased personal access and the familiarity with online worlds as spaces for play and interaction, all suggest that the divide between 'physical' and 'virtual' presence may be increasingly blurred over the next few years.[28] This does not imply the death of physical co-presence (previous increases in virtual communication have in the past driven demand for increased face-to-face communication[29]), merely an increasing acceptance of and familiarity with remote interaction as an everyday part of personal and professional life.

Fourth, we will increasingly take it for granted that we are working and living alongside increasingly sophisticated machines.

Our understanding of what we mean by 'machines' may change as non-human entities are more radically embedded into human bodies, and machines become semi-autonomous actors in social networks.[30] Over the coming two decades, people are likely to become increasingly accustomed to machines taking on more roles across civic society, the workplace and in the home. The complexity of these technical networks will also increase exponentially, as systems are designed to be adaptive and self-repairing, as systems are increasingly made up of increasingly complex components, and as these components and systems themselves are networked with other systems, for which they were not designed.[31]

Fifth, networks remain an important metaphor for personal, social and institutional capital.

Networked and distributed forms of organization are likely to underpin institutional and organizational arrangements because they offer flexible, scalable and survivable systems.[32] Network organization allows organizations to rapidly out-communicate those outside them, and to rapidly adapt to change.[33] Such forms of organization change the relationship between those within them from the relationships familiar in traditional hierarchical organizations.[34] The capacity to manage and mobilize social networks will also form an important part of personal social capital, and there will be increasing demand upon public organizations to build this capacity.

Sixth, biosciences will produce unpredictable breakthroughs but important new stories about ourselves.

Massive computing power opens up the capacity to observe and intervene at a molecular level in the brain and the body in a range of disciplines with potential implications for education, from neuroscience, to cosmetic pharmacology, to genetics.[35] Historical precedents suggest that while the practical applications of such developments are highly uncertain (ranging from paradigm-bustingly profound to disappointing damp squibs), we can be confident that they will generate a new set of (sometimes misleading and simplified) popular narratives to account for human behaviour. Of most significance for education is the likelihood that these sciences will lead to the reintroduction of the biological into accounts of educational attainment and purpose.[36] New institutional relationships between social sciences (including education, psychology and sociology) and physical sciences are likely to emerge and form the basis for new knowledge, policy making and practice.[37]

Seventh, population is ageing globally.

Declining fertility and increasing longevity look set to produce a globally ageing population. As Sarah Harper argues, 'By 2030, half the population of Western Europe will be over 50, one quarter of the population of the developed world will be over 65, and one quarter of the population of Asia will be over 60.'[38] Although the picture is of a global 'century of maturity', late life health and wellbeing will be patterned by significant inequalities both within countries and globally, with some groups suffering potentially radically abbreviated lives compared with others able to significantly extend late life activity.[39] These ageing patterns are also likely to influence policy responses to demand for international migration caused by environmental degradation and resource scarcity; and to influence international demand for skilled labour, increasing the international movement of people of all economic levels.

Eighth, energy, mineral resources and climate warming will remain significant issues.

The world's energy consumption continues to rise at an alarming rate even as commentators argue that we have passed the point of Peak Oil.[40] Minerals used in many technologies are implicated in civil war struggles.[41] At the same time, a 2°C temperature rise is already in train based on historical levels of CO_2 in the atmosphere.[42] All of these factors will play constraining roles in the development of socio-technical practices. At the present time, agreement at international level on carbon reduction has not been secured and it is not clear that alternative energy resources will be sufficient to replace fossil fuels. International water and food policies are increasingly areas of international contention as such resources become more stressed.

What futures can we anticipate in these circumstances? One reasonable response based upon historical precedent, current indications and an assumption that humanity is not suicidal[43] would be to assume a 2°C temperature rise by the mid 2020s, with strategies in place to prevent further rises. Such a rise would require nation states in temperate zones to adapt to frequent extreme weather events, to invest significantly in domestic energy and food security and to require significant energy reduction.[44] This rise would also require wealthy temperate states to make decisions about immigration and levels of support for populations living in poorer or more stressed environmental zones in which the costs of adaptation may not have been met. A critical political question will be whether we seek to create collective or national responses to these changes, rather than whether we will respond at all; about that, there will be little choice.

Ninth, we are starting from a base of radical national and global inequalities.

Just as socio-technical development is embedded in material and resource constraints, so the socio-technical developments of the next two decades are also embedded in historic socio-economic conditions. The contemporary period is one that is characterized by a rapid two-decade growth in income inequality in many countries, in particular the UK and the USA.[45] Social geographer Danny Dorling, for example, points out that wage inequality in Britain stands at the same level in the contemporary period as in 1854 when Charles Dickens wrote *Hard Times*.[46] These existing patterns of inequalities within and between states will provide radically different experiences of socio-technical development for different groups over the coming two decades. They will disrupt accounts of smooth generational change or technological progress, and have the potential to create radical divides between different groups' experiences of what it means to live in the twenty-first century.

Outline of the book

It is on the basis of these assumptions that I argue that we need to rewrite the relationship between education, socio-technical change and the future if we are to ensure that socio-technical changes of the next two decades do not simply serve to produce futures of profound inequality and environmental degradation.

There are already those, today, who argue that the emergence of a rich educational ecosystem outside school walls, the potential to 'access' learning remotely and the recognition of young people's informal learning in digital cultures is doing away with the need for physical institutions like schools. When we look at the range of plausible trajectories for socio-technical change over the next two decades, however, I argue that rather than heralding the demise of the school, these changes make a physical, locally connected school even more important (Chapter 1). The local school will be important because we will need to create accessible spaces where we can work out how to cope with the disruptions to intergenerational relationships that are promised by ageing populations, environmental degradation and rapidly changing socio-technical practices (Chapter 2). It will be important because we will need to create spaces where we can explore how to live with the potentially radical diversity offered by the capacity to augment our intelligence and our bodies, and to integrate biology with computing (Chapter 3). The local school will be important because we will need curriculum and pedagogy that teach us how to live with our collective, multi-modal and sometimes dangerous knowledge resources. To do so, we will need to have embodied educational relationships that foreground the connection between our knowledge and the lived impact of our decisions upon people (Chapter 4).

The importance of the local school becomes particularly visible when we look at the expectation amongst many that current trends will play out to produce economic and social futures of profound inequality and environmental degradation. If we are to challenge such a trajectory, we need to create schools that are capable of supporting communities and students to come together to imagine and build sustainable futures for all. Such viable alternatives[47] will need to draw upon and contribute to the resources of local communities, and schools will need to act as engines for economic change in their neighbourhoods (Chapter 5). The local school, then, needs to act as a powerful democratic resource and public space that allows its students and communities to contest the visions of the future that they are being presented with, and to work together through the spaces of traditional and emergent democratic practice, to fight for viable futures for all (Chapter 6).

Such a school would not be the 'future-proof' school familiar from the dominant myth of the future in education, seeking simply to adapt itself to change and prepare its students for their role in the knowledge economy. Instead, it would be a future-building school, determined to act as a powerful prefigurative space for fair socio-technical futures. It would act as a public space for a community's conversation about the future. It would see itself, and its students, as interdependent communities, technologies and ecosystems. And it would act as a laboratory for imagining, testing and realizing alternative futures (Chapter 7). Over the next 20 years, such a school could plausibly be built drawing upon the changed socio-technical resource we will have at hand, and building upon the new relationship between a school and its wider educational ecosystem (Chapter 8). When we look around us today we can see that there are educators, researchers, activists and policy-makers around the world who are already beginning to build such a school. They are showing how new curriculum, governance arrangements, technical systems and pedagogies can go a long way towards achieving such a change in the relationship between the school and the future. These examples act as powerful resources for optimism about our potential to create such a school, and show how schools can play a powerful role in tipping the balance of socio-technical change in favour of sustainable futures for all of our students (Chapter 9).

Health Warning 1

This book is concerned with rethinking the relationship between socio-technical change and educational futures. It doesn't claim or seek to address 'The Future' in all its complexity. I will not, for example, be talking about some subjects beloved of many futurists – flu pandemics, asteroid strikes, the possibility of settling on Mars (much though these are sometimes very useful prompts for unsettling assumptions and for creative reflection). I will also not be talking about those areas that are often the concern of political or military futurists – global war, relationships between faith and science, the battle for scarce resources – although these will, of course, play a role in shaping educational contexts and values over the coming years. Rather, this book is focused specifically upon trying to think about how technological and social development may play out in areas that are understood today as intimately concerned with education – how we might think about knowledge, how relationships between adults and children, teachers and students might change, what it might mean to educate 'citizens'.[48]

Health Warning 2

Although I have restricted my attention to the future of education in the context of socio-technical change, this still encompasses very diverse issues. It includes, for example, questions of contemporary democratic practices as well as discussions of possible implications of biosciences; it includes research in the learning sciences as well as development trends in the computing industry. Because of this breadth of coverage, there will necessarily be those who, on reading sections related to their area of expertise or in which they are particularly interested, might wish for more nuance or depth. Those seeking more detailed discussions of the issues and developments described in each chapter are encouraged to explore the endnotes, where links are made to more detailed sources. I hope, however, that exploring this broader range of issues will allow us to get at the repeated patterns of risk and opportunity presented by the different socio-technical futures being envisaged by researchers, teachers, developers and activists at present. I hope also that such a broad approach will make it easier to identify common ground and to build alliances between those of us, whether researchers, educators, developers, scientists, parents or activists, usually concerned with just part of this broad picture. If we are to tip the balance of socio-technical change in favour of social justice, after all, we will need to work together.

Chapter 1

Is there a future for schools?

For fear of stating the obvious, any consideration of the relationship between education and the future needs to acknowledge that educational institutions cannot be considered natural and unchanging phenomena like the cycles of the moon or the movements of the sun; they have not always been this way and they will not always be this way. Rather, they are the temporary and contingent products of complex cultural, technological, economic and political contexts. Indeed, the contemporary period of mass education is a very recent product of human history and, given levels of absenteeism and exclusion today, cannot itself be seen as a secure and universal experience.

Schools themselves, therefore, cannot be seen as an unchanging detached vantage point from which to observe history passing and in which we can prepare in comfort for new futures. Instead, our understanding of what counts as a 'school', a 'teacher' and a 'curriculum' may also be unsettled as new socio-technical practices emerge.

The next decade promises to bring some significant challenges to the way we think about schools. First, children's participation in digital cultures raises a set of questions about how and whether we should police the boundary between formal education and informal learning. Secondly, the potential to set up online schools combined with an impoverished national debate about education is opening up the possibility for a fragmentation of state education, raising questions about who should govern schools. Thirdly, the 'ecosystem' of education outside the school is becoming increasingly complex, as new folk educators are beginning to make their presence felt and as workplaces become sites for formal accreditation of learning, raising questions about the institutional and economic arrangements that should underpin education.

All of these developments have the potential to challenge the monopoly of schooling over educational processes. They have the potential to radically unsettle our understanding of where learning happens and to widen the resources that schools have available to support teaching and learning. Such developments, however, also open up the possibility that schools will not be able to play the increasingly important role of acting as a democratic public resource to support communities in responding to changing times.

Educating the 'new millennials' and 'digital natives'

In 1998, I spent a year interviewing families about their use of new technologies in the home. This was the period when the home computer was being sold with a vengeance into the domestic market as an educational tool, and at that time we were astonished to find that nearly 80 per cent of the children in the UK had a computer of some sort or another at home. This was the height of the digital encyclopedia boom, when Encarta reigned supreme, and when we still asked questions on our surveys not about internet access, but about whether people had a 'modem'. As educators and researchers, we and others were trying to grapple with the implications of these new technologies for children's learning. What did it mean that children now had access to digital information resources in the home and to creative production tools? Were we witnessing the birth of a new generation who would require radical changes to educational policy and practice?

As each new technology and each new generation of learners has arrived (we were concerned then about 'digital natives', today researchers study 'new millennials'), researchers and educators have been asking what these new digital resources for children's informal learning might mean for the future of schooling.

The study I was involved with then was just one of many that, over the last three decades, have seen a flowering of research into children's informal digital learning cultures.[1] This research takes in the various waves of new technologies – from the arrival of the games console via the personal computer, the internet and now the most recent flourishing of social software. Over this time, there have been remarkably consistent findings from these studies. These consistent findings imply that, rather than needing to be buffeted by the perception of waves of change, a consistent set of challenges emerges for educators from this landscape.

First, the study of young people's learning with digital technologies outside school makes visible how different children's informal learning is from schooled learning. There has been consistent evidence that young people come to learn to use digital environments by trial and error, messing about, fiddling around. Rather than following a 'curriculum' led by an expert, learners out of school are supported by just-in-time help from peers, siblings and adults. In these environments, their learning is driven by their own interests and friendships. Such learning can have a passionate intensity that can support them through periods of repetitive practice and commitment over long periods of time. Learning in these settings also involves playing with and exploring different identities, trying them on for size, exploring what these identities require in different contexts and communities.[2]

Recent studies looking at a wide range of non-digital informal learning activities also identify very similar patterns,[3] and the few examples we have of historic informal learning practices also demonstrate the potential for young people to 'self-educate' in environments where they are encouraged, supported and able to pursue their passions.[4]

The changing digital landscape might therefore be understood not as a source of radically new approaches to learning by young people, implying some fundamental generational change. Instead, we might conjecture that access to digital technologies amplifies the processes of informal learning that have always taken place outside schools. It lowers the barriers to access to information about emerging interests, it allows easier access to communities that are dedicated to those interests, and it offers resources for experimentation, play and feedback. For those children with access to digital technologies outside school, such resources have the potential to intensify the impact and reach of their informal learning.

Secondly, despite the rhetoric about generational change emerging from exposure to digital technologies, profound differences between young people consistently show up. The presence of digital technologies in the home has not made all children more creative, more entrepreneurial, more social or more stupid, any more than the sales of *Encyclopedia Britannica* or comics in the early twentieth century made all children cleverer or dumber.[5] Nor are all children involved in the same sorts of activity online; they are not all avid games players, social networkers, bloggers or happy slappers.[6] The expert development of competency in these settings, moreover, is fostered by parents, peers and others in the informal learning setting. The development of expertise is neither innate nor inevitable.[7]

The rhetoric of generational change obscures the significant differences between young people in terms of their types of access to and use of digital informational environments. Family cultures, peer cultures, access to material and economic resources, all shape the ways in which young people participate in digital spaces, with familiar socio-economic patterns playing themselves out particularly around children's levels of access and participation. Such diversity in practice is likely to continue making it problematic to argue that there is a single form of 'media literacy' or 'information skills' that might act as a consistent benchmark for youth participation in digital environments, and will continue to raise questions about what equity of participation in these spaces might look like.[8] Over the next two decades, then, we will need to pay attention as much to the differences between individuals within the same age cohorts as we will to the differences between generations. And we will need to recognize that the informal learning landscape is a space where existing patterns of inequalities structured around ethnicity, gender, educational capital and income continue to be played out.[9]

Thirdly, while there is significant diversity in types of participation, there are some activities that young people are less likely to stumble upon or become expert in without explicit encouragement and teaching. The development of mathematical and scientific understanding, for example, comes up much less frequently in reports of children's online activities than the development of new literacy practices.[10] At the same time, the development of critical literacies also seems to require more support. For example, the critical reading of online information or the perception of digital environments as designed products, and therefore open to redesign, may require explicit teaching and encouragement.[11] For young people to move from roles of participants in digital spaces to critical readers and active agents usually requires bridges to be built between participation, critique and production. The breathless rhetoric of generational change needs to be tempered, then, with an awareness of the difficulty for all generations and age groups of developing complex conceptual and critical skills.[12] These do not just emerge through participation in digital spaces, they need to be fostered and supported by more-expert others, whether teachers or other participants in expert cultures.

These consistent findings from several decades of research provide some pointers towards the probable 'impact' of new millennials or digital natives over the next few decades. While the majority of students will be coming into schools with expectations of the playability, sociability and accessibility of information, such too are likely to be the changing expectations of more and more adults in the school setting (the digital natives are now the teachers). The more important issue is the possibility that the increased visibility and reach of informal learning practices threatens to deepen the divisions between the informal learning cultures of different groups of young people outside school. *The challenges educators will face, then, are not those of responding to a single overwhelming flood of new generational practice, but of deciding how to respond to very visible different experiences of learning outside the school setting. This is a very old problem in a new form.*

Competition and fragmentation

The contemporary period sees increased disaffection with mainstream education provision being voiced from a number of different quarters. Children's rights campaigners and psychologists are among those pointing to high levels of anxiety, depression, self-harm and reported stress amongst young people. They point to cultures of high-stakes testing and individualized competitive performance cultures and argue that these practices will simply result in the nurturing of generations of highly dependent individuals, lacking in resilience, confidence and self-esteem.[13] Others argue for the need to return to education built on close and sustained human relationships or an education more closely concerned with interdependence with nature.[14] Others, mindful of the state's potential to seek to mould compliant future citizens, resist the incursion of education into areas such as the development of self-esteem and 'happiness' skills and argue, instead, for a return to education systems characterized by strict hierarchies of knowledge and disciplinary boundaries.[15] Observers of contemporary shifts in the digital landscape argue for schools structured around 'twenty-first century skills' and cross-curricular projects.[16] Those who foresee profound environmental catastrophe call for an education for survival.[17] All of these observers make demands for a new approach to education.

Such a questioning of educational purpose would normally form part of a healthy public debate about education's role and purpose.[18] Over the last 20 years, however, public debate about educational aims and purposes has been eroded by a managerial analysis of educational 'attainment', governed by obsessive concern with relative positions on various league tables, as though such tables (as

Danny Dorling points out, designed by economists) were in themselves a meaningful measure of educational success.[19] Such a hollowing out of public debate and its reduction to neurotic comparison of statistical evidence has changed the quality of discussion about educational purpose from a debate about 'what education should be for' to a search for 'what works to get people up the league tables'.[20] Over time, servicing the data has itself become the purpose of education, whether for students seeking to become a 'level 4' or nations seeking to position themselves higher up the international league tables. The results of this audit culture in the UK are well documented. The Cambridge Review of Primary Curriculum, for example, demonstrated the effect that such processes have had in reducing the breadth of curriculum;[21] while for educators, the loss of professional identity and reduced investment in teacher learning and research is clearly visible.[22]

One important consequence of this changed focus to a concern with national targets is the subsequent reduction in the autonomy of schools to explore their educational purpose with their community. This means that it is hard for both parents and educators to publicly debate the criticisms of education described earlier, or to explore the balance between these competing educational demands with students.

In this vacuum such criticisms are increasingly finding a public voice in requests by different groups with competing visions of education to simply 'opt out' of state education. These requests are being translated into ever higher levels of tutoring and home schooling in the UK and USA[23] and the flourishing of 'alternative' educational approaches, such as Steiner, Montessori and Forest Schools.[24]

For those children and families without economic, educational and social resources to facilitate such a withdrawal from public education systems, however, disaffection or disillusion with the purposes and practices of mainstream education can often only be expressed by absenteeism. This leads in the worst cases to criminalization of the parent for failing to ensure their child attends school and, too often, to criminalization of children who seek other forms of education in gangs and on the street.[25] In the UK 7.5 per cent of pupils on free school meals are persistent absentees. In the USA, similar patterns emerge:

> drop-out rates now amount to close to 35 per cent of those who begin public schools in the United States. Of special urgency is the surging gap between the wealthy and the poor, a gap that correlates in both directions with educational levels. Youth from impoverished backgrounds are statistically most likely to drop out of school; high school dropouts earn less than those with a diploma, and significantly less again than those with a university degree.[26]

In the UK and other countries, the strategy of opting out of a collective debate about education is being given policy sanction with the establishment of the highly contentious Free Schools legislation. This allows those who wish to seek alternative education practices and who can demonstrate sufficient demand, to be provided with public funds to set up their 'own' schools. This, by itself, does not necessarily prefigure the breaking up of state education systems, as the difficulty of finding premises and setting up new buildings is prohibitive of all but the most engaged parents and communities. In this context, however, the growing respectability of online and remote education may begin to play an interesting role.

New wholly online schools are being established by independent charities, parents and commercial organizations.[27] In the USA, by 2005 twenty-four states had statewide virtual schools, with estimates of between 328,000 and 700,000 students enrolled in programmes. Some states have made participation in online courses a prerequisite for graduation.[28] These schools can offer mainstream education for students seeking to be part of a specific community; the LBGTQ school, for example, is an online school that seeks to create a supportive environment for Lesbian, Bisexual, Gay, Transgender and Questioning students and which offers a mainstream educational provision. Or they may offer, like First College, one of a number of wholly online schools in the UK, an alternative to 'mass industrial' models of conventional schooling by ensuring that there are small group sizes and close relationships between staff and students.[29]

The Open University, of course, offers a 30-year case study of the possibilities of 'virtual' educational institutions. While the OU has long committed itself not only to provision of expert tuition but also to pastoral care, other wholly online universities are taking a different perspective. Institutions such as Phoenix University, for example, have seen over 30,000 students graduate since inception and are single-mindedly focused on a programme of tuition and support rather than developing the wider experience of university life online. Countries such as Turkey and China have the largest wholly online universities, suggesting that such models may be providing alternative routes to widening participation in HE in such emerging economies.[30]

Most of these institutions are seeking to achieve (in the main) traditional educational goals through wholly online means. This does not mean that there is no education institution any more (teachers, lecturers and administrators are all still present, they are just playing a role backstage and online). Nor does it mean that educational practice and purpose are radically changed; formal assessment, prescribed curricula and traditional educator–student relationships still pertain in most cases. They do, however, demonstrate a growing tendency to see education not necessarily as a face-to-face activity, but as something that can happen remotely.

The ability to set up online educational resources that enable a much wider potential pool of students to participate at least partly remotely, increases the viability of setting up educational institutions that reflect the values of different organizations, parents groups and community associations. For the first time, policy framework and funding regulations are becoming aligned with the socio-technical practices that allow economies of scale which make it feasible to imagine the creation of large numbers of alternative education institutions.

What such a flourishing of alternative institutions might mean for education provision, however, is the subject of heated debate. One as yet unsubstantiated vision suggests that releasing schools into the control of parents will lead to the creation of education institutions ever more deeply connected with and accountable to their 'stakeholders'. Another suggests that these developments open up the possibility of branded chains of privately run and publicly financed schools becoming a very familiar part of the education landscape. As the capacity to provide education at a distance becomes a familiar part of educational practice, branded chains may develop into international organizations, offering a mix of face-to-face and online provision in complex hybrids of public-private provision across different countries. The Teaching English as a Foreign Language sector is one place to look to see how such a trajectory might play out.[31] We are already seeing the development of branded chains of schools in the UK. Such a model might radically reduce the capacity of schools to engage in educational debate with their local communities, as policy, curriculum and pedagogy would be determined elsewhere.

A new educational ecology[32]

A large number of public education institutions, particularly at university level, are today making publicly available course materials and resources for anyone to use, not simply their own students. Famously, MIT has made its course content available online through its Open Courseware programme with the result that, anecdotally, more students are said to be learning using its materials in Africa than on campus. MIT is not alone in this; the UK's Open University has its Open Learn programme and Carnegie Mellon in the USA has developed its own Open Learning initiative. The development of platforms such as iTunesU and the MiroCommunity have also led the opening up of access not only to text-based materials, but to the lectures and workshops at the heart of university life. It is now possible to search for, and watch from home, world-leading lectures from top academics who would previously have been speaking only to the students in their lecture halls.[33] Museums and galleries are also increasing their online educational offerings and using web spaces to provide online access to museum archives and collections, to host lectures and run forums for discussion, as well as using the Web to involve the wider public in a range of citizen science or democratic curating activities.[34]

New services are also emerging that specialize in making public intellectuals from academics, designers and other knowledge workers. The TED website[35] was based originally on a select invitation-only conference to which leading researchers, industry figures, politicians, activists and artists around the world were invited to give 'the speech of their lives'. Now, it is an online phenomenon bringing together thousands of short, highly engaging and accessible presentations on big ideas in areas ranging from astronomy to microfinance. Increasingly, the site is evolving to act as a portal for lectures from other events and institutions, and uses social networking sites to promote its latest lectures and encourage debate around the ideas emerging.

The Web is also populated by thousands of more specialized and less professionally produced videos made by a new groundswell of what we might call 'folk teachers'. These individuals have particular skills that they thoughtfully and precisely document and then post on YouTube or similar sites for everyone to access. Do you need to learn how to turn a heel when knitting a sock, how to manage a tricky bit of fingering on the guitar, how to bleed a radiator? All of these are the subject of short, helpful videos and guidance on these sites. They can be watched over and over again, paused and fast forwarded to allow viewers to get a careful handle on the problem at hand. In some cases, they are also the subject of comments from viewers, and links to related videos that develop ideas further. Some folk educators take their contribution further than others. Take, for example, the Kahn Academy.[36] This massive online resource bank of educational resources in maths and sciences is the product of one man's obsession. It seeks 'to use technology to provide a free world-class education to anyone, anywhere' and consists of over 1000 video tutorials supported by software that generates problems and gives student feedback. Salman Kahn, a former hedge fund worker and author of the tutorials who set up the website in his spare time, describes himself as a 'teacher to the world'.

One-way demonstrations, lectures and educational materials can be complemented by services that allow users to ask questions and get rapid responses. Sites such as ChaCha.com, for example, use a combination of 35,000 human respondents and smart data-mining to provide answers to questions ranging from the philosophical to the practical. More community-focused problem-solving sites include stackoverflow.com, a Q&A site for the web developer community where people can post problems and get suggestions and examples of previous solutions; or ask.metafilter.com which, like ChaCha, is a generalist site for question posing. As the capacity to more intelligently interpret questions develops and is combined with ubiquitous and location-based services, we would expect the answers to such questions to become more sophisticated, more aware of context and user history, and more likely to provide a meaningful contribution to dialogue.[37]

Potentially more radical is the exploitation of the online environment to realize the dreams of some democratic educators to de-institutionalize education entirely in favour of the creation of a learning *society*. Services such as the 'School of Everything', for example, are explicitly inspired by Ivan Illich's ideas about deschooling society, and offer services that allow would-be learners and teachers to find each other and to meet up without the aid of a mediating physical institution that specifies curriculum and pedagogy. Through this site, individuals and organizations can advertize what they are willing to teach, allowing others to contact them to set up face-to-face learning opportunities. Individuals and groups can also find venues to meet up for learning groups. Such practices begin to normalize the idea of teaching as a human capacity rather than a professional identity, and learning as an everyday part of life rather than a specialized set of procedures taking place in certain specified places.[38] These developments start to make visible the potential wealth of untapped learning resources in a community that are rarely drawn on in schools.

Such services suggest a need for a new story about the relationship between public services 'providers' and 'the public', between schools and communities.[39] In sectors outside education, the idea about what makes for successful public services has been changing. In health and policing, for example, citizens are seen to play a much more active role, in which they are seen as 'co-producers' of the services. Indeed, the idea of what counts as 'security' or 'health' has changed from something provided by professionals seeking to 'fix' a problem, to something that can only be produced by the active involvement of communities and patients.[40] Communities, rather than being seen as bundles of needs, are recognized as being powerful resources for effecting change themselves if public service organizations rethink their role as one of providing a platform and support.[41] These emergent ideas have led to a raft of initiatives from community policing to shared decision making in medicine.[42] In education, they open up the potential for seeing communities outside the school as critical in achieving education. They are potential partners who could contribute to the educational process. In this perspective, an approach to education that does not seek to engage with and harness the capacity of this wider constituency is unlikely to be successful.

The development of a rich online education landscape, the increasing visibility and accessibility of folk educators, and the changing scripts for public services have the potential to open up new relationships between schools and their communities. These new relationships would be premised upon a search to understand the roles that parents, students, community and cultural organizations and online educators might play as co-educators. They would also be premised upon a rethink of the role of the professional educator in an environment in which student access not only to information, but to expert lectures, to problem-solving groups and to peer learning communities is theoretically possible outside the school walls.

Learning and working

The relationship between the school and the workplace is also under negotiation as young people are beginning to question the 'return on investment' of traditionally 'high-status' educational routes. Emerging concerns about the financial cost of higher education in particular and the declining optimism about a return on that investment, underpin instances of middle-class student protest and resistance. As one American university student argues in his blog:

> We work and we borrow in order to work and to borrow. And the jobs we work toward are the jobs we already have. Close to three quarters of students work while in school, many full-time; for most, the level of employment we obtain while students is the same that awaits after graduation. Meanwhile, what we

acquire isn't education; it's debt. We work to make money we have already spent, and our future labor has already been sold on the worst market around. [...]What we learn is the choreography of credit: you can't walk to class without being offered another piece of plastic charging 20 per cent interest. Yesterday's finance majors buy their summer homes with the bleak futures of today's humanities majors. This is the prospect for which we have been preparing since grade-school.[43]

In the context of economic recession, such criticisms are only infrequently leading to organized protest. More often they are stimulating a debate about the relative merits of academic versus vocational education, and fuelling an increase in interest in apprenticeships and on-the-job training.[44]

At the same time, employers are also beginning to more explicitly define an educational role for themselves. Many of the major multinational corporations already have corporate 'universities' with Deans, faculties and programmes of courses and training ranging from personal development (such as t'ai chi courses or craft skills) to recognized qualifications critical for career progression, with some granting degrees in their own right. See, for example, Barclay's University which aims:

> to empower our people to take charge of their own learning and development and to help them prepare for tomorrow's challenges. The creation of Barclays University reflects two emerging realities. First, as the pace of change continues to accelerate, our people must be able to keep up. Second, people need and want more control over their careers and lives. That is why Barclays University offers an integrated range of learning channels, from traditional face-to-face training through e-learning to personal study.[45]

Corporate universities numbered over 2400 in 2002, and were forecast to overtake the number of private universities in the US by 2010.[46] Their relationship with traditional universities is complex. In some cases the corporate university acts as a portal to traditional university or college courses that are simply restructured to meet the needs of the company; in other cases the courses are internal training and development. In areas such as telecoms, companies already retain exclusive rights to certify individuals in areas related to their own products; Cisco, Redhat and Microsoft, for example, all offer their own programmes of training and accreditation. Whether these corporate universities will come to compete with, overtake or actually drive up interest in lifelong learning amongst workers and encourage participation in universities more generally is far from clear at present.[47]

Commercial companies are also being accredited to offer training and qualifications in areas previously limited to schools and colleges. In the UK, for example, McDonalds, Network Rail and Flybe have been given formal powers to accredit learning by school students on placements.[48] At the same time, new relationships are developing between schools and commercial organizations. Sponsorship of schools to create close links with 'business' has been part of the

UK's education landscape for at least the last decade and has been a core part of university life for many more years. The relationship between school and industry is becoming more complex; schools are being seen as resources for the creation of economically useful knowledge and intellectual property. There is, for example, anecdotal evidence of major companies investing in schools as research labs.[49]

The disappearing school?

The education landscape is becoming highly complex. It comprises professional educators working in schools and universities; it comprises community and folk educators sharing their expertise for their local communities and their wider interest communities; it comprises employers seeking to enhance employees' contribution to their business and to generate new research and knowledge; it comprises professional educators taking on new roles as content providers, freelance lecturers, tutors and community educators. It also comprises some students increasingly able to mobilize personal digital resources to participate in learning communities. These individuals and groups are also acting from diverse motivations – altruistic, commercial and for reciprocal benefit.

This complex landscape brings risks to education professionals that are familiar from other sectors, such as the casualization of employment and the introduction of competition for professionals from amateur hobbyists. It also calls for a re-imagination of the school. One suggestion is to reconceive of the school as a 'mobilizing network', able to draw together and harness diverse educational resources for its students.[50] Such a mobilizing institution would see itself not as a traditional education institution – the sole site of knowledge and authority – but as the means by which students can be enabled to participate in and mobilize these learning communities.

This wider educational landscape, when combined with a discussion of ageing populations, also begins to suggest a marginalization of the school as the focus for educational policy-making, as one of the founders of the School of Everything suggests:

> for the school system to be the main thing we think about when we discuss education policy is outdated. Schools will be ten per cent of education policy in twenty years' time. Learning will have to focus on helping you continue to learn throughout your life.[51]

Taken to their logical extreme, such discussions are leading to suggestions that the school itself should simply be dissolved into the learning landscape and replaced by personalized learning environments:[52]

> Announcing that compulsory schooling will end for all children by 2020 should provide a powerful catalyst for the development of alternative institutions that unbundle the five functions of schools – custody, behaviour,

cognition, socialization, and screening. This process will need to be community driven, since the way different communities will want to address child safety and the learning processes for their community will differ. Ministries of Learning will focus on how to support the shift from the management of large factory schools to the provision of resources for the local unique creation activities that bring together generations and tasks to create ongoing learning processes. The Ministries of Learning will also play an active role in the development of the many different evaluation and reputations systems, working to ensure that the summative and formative assessment appropriate to the diversity of what people know are addressed. Equally important will be the effort to ensure that there is sufficient transparency in how people learn and that the different pathways can be shared on the basis of comparing people with similar attributes and aspirations. Major milestones: By 2015 half of high school students have opted out of the compulsory system. By 2020 the old classroom school is a historical vestige.[53]

In defence of a school

These developments open up radical new futures for schools, teachers and the relationship between schools and communities. They open up the possibility of schools fundamentally detached from place and connected only by shared educational values. They open up the possibility of schools radically distributed across cities and workplaces and fragmented into millions of personalized learning environments.

So why argue the case for 'a school' even as it becomes theoretically possible for the first time to equip individuals to wrap their educational resources around themselves and to personalize their learning to meet their own needs? The oppression of standardized teaching and curriculum, and the exclusionary and sorting practices of schooling, after all, might be overcome by the use of digital technologies to allow individuals to construct their own educational pathways from a range of different education providers and resources. And indeed, for some children, their survival is predicated upon their withdrawal from hostile schooling experiences.[54]

The reason that I think we need to continue to invest in the school as a physical space and a local organization, is because I believe that it may be one of the most important institutions we have to help us build a democratic conversation about the future. A physical, local school where community members are encouraged to encounter each other and learn from each other is one of the last public spaces in which we can begin to build the intergenerational solidarity, respect for diversity and democratic capability needed to ensure fairness in the context of socio-technical change. Moreover, the public educational institution may be the only resource we have to counter the inequalities and injustice of the informal learning landscape outside school. The school is also potentially the most powerful local institution we have to help resist possible futures of breakdown and dispossession that I will describe later.

Far from being irrelevant in a world of digital networks, the local is an important sphere for achieving change that impacts on people's lives and for building children's social and educational resources. It is often at a local level that substantial budgets are allocated and decided, often in ways that are determined by special interests. Face-to-face meetings encourage relationships of reciprocity and care; acting at the local level may encourage greater participation because people care more about what happens in their own areas; and the local is a site in which differences of age, ideology and religion cannot be avoided. The local, in other words, is a place where we are forced to learn to live together and in which important decisions are made.[55] All of these reasons suggest the need for a public education institution rather than a landscape of atomized, personalized learning environments.

There are also other, equally important reasons: not least that while everyone learns and everyone teaches, there is such a thing as expert professional knowledge in education. Those who have specialist disciplinary knowledge of a particular subject may be lousy at helping other people understand it. There is a powerful argument for retaining schools as sites for important professional learning amongst educators, as a network through which insight into learning sciences can be shared, and as important resources to enhance the overall quality of teaching and learning in the wider educational ecosystem. Finally, barring revolution and complete breakdown, there will continue to be a need for social institutions that provide care and protection for children, and such an institution is likely to be tasked with an educational role. In that case, we may as well ensure that it works well.

Given these concerns, *we would do better to re-imagine and rethink the role of the school than to proclaim its impending doom*. Of course, these concerns also suggest that we need to take a long hard look at whether schools live up to their responsibility in these areas; whether, for example, they really act as a powerful force to counter injustice, whether their professional practice really encourages the sharing of knowledge, whether they really are enabling communities to build the knowledge and resources they need to imagine better futures and work to build them.

It is therefore the time both to defend the idea of a school as a public resource and to radically re-imagine how it might evolve if it is to equip communities to respond to and shape the socio-technical changes of the next few years.

The trajectory of this evolution will be dependent upon schools' responses to five major challenges – how they adapt to changing intergenerational relationships, how they address the networked individual; how they engage with new conceptions of knowledge; how they locate themselves in relation to growing inequalities; and how they see their roles as actors in democratic debate. It is to these five challenges that I now turn, beginning with the unsettling of traditional intergenerational relationships.

Chapter 2

A new generational contract

At the heart of the educational enterprise are human relationships. Whatever educational philosophy we adhere to, whether faith in streaming and grammar schools, radical anarchist traditions or modernist school improvement perspectives, the people engaged in the educational encounter are seen as central to shaping the meaning and success of the experience. So much so that one of the most commonly expressed fears about the relationship between education and technological change is the idea that we may one day replace educators with machines and that the essential humanity of the encounter may be lost.

One of the most important of these human relationships is the relationship between adults and children. If we want to understand the implications of socio-technical change for the future of education, we need therefore to explore how socio-technical practices may be unsettling and reshaping our expectations for adult-child relationships, and the sorts of risk and opportunity that such new expectations may pose for children.

The standard model of childhood

The western model of education can be understood as being built upon a relationship between adults and children commonly referred to as the 'standard model' of childhood. This model is usually understood to have emerged from the socio-technical changes of the industrial revolution, which called for a large body of educated labour and required the separation out of children into educational institutions away from the labour market. Childhood was seen as a time for careful investment that needed to be protected from malign influence and carefully nurtured until reaching adulthood.[1]

These changes produced education systems that detached children's learning from the lived experiences of communities and carefully determined which adults children should encounter. Often they were organized around prescribed and predetermined curricula and characterized by pedagogic relationships that saw the teacher as conveyor of knowledge and understanding to the 'empty minds' of children. As children were separated from the formal economy, new stories were told about childhood as a time of vulnerability, a time of innocence, a time of dependence. And reciprocally, these stories about childhood also produced particular stories about adulthood as a time of labour, of secure identity and of expertise. In this story, adulthood became the 'end point' to which childhood aspired. The institutions and the narratives of childhood therefore became mutually reinforcing. Such a model of adult–child relations brings risks to children – their rights can be overlooked as they are seen as less than fully formed humans; but also benefits – children are invested in, protected, cared for.[2]

Notwithstanding its dominance as a common-sense story of childhood, however, the standard model of adult–child relations has been under threat pretty much since it first came to underpin educational and familial institutions a couple of hundred years ago. Not least because, as research in the sociology of childhood has taught us, the idea of children as lacking agency, as not shaping their world in active and meaningful ways, is pretty hard to sustain; but also because children have historically resisted their representation as 'less than' real people. The children's strikes of the 1930s, for example, make it hard to sustain a view of children as 'naturally' incapable of being social actors. Moreover, as each new wave of technology has emerged – cinema, television, video, computer games, the internet – so too has it been heralded as breaking down the cocoon separating children from malign influence.[3] The standard model, therefore, has always looked pretty shaky as a description of childhood from the perspective of children themselves. Over the last 30 years a number of factors have combined that disrupt this model of childhood still further by requiring a reconceptualization of children not as 'less than adult' but as social actors in their own right.[4] The 'discovery' or targeting of young people as a consumer group in the 1980s and the development of a Children's Rights Agenda, enshrined in the UN Convention on the Rights of the Child, for example, began to offer children forms of economic and judicial citizenship that required that their views be taken seriously by adults.

The relationships between adults and children of care and control, of responsibility and restriction that underpin contemporary education can be understood, then, not as natural relationships, but as contested and negotiated products of their time and their culture and as subject to change. In these negotiations, new technologies and new socio-technical practices are harnessed to create different forms of adulthood, childhood and family.

'Digital natives' and 'lifelong learners'

At the turn of the century, as digital technologies were being presented by politicians and industry alike as heralding a new 'information society', children's reportedly intuitive capacity to learn to use these powerful symbolic new tools began to provide a new language for talking about adult–child relationships. New and powerful domestic technology and computer games industries emerged which produced images of young people as masters of the new symbolic order. And as the internet took off, adults were presented with stories of child entrepreneurs making fortunes and were encouraged to buy computers for their children in order to allow them to compete in this new world.[5]

In this context, the now familiar ideas of the 'digital native' and the 'digital immigrant' were born, which described children as natural citizens of the new world order, and adults as analogue impostors, trying to keep up.[6] Researchers and marketers described computers, the all-powerful symbols of the newly globalizing economic world, as 'children's machines', and even shiny new Prime Ministers-in-waiting professed themselves astonished by children's capacity to enter into this new world:

> Ask me my three main priorities for Government, and I tell you: education, education and education.

> The first wonder of the world is the mind of a child.

> I sometimes sit reading a paper or watching TV, and look up to see my children at a computer, and marvel at what they can do; using that computer as easily as we read a book.

> (Tony Blair in 1996)

The idea of the digital native was used as a basis for questioning the sorts of learning, knowledge and practices that schools should value, as a basis for making visible children's rights to have a say in their education and as a basis for questioning teachers and schools' claims to design education based on tradition and precedent. The time had come, many advocates for this perspective argued, for a radical rethink of education – and looking to the way in which children were playing, learning and living with digital technologies would help adults learn how to adapt.

Like many other narratives of children's agency or calls for educational reform, however, this idea might easily have been relegated to the familiar realms of 'alternative' discourses of education if it were not for the fact that, at the same time, ideas about adulthood were also changing. Indeed, the same sorts of people who were heralding children as the natives of a new digital world were often calling for adults to take on new roles in contemporary society. Adults were being asked to become flexible, adaptable and responsive to change in the context of a fluid and rapidly changing 'post-industrial knowledge economy'. Adults were told that they were increasingly responsible for making their place and role in the world on an ongoing basis, rather than taking up employment for life.[7]

In this context, industry and politicians recast as strengths to which adults should aspire the attributes of childhood that had previously been seen as vulnerabilities: playfulness, fluidity, adaptability, malleability, all became desirable attributes for the new knowledge worker. In contrast, the traditional attributes of 'old' adulthood – constancy, stability, experience, expertise – were seen as potential risks and barriers to adaptation and change. Rather than seeing childhood as a time of incompetence, therefore, adults were encouraged by companies such as Lego to take children as their models in order to survive in this new world:

children are our role models. Children are curious, creative and imaginative … lifelong creativity, imagination and learning are stimulated by playful activities that encourage 'hands-on and minds-on' creation, fun, togetherness and the sharing of ideas. People who are curious, creative and imaginative, i.e. people who have a childlike urge to explore and learn, are best equipped to thrive in a challenging world and be the builders of our common future.[8]

For at least the last ten years we have seen new ideas of childhood and adulthood circulating that threaten to disrupt the standard model of adult–child relations upon which most educational institutions are premised. They destabilize adult expertise and promote images of children as socially and technologically competent in the all-important spaces of the new digital networks.[9]

Ageing populations and beanpole families

These ideas are, today, being joined by another powerful narrative of change focused on the potential implications of population ageing and a new uncertainty about the security of the intergenerational contract.

Over the next couple of decades Western populations are unlikely to be characterized by the familiar pyramidal structure of masses of children and relatively few elders in which the standard model of childhood was born. Instead, there is a large bulge in the population graph as baby boomers make their way into and toward retirement. There is also a decline in fertility. By 2030[10] demographic forecasts suggest that half the population of western Europe will be aged over 50, with significant numbers expecting a further 40-year life expectancy. This changing demographic also sees a significant rise in the number of people who are living what would now be considered exceptionally long lives, as Leeson argues: 'in 2006, there were 10,000 people in the UK aged 100 years and over. By 2056, this number is expected to increase to an astonishing 286,000 and to around 1 million by the end of the 21st century.'[11]

Decreased fertility combined with increased longevity tends to change the typical structure of the family, giving rise not to the 'short fat' families of multiple siblings and few generations which easily support the intergenerational contract, but to 'beanpole' families of multiple (four to five) generations with small sibling groups. At a population level, such a demographic shift means that the ratio of workers to retired people in the population would significantly decrease, heralding stories of late-life dependency and competition for shrinking public resources as tax receipts decline.

Longer life does not, however, always imply dependency. New stories about late-life activity are increasingly visible in the media and in business as older age groups mobilize, collectivize and start to challenge dominant representations of themselves as dependent and burdensome. New stories are being told that show older individuals as positive resources for society either through paid work, or through voluntary and social activity. At the present time, for example, the contribution through voluntary activity to the UK national economy of the two oldest cohorts is calculated to be in the region of 18 million hours per week or £4bn per annum.[12] Older adults are also, often, actively involved in caring. In the UK in 2003 over 50 per cent of the UK population were grandparents by the age of 54, meaning that over a third of a lifespan, on average, is spent being a grandparent; 26 per cent of grandparents were involved in some form of care for their grandchildren, while over 60 per cent of grandparents saw their grandchildren at least once a week.[13] As 'retirement' looks ever longer, people may also wish or be forced to keep working for longer to provide financial security into old age or to gain the social benefits of participation in the workplace. Late life is becoming a site for both active consumption and continued employment.

New relationships are also being negotiated in family homes as technical and social trends converge to drive ever-increasing use of the home as a workspace:[14] broadband connectivity; easy and cheap video conferencing; secure cloud computing systems allowing access to files and information that is normally based in 'the office'; less stable employment and increased freelance or short-term contracts; business cost-cutting around real estate and the emergence of hot-desking in offices. The need to combine caring for children and older relatives with working also comprises a 'pull' to physical presence in the home. These drivers are beginning to see a reconfiguration of some homes not as a site of leisure (albeit that this was only ever the case for a limited number of people) but as a space in which parents, children, grandparents and friends negotiate the complex demands of family with working in the formal economy.[15] Such a merging of working and learning practices may mean that, for some, the future spaces of the family home start to look more like a pre-industrial household economy, in which not only working and domestic life were blurred, but where the roles of family members were not so clearly defined into those related to the 'market' or to the 'domestic' economy. As demographics shift and technologies allow for new forms of connection, such a negotiation may produce family roles and relationships that are far from familiar today.

Longer life in beanpole families offers complex narratives of adulthood and intergenerational relations. The linear route through a progression of stages of schooling, working, followed by a short retirement of leisure is being replaced by a longer life comprising overlapping stages of retirement, working, learning and caring.[16] Great-grandparents may be called upon to act as primary carers for children, grandparents may be involved in retraining alongside their children and mixing care and work much later in life. And as we live longer, the challenges of maintaining a lifelong relationship also become more visible, causing us to move into and out of more relationships, and bringing stepchildren and parents into the mix of support and commitments we need to negotiate.[17] Future families, and relationships between family members, are likely to be characterized not by taken-for-granted stable family 'roles' but by complex negotiation between family members about what it 'means' to be a parent, a teenage daughter, a grandparent.[18] For those who manage these negotiations, however, the prospect beckons of intensified intimacy and shared experience after a life together of 70 or 80 years.[19]

Class, income and culture may lead to very different intergenerational and family relationships. Already, middle-class grandparents in the UK are less likely to contribute face-to-face care to their grandchildren as they are likely to live further away; they contribute, however, more in terms of gifts and economic support. Middle-class families are also more likely to be able to work from home.[20] At the same time, there are likely to be profound differences in the degree to which different socio-economic groups and professions are able to equip themselves effectively for a longer period of later life; while some grandparents may be active, looking for creative and personal fulfilment and economically secure, others may be suffering from ill-health, required to work later in life to generate income and highly dependent upon the state or others for their welfare. Similarly, family make-up and relations of intergenerational care seem to be patterned along cultural and ethnic lines, as around 66 per cent of British resident Indian elders live with one of their adult children, compared with just 15 per cent of white elders.[21] What the future family looks like in the context of demographic change, therefore, will be inflected profoundly by questions of family income, family cultural and religious values and by family health.

For all of us, however, living together for longer across multiple generations opens up new challenges of 'translation' across the socio-technical norms and assumptions of different age groups. The experience of watching *Mission Impossible 3* with my own grandfather brought this home: as we watched the unfolding tale of spies coordinating their activities across the globe, accessing remote information and talking to each other through Bluetooth headsets, it became clear that he simply couldn't understand the story, because he couldn't understand the media of communication that were taken for granted in the storyline. Spies, yes, these were familiar; dark forces from across the globe, he knew about those; but the idea that they should be able to simultaneously coordinate their work across time and space in this way seemed, to him, despite his training as an engineer and a pioneer in his own way in his day, to be profoundly implausible in his 75th year.

As socio-technical practices change over the next couple of decades, we need to ask what children in 20 years will see as a 'natural' storyline and what we will see as absurdly outlandish as we get older. More importantly, what social relationships will we need to develop to ensure that we can translate between generations, to ensure that we can negotiate our different ideas about 'common-sense' socio-technical practices. The current differences between generational attitudes towards privacy online, in which younger generations seem much more comfortable sharing what might previously have been considered 'private' information, for example, provide an insight into the sorts of flashpoint that may arise. Others are likely to emerge. These differences in taken-for-granted techno-cultures have the capacity to open up divides between generations. As Mimi Ito and her team argue, however, while the concern about generational divides is often about potential differences in values, it is more often the case that values are shared across generations but enacted differently through different socio-technical practices.[22]

As well as opening up the possibility simply for vast chasms of mutual incomprehension between multiple generations, such differences are also an opportunity to encourage intergenerational learning and exchange within families, with younger family members inducting older members into specific socio-technical cultures and older adults inducting younger members into family traditions, values and cultures. Already today it is commonplace to find grandchildren acting as important teachers for grandparents to introduce them to web technology, and precedents can be found in the roles played by younger children in citizenship education and adjustment for older family members following migration.[23]

The socio-technical networks in which many families are implicated are now also unsettling the familiar role of adults in cocooning and protecting children from the outside world. Instead, the boundaries between public and private, between work and lifeworld are being renegotiated as families appropriate new digital technologies. Over the last ten years, for example, the capacity to network the child from the home, to allow her to connect at any time, in any place, to anyone, has created a new set of spatial relationships in which children are understood to be intimately networked with their peers and others even from the spaces of the home. In the past, parents may have been able to have what Mimi Ito calls an 'ambient understanding'[24] of their children's interactions through the single family telephone. As personal and mobile devices proliferated in many households each family member has come to act as their own communications hub, managing their relationships with the wider world through their own devices and wrapping a 'personal cloud' of contacts and relationships around them as individuals. Parents may now seek to access their children's social networks, and such access may be possible subject to negotiation, but they have a much more limited role in mediating such networks.[25] The walls of the family home are increasingly porous, as children are able to construct their social networks around themselves, networks that may stretch far beyond the immediate neighbourhood or school.

Salesman, disciplinarian or competitor: what role for adults?

Over the last few decades we have seen a profound unsettling of traditional adult and child relations. The tools that are being used, the communication patterns enabled, the organization of time, all have gone some way to disrupt mid-twentieth-century 'typical' roles for the adult and the child. The patterns of population ageing over the next decade promise to increase the complexity of adult roles, diversifying the adults involved in children's care, the relationships between them, and the responsibilities that they have for and to each other in the home.

The response that education should take to such changes is highly contested and increasingly politicized, and likely to act as a site of significant debate over the next decade. The relationships that we seek to create between adults and children, after all, structure everything from governance, to pedagogy in our schools.[26]

One response to the idea of the 'digital native' is to see young people as independent and discerning consumers. Children's seeming ability to master and make decisions about digital cultures is taken as a basis for reconfiguring education around the idea of the intelligent child consumer able to select from a variety of different offerings. As social commentators Charles Leadbeater and Tom Bentley observe:

> Young people are far more avid and aware consumers than they used to be. This culture is bound to have an effect on how they view education. Many secondary school age children now have mobile phones for which they can get 24/7 telephone support, different price plans, equipment and service packages. They are used to a world in which they can search for, download and share digital music on the Internet.[27]

> Young people have a far wider range of distractions and alternative pursuits on offer than ever before. The growth of multi- and mass media, including computer games, pop music and the Internet, as well as the proliferation of retail and consumer goods, and leisure activities and facilities, means that young people choose between an increasingly wide range of alternatives. ... Information is accessible in ways which older people are still struggling to get to grips with, while the young, more often than not, take to them like ducks to water. Educational institutions must compete with a dazzling array of alternative information, distractions and sources of motivation and example. ... Whether we think that teachers ought, in principle, to have to compete with such influences on their pupils' attention, they already do.[28]

This perspective implies that the new all-consuming, all-independent children with their rich digital cultures and independent communications networks cannot be engaged other than through manipulating their desires and attentions. This line of thinking manifests itself in a vision of adults as salesmen, seeking to 'market' their values to children in the face of distractions from other, less desirable cultures.[29]

Such a vision of adult–child relations positions teachers and parents as fighting for children's attention against the distractions of popular culture. It is a relationship in which the child is conceived of as consumer and the responsible educator's role is to use all the tools and tricks of digital cultures to appeal to the child, to seek to grasp their attention. In these visions of the child as digital consumer, the challenge for educators is constructed as one of ensuring that the 'offerings' of education are able to compete with the 'distractions' of the digital age. The role of the state, and of adults, is to ensure competition to enable consumers to select from the widest range of possible choices. Zygmunt Bauman describes this relationship as 'a gradual yet relentless replacement of the orthodox teacher–student relationship with the supplier–client, or shopping mall–shopper pattern'.[30]

There are evidently significant problems with this approach. For adults, it undervalues their experience and knowledge. For children the risks are greater: not only does it hollow out children's identity as social actors to one that is solely concerned with consumption, but it obscures the factors that allow even such a hollow identity to be built: namely, access to the material and economic resources that allow children to participate in digital cultures.[31]

A competing response to the unsettling of traditional adult–child relations is to seek to reinstate and reclaim the rights of adults to wholly determine children's educational experiences. The UK's Conservative Party, for example, seeks to reinvigorate a language of adult responsibility for education. Such a responsibility, however, is presented at the expense of recognizing children's rights and talents, as Michael Gove, then Shadow Secretary of State for Education (2009) makes clear in his celebration of one particular 'ideal' school:

> Because what Sir Michael does is deliver what every sensible parent knows is needed in our schools.
> He insists on a proper uniform – with blazer and tie – respect for authority, clear sanctions for troublemakers and no excuses for bad behaviour.
> He sets classes by ability – so the brightest can be stretched and the weakest given special support.
> He teaches traditional subjects in a rigorous way and when the bureaucrats try to insert the latest fashionable nonsense into the curriculum he tells them where to get off.
> There are fantastic extra-curricular activities, proper competitive sports and an amazing team of teachers – who work into the evenings and on Saturdays to give their pupils the best possible chance in life.
> Why isn't every state school like that?
> It's my job to make sure they are.
> So where do we start?
> Well Sir Michael would tell you – with discipline.
> …
> We'll develop a Troops to Teachers programme – to get professionals in the army who know how to train young men and women into the classroom where they can provide not just discipline – but inspiration and leadership.[32]

This particular 'ideal' future school is also designed to offer transparent classrooms, no corridors, and to enable the head teacher to see into 'all the nooks and crannies' of the school in a context in which 'care' equates to total surveillance.[33] Future relations between adults and children in this vision are disciplinary, both in terms of management of behaviour (by adults, of children) and in terms of knowledge (knowledge is presented as the property of adults, and children will be introduced gradually into its secrets). This particular future vision for adult–child relationships restates the separation of the child from society, and reproduces the conception of children as without rights and without voice.

Public debate about education for the foreseeable future seems likely to be characterized by a debate between these two visions of the future of adult–child relationships, neither of which provides a particularly compelling future for children.

These are, however, in the main debates *about* children amongst *adults*. Children's own voices are rarely heard. A significant disruption to this pattern, however, may come during the next decade in the form of challenges to the legitimacy of adults to take decisions on the part of children. Such a challenge to adult legitimacy would be premised upon a perception of adults and children having different and competing interests as increasing demands are made upon public resources, and as anger over the implications of adult neglect to prevent climate chaos intensifies.

The continuing failure to reach an international political agreement for legally binding limits on carbon emissions and the impoverished imagination that sees carbon trading as a coherent strategy, mean that young people growing up today will, barring miracles, be growing up with the legacy of a warming planet and the inevitable human, economic and material costs that this will bring to us all. We are already beginning to see generational divides mobilized in debates on the causes and responsibility for climate change. The film *The Age of Stupid*, for example, specifically points the finger at contemporary adulthood's failure to act in response to unmistakable warnings of climate warming.

At the same time, an ageing population combined with restricted public resources in the wake of the 2008–9 economic crisis also begins to set up generational needs in opposition to each other,[34] as a recent report from the Brookings Institute argues:

> Right now, the intergenerational contract favors the old at the expense of the young. It operates under the premise that the wide base of working-age Americans can, and should, support the relatively small number of Americans in retirement. But over the coming decades, there will be far more older Americans, including many in their sixties and seventies, who can work and who, with proper planning, should have sufficient assets to contribute far more to supporting themselves than was possible in the past. ... And a country that gives priority to its elderly over its young is arguably a country that doesn't have much of a future.[35]

These combined factors – population ageing, climate disruption, limited public finances – fuel the potential for intergenerational conflict. Already today there have been demonstrations in Germany by students in protest at allocation of public finances to pensions and cuts in student budgets. Organizations are being established to fight for 'intergenerational justice', often around flashpoints such as access to housing in the UK, or to education in Germany.[36] Some politicians are equally stoking up concerns about the 'legacy' of the baby boomers, casting that generation as a particularly selfish and reckless 'golden generation' who have surfed the waves of economic growth, used up the environmental resources, and left little for their children and grandchildren,[37] while newspapers are beginning to see the potential for intergenerational conflict to make a good news story: one recent headline read, 'This is not youthful rebellion. We see the catastrophe ahead. Climate change has provoked a war between the generations. Younger members of the government need to choose their side.'[38]

In these narratives, adults and children, older generations and working adults are produced in relationships of competition and conflict. In this context, the intergenerational contract in which care is collectively passed down the generations at the start of life in exchange for reciprocal care at the end of life, begins to be unsettled as generational interests are seen to be competing for scarce resources rather than complementary. In this context the collective intergenerational contract that has underpinned the expansion of mass education looks increasingly fragile.[39] The legitimacy of adults to act for and on behalf of children, to stake a claim to the moral high ground and to shape educational decision-making in these contexts, may be hard to sustain.

A new contract between generations

None of these trajectories are either desirable or sustainable. All of them present serious risks to those who depend upon the existing standard model of childhood or the existing intergenerational contract to provide relationships of care and support. In all of these futures, those children and adults who are already most vulnerable may suffer most. The idea of adult as salesman assumes that all young people have the resources to support informed decision-making, it provides no resources and support for the child unable to 'work the system'. The disciplinary adult tends to privilege those values, behaviours and knowledges that are already the preserve of dominant groups and interests, and to offer security at the expense of human rights. The competitive model erodes relationships of care that are critical for protecting the most vulnerable, whether young or old.

How then, can educational institutions respond to changing adult–child relationships in ways that prevent them from amplifying existing inequalities? I would argue that, just as the changing adult–child relationships of the industrial revolution inspired a new educational imaginary that underpinned the growth of mass education, so the changing adult–child relationships of the twenty-first century now also require a new educational imaginary. This educational imaginary needs to be premised upon two important principles: a commitment to building intergenerational solidarity and a recognition of what constitutes powerful learning environments.

An education for intergenerational solidarity would recognize that vulnerable children and adults might have more in common with each other than with people of the same age group, and that the solutions to their problems might be better dealt with across generations. An education for intergenerational solidarity would recognize that some challenges are collective and impact all of us, young and old, and require collective responses. An education for intergenerational solidarity would also recognize that in conditions of rapid technological development, no generation has a monopoly on expertise or understanding and that the need to learn, try things out and change is a property now of all age groups. If our urgent challenge is to learn to live well in changing socio-technical environments, we need to draw upon the expertise of all age groups to do so. We cannot afford to lose the experience and insight of the older generations, or the capacity for new ideas and rapid appropriation of new tools of the younger generation. We cannot afford to allow only certain age groups to take on positions of responsibility, or to relegate others to the scrapheap. We need, instead, to create powerful learning environments that build intergenerational solidarity.

The second principle is the commitment to building powerful learning environments to support intergenerational solidarity. This is premised upon the recognition that powerful learning environments are more than intergenerational transfers of knowledge and that we can therefore be more flexible and creative in the roles that we ask children, teachers and other adults to play within them. Much of the anxiety surrounding changing adult–child relationships, for example, relates to its disruption of what Keith Sawyer calls the traditional 'banking' model of education, which assumes:

> … that knowledge is a collection of facts and procedures
> … the goal of schooling is to transfer facts and procedures
> … the teacher is the individual who possesses these facts and procedures and whose mission is to transfer them to students
> … the success of schooling can be determined by administering paper and pencil tests that determine how many of these facts and procedures the student has internalized.[40]

The broad direction of research in the learning sciences over the last 50 or so years, however, suggests that this 'banking' metaphor is misplaced. Instead, learning is profoundly social and situated. The development of knowledge and understanding is first produced in interaction with others and then internalized. It is developed through participation in meaningful activities, first as novice then, after time, as expert. It is developed through activities such as playing, fiddling around, copying, watching; and supported by guided participation when needed. It involves just-in-time support when necessary and is characterized by fluid roles where individuals may be both experts and novices, teachers and learners at different times. It involves the exploration and development of identities and emotional engagement with activity. Powerful learning takes place in the context of the rich resources of the activity, with material, conceptual and human resources to hand. Progress is measured against mastery and personal goals rather than decontextualized from practice. Such approaches to learning have been identified not only as characteristic of a range of different societies and cultures, but also as properties of highly economically and symbolically successful groups.[41]

If we do not need to rely on the banking metaphor as a basis for the design of powerful learning environments, and we understand learning to be a different and richer process of meaningful participation in practice, the anxiety over changing adult–child relationships can be mitigated. This means that we can begin to open up the possibility of adults and children together playing varied and fluid roles in the educational process, while recognizing the asymmetry in experience between generations. It opens up the possibility of designing educational institutions that allow old and young to learn together how to live with rapid socio-technical change and how to tackle the profound challenges posed by the next quarter-century.

Where the last century saw the rise of mass formal education, this century therefore needs to see the rise of intergenerational learning environments. We need to create educational relationships where teachers, parents, children and grandparents can come together as 'co-conspirators'[42] to learn from and collaborate with each other. We need to create institutions that enable people of different generations to learn together to understand and overcome those challenges that are of common concern to all. In so doing, we will begin to create the relationships and institutions that can underpin a multi-generational conversation about the future.

Chapter 3

Being human

Educational goals are informed by ideas about the types of people that education is intended to produce. Since the inception of mass education of children by the state, education has historically been concerned, for good or ill, with attempting to shape, discipline and mould individuals to become productive workers and responsible citizens or, from more emancipatory perspectives, to enable children to become 'fully human'. What counts as a responsible citizen, a productive worker, or a fully realized human being is, of course, the subject of some debate. The idea of education as a process concerned with the development of the person, however, is not.

When we look at the emerging socio-technical practices of the next two decades, however, what might these mean for the sorts of people who will be engaged in the educational encounter? As we develop a range of new technologies and tools that allow us to intervene in the body, to manipulate and enhance the senses, what might it mean to be 'fully human' in these contexts? As we create new tools and technologies to project and record our identity and to hold our memories, what new ways of being human might open up to us?

Of course, people have always developed and used tools to enhance their capabilities. From our earliest history we have worked on and adapted the artefacts around us to enhance what we can do. We have also been creative in our tool use, rather than slaves to some predetermined design. Just because something is designed for one purpose (a set of steps for walking down) doesn't mean we can't imagine its use for another (an arena for demonstrating skateboarding skills or a space for hanging out). We have the capacity to adapt what we develop for a wide range of uses far beyond the imagining of their original inventors, not least for enhancing pleasure or play or for creating carnage and violence.[1]

Not only have we changed our environment by creating tools from it and by using these tools to shape it, but these tools have reciprocally changed us as we have come to adapt to them, rely on them and develop ways of working with them. We change our bodies to mould to the demands of our tools (consider the aches from using a computer for too long or the muscles we develop from wielding a mallet). We also change our social structures and expectations (consider how our ideas about a sensible distance for a commute have changed over time as our modes of transport have become faster). These practices then become part of wider socio-technical systems to which we become accustomed and in time, come to depend upon. The city, for example, is a familiar socio-technical system in which many of us live oblivious of our dependence on the water, sewerage, electricity and transport systems that meet our day-to-day needs. These changes, these adaptations of ourselves, our bodies, our expectations and our aspirations, happen slowly and incrementally. We do not see a sudden emergence of a new techno-culture overnight. Instead, the future comes slowly, one day at a time, and it is slowly, one day at a time, that we adapt our bodies, our expectations and our social practices to create new cultures through the tools we develop.

Such changes, as we adapt our sense of selves to the new tools we create, raise interesting questions for educators. They require us to ask, in particular, what sorts of augmentation of the self are desirable or valuable. And how will we manage the augmentation of the self in schools in ways that are equitable and democratic.

Improving on evolution?

The boundaries of the individual are being fractured and transformed in interesting ways through emerging socio-technical practices. Many of these are taken for granted, others cause more of an instinctive shudder of disquiet. One of the latter is the biological augmentation of the individual, the breaching of the human–machine boundary.

The idea of biological augmentation seems strange, but people have been doing it for centuries. Different cultures have been augmenting the body through jewellery, make-up, clothing, diet, contraceptives, glasses, contact lenses, hearing aids, and innumerable other delightful or practical adaptations, for years.

Such augmentations are beginning to take on a digital character. For quite a few years, Western medicine has led many of us to take it for granted that it is possible to embed digital technologies into the body. Pacemakers, for example, are a relatively commonplace medical intervention, both for the heart and, more recently, for the brain to manage some forms of Parkinson's disease. Cochlear implants (devices to allow deaf people to hear and that integrate human biology with computers) are beginning to become routine. Such tools are intimate augmentations of the human body, blurring the boundaries of biology and machine. The integration of computing and biology is also being driven by the prosthetics industry, fuelled, not least, by the wars in Iraq and Afghanistan. In this field we are beginning to see researchers developing artificial limbs that are fully integrated with human nervous and muscular systems and equipped with sensors to enhance feedback about touch and grip.[2] Commercial and public labs are working to create 'skin' that can sense and respond to touch, giving the possibility of new limbs that feel real;[3] and to develop ocular implants, connecting the retina with cameras and computers, to correct blindness. Researchers are developing systems for neural control of prosthetic limbs even in cases of severe nerve damage.[4] The prosthetics industry is becoming increasingly capable of overcoming significant physical disabilities and creating not only functional but desirable augmentations to the body.

As with many medical developments, what was designed initially for corrective purposes is already being appropriated for other pleasurable or subversive means. Bionic prosthetics are being used by artists and designers, for example, to develop beautiful body jewellery that uses skin sensors to measure symptoms of arousal and changes colour accordingly.[5] In 2009, Rob Spence, a film-maker who lost an eye in an accident, decided that he wanted to replace that eye with a miniature camera to allow him to record everything that was going on around him.[6] Textile designers are experimenting with intelligent and autonomous fabrics that respond to environment and to the body and to encounters with other people in complex, unpredictable and sometimes beautiful ways.[7] The enhanced body of the future may not be the uniformly 'correct' body of medical textbooks, but weirder, more wonderfully, more playfully enhanced. It is in the sports arena that we are starting to see some of the sorts of debate that this is likely to prompt. Why, for example, is it OK for some sportsmen to have laser surgery on their eyes (Tiger Woods, for example) while others taking steroids or using prosthetics are barred from participating?

These physical prosthetics are pretty easy to see. Less visible, however, is the use of 'smart drugs' taken to enhance cognitive function. Take, for example, the increasing frequency of use of Provagil/Modafinil. Designed for people with sleep disorders, this drug is now increasingly being used for cognitive enhancement. High school and university students are frequently reporting using Ritalin and Adderall (initially designed for people labelled as having Attention Deficit Hyperactivity Disorder) to help them concentrate and study for longer. Already today some commentators are reporting that the intersection between subcultures of drug experimentation and a highly charged and individually competitive economic culture can make the use of such drugs feel obligatory rather than optional,[8] while parents are reporting that they may feel pressure to encourage their kids to take them.

> When asked whether healthy children under the age of 16 should be restricted from taking these drugs, unsurprisingly, most respondents (86%) said that they should. But one-third of respondents said they would feel pressure to give cognition-enhancing drugs to their children if other children at school were taking them. Morein-Zamir found this coercive factor very interesting. 'These numbers strongly suggest that even if policies restricted their use by kids, pressure would be high for parents,' she says.[9]

Where such conditions prevail, pharmaceutical companies are likely to continue to invest in developing drugs able to confer cognitive competitive advantage, and people are likely to experiment with these in ways that push the boundaries of their use. Substantive debates about the use and regulation of such drugs, given the uncertainty about their long-term implications for mental functioning, will doubtless ensue.[10]

As in the 1960s and '70s, such debates could lead to non-pharmacological cultures of experimentation with cognitive enhancement. Developments in brain imaging,[11] for example, make clear that significant brain activity precedes associated conscious experience. For example, it is possible for the brain to register 'seeing a picture' without conscious recall, and much of the process of information monitoring and scanning of our environment is taken for granted and routinized in social contexts. At the same time, experiments in this field also suggest that complex decisions can be made without or prior to awareness of decisions and in some cases, better decisions are made without conscious attention.[12] Such developments challenge the assumption of the primacy of the rational, autonomous, information-assessing individual that current 'smart drugs' are used to enhance, and instead require us to rethink our processes of building understanding and knowledge as also encompassing the unconscious, emotion and intuition. Finding ways to enhance or draw upon the unconscious may therefore become an important alternative site of investment. Sohail Inayatullah, for example, points out that meditation is already becoming an important strategy for cognitive enhancement in some Eastern universities.[13]

These developments, however, are 'post-hoc' improvements or additions to the human body. In contrast, the massive processing power of computers opens up radically new ways of working on the human body through genetic engineering.[14] This science offers a new way of 'seeing' the human body and of enabling us to act upon it. As Bruce Sterling, the science fiction writer, designer and communicator of science argues: 'Genetics … is a cultural point of view. … It's a matter of seeing the once-secret productive engines of nature, envisioning that as an industry, and understanding the broad implications.'[15] This 'point of view' may lead to a new common-sense starting point for intervention in the body.

We are already seeing ever earlier starting points for interventions into the body. Already, mothers are enjoined by policy-makers and a growing parenting industry to give up smoking, eat well, take appropriate exercise and play Mozart to the foetus before birth. The relocation of the reproductive process from the body to the test-tube, however, combined with the new capacity to intervene at the genetic level, opens up the opportunity to manipulate the biological material of the child pre-conception. Such a manipulation is currently used correctively, to avoid debilitating hereditary conditions. Genetic profiling is already becoming more routine and there are researchers and commercial companies advocating that a genetic profile should be a taken-for-granted part of an individual's general medical health kit.[16] In these conditions we might expect that the familiar trajectory of medical care from corrective to elective process is likely to widen the application of pre-conception and pre-birth intervention, raising a host of legal and ethical questions. There are those who argue that such an intervention is a moral imperative as it offers the chance to 'enhance evolution'.[17] Such arguments evidently raise profound questions about the starting point for human rights as well as the risks involved in 'hard-wiring' genetic changes pre-birth. As Sterling, again, semi-humorously points out, there may be some counter-intuitive drawbacks to being genetically 'enhanced':

You finally reached young adulthood only to find yourself obsolete. There are already better, faster, and cheaper ways of doing whatever it is that you were genetically altered to do. And these alterations are probably not inscribed within human eggs, the way your alterations were. That is a hopelessly slow and clumsy way to handle the power of genetics. You are stuck with hardwired genetics inside your own flesh.[18]

The question of intergenerational justice also raises its head here – at what point could such early interventions be seen less as concerned parenting, and more as an attack on the human rights of the future person?

The dream of the single identifiable gene that could turn on and off human traits has, however, faded in recent years, to be replaced by a much more complex account of genetic effects: genes are annotated, they are redundant, they make a difference in context with other genes.[19] The social and the contextual are increasingly seen as important factors in accounting for the effects of genes and in determining whether they do, in fact, matter. Manipulation of genes is also increasingly seen as involving trade-offs and unintended consequences. Enhancement of memory in mice, for example, also led to greater pain sensitivity.[20]

It is perhaps at the end of life where genetic science may be most significant in changing our sense of identity. The field of pharmacogenetics, for example, that enables the precise tailoring of drug treatments to individuals' specific characteristics is seen to hold out the possibility of achieving significantly more successful medical interventions. When combined with the potential of farming body tissue and parts as replacements for defective organs, and the longer-term promise of highly precise nano-robotic surgery, these biosciences are seen by some to hold out the potential for new human biological futures. In some accounts they promise radically prolonged life to those who can afford it, with individuals 'surfing the waves' of medical developments over the coming years to become 500 or more years old.[21] In even the least dramatic accounts, the child entering school in 2011 is seen to have a good likelihood (if they are born socio-economically and environmentally lucky) to live into their second century.[22]

The 'individual' in these futures, is not only the person but the person plus a highly sophisticated and powerful set of potential capabilities, some of which may be radically embedded in the body, some of which generate a massively rich digital identity and footprint, some of which offer cognitive enhancement and longer lifetimes. These sorts of augmentation promise to make debates about the use of calculators in school seem trivial and offer a potential for radical and massive amplification of inequalities between different students. Taken-for-granted longer life, of course, brings a whole new dimension to the challenges of lifelong learning.

The non-forgetting human

Today it is probably cheaper, for the first time in human history, to capture information and keep it than it is to decide in advance what we want to know, or to work out carefully what we want to keep.[23] Consider Gitte Stald's study of young people's use of their mobile phones, and the ways in which she says these are now used as 'lifelogs':

> The sim card in your phone could be seen to contain the story of your life (at least at the present time): not just text messages, photos and videos, but also chosen or given tokens such as icons, ring tones, music lists; and the diary, address book, alarm clock all save and display the experiences and activities of the user as they have been mediated and captured by the mobile. As one of the sixteen-year-old boys says: 'Actually I would ten times rather lose my mobile than my sim card because that is where you have all the important stuff.'[24]

The advent of cheap digital memory, for many of us, has changed where we focus our energies. We think less carefully about what we record and why, and about what we save or throw away. In principle, we can capture pretty much everything and keep it. Think about how you manage your email account; it would take more time to go through your sent emails and decide which should be kept and which discarded, than to just keep everything and ensure that your search functionality is up-to-date.

Microsoft, a few years ago, developed the SenseCam; this device, hanging round a wearer's neck, would take a photo every 5 seconds and store this as a record that allows the user to skim quickly back to particular times of the day.[25] Designed initially to support adults suffering from dementia, it also shows how capturing immense amounts of data about our lives has the potential to become taken for granted. Similarly, the devices that allow the tracking of children's movements by concerned parents, or the frequent use of 'tagging' as a means of securing prisoners on early release, are just two of the examples of the day-to-day recording of information that becomes possible when we embed digital technologies into our lives. Games are also being made of the sharing of location-based data – FourSquare allows people to compete to become 'mayors' of locations in local areas, based upon frequency of visits. Sharing location becomes part of what it means for some people to be 'friends' with others, as services such as Dopplr allow users to see where people they know and work with are on a day-to-day basis. All of these services, along with the 3.2 million CCTV cameras in the UK[26] and the rise of reality and surveillance TV entertainment, begin to build familiarity with the idea of constant capturing of personal data, from images of what we can see, to our location.

And it is not just our physical data that many of us constantly record; as we shift away from cash to card transactions, for example, our financial data is recorded for a later date; our phone calls are logged by cell location. Today, some of us are 'delighted' to see our friends' automatic updating of their running routes and times on our social networks. It would not take much imagination to suggest that the sort of people interested in sharing this with the world, or at least tagging it for their own personal benefit, may also come to see it as normal to share their heart rates during the run, the air pollution levels at different stages, their digestive state prior and after the run, and the various tunes they had playing at the same time.

The augmentations that we taken for granted today – mobile phones in particular – capture histories of our movements and interactions. A recent project called BlueFish[27] was set up to make visible to passers-by in a city street just how much data was being captured about them through their mobile phone. On a big screen showing a cartoon aquarium, as you walked past, a friendly cartoon fish would pop up. This fish would have your phone's Bluetooth name and would bob around the screen saying that your phone had been seen at such and such a place in the company of another (named) phone. Working on Bluetooth scanners, this system playfully showed the information that is easily captured today as we walk around the city streets. These Bluetooth scanners are being used widely in our cities to capture such information. As other sensors and devices are added, what other ambient information will be casually collected on our movements?

In another project, artist Christian Nold placed sensors on volunteers' fingers that capture heart rate and galvanic response, and asked them to walk round the city wearing the sensors and carrying GPS devices. The project then produced individual and collective maps of the city, and provoked a range of debates over what constitutes high-intensity or peaceful city environments. Just as interesting as the project itself, however, was the fact that Nold was subsequently approached by companies eager to appropriate the technology and use it for commercial purposes.[28]

And it is not, of course, just sensory or ambient data that is increasingly recorded – instead, information and ideas that might previously have been private or locally circulated amongst friends or peers are now available to all. The age of social software encourages 'mass self-communication', the ability to record, in public, the ideas and information that might previously have been part of a personal archive.[29]

As the capturing of information becomes ever cheaper, as the sites for communication proliferate and as sensors and speck computing[30] make the form of collection more diverse and more location-specific, data trails flow out behind each of us like slipstreams. Once the recording costs are low enough (and they already are) and the search systems are good enough (and they're getting that way) it's not a great stretch of the imagination to see that this ambient information-gathering environment will produce an intimate archive of the physical and cultural minutiae of our everyday lives. It will record our bodies, our environments and our interactions just as a background hum while our attention is elsewhere. *The individual becomes not the biological person alone, then, but the person plus a shareable, searchable, detailed history,* distributed across personal, collective and commercial settings, more detailed than the person's memory alone and more accessible by others.

When biology meets computing

While the augmentation of the self with digital or biotechnology leaves our ideas of what counts as a person relatively intact – it is still the person *plus* the technology

– there are some developments envisaged today that over the longer term raise a series of more interesting questions about what will constitute the boundary between humanity and our machines.

First, we are already seeing the development of bio-computing (the shift from using silicon to using biological material as the basis for building computers). Recently, although at a very basic level, there have been experiments in which slime mould has been used as a control system.[31] There is also substantial investment and excitement around the possibility of DNA computing (computational devices built from DNA material), not least because it seems to require radically reduced energy consumption. Such developments begin to allow us to ask the question – at what point will we begin to consider machines 'alive'?

Secondly, the capacity to engineer at a microscopic scale is developing. This not only opens up the possibility of biological engineering (building machines from biological/biochemical material) but also potentially allows the development of very small-scale devices – including sensors and other computational devices – that could be embedded in, and in time become an everyday part of, human bodies.[32] As computer processing power is expected to continue to increase, such embedded devices would potentially make massive informational power routinely and intimately available to humans (as contemporary brain controlled interfaces are already beginning to demonstrate).

Indeed, there are those today who see these sorts of development as harbingers of radically new ways of being human within the next 50 years. These individuals and groups are already actively working towards the goal of merging human and machine intelligence[33] and relish the arrival of what they have called 'The Singularity' with, as some commentators have observed, the same enthusiasm as some fundamentalist Christians look forward to 'The Rapture'.[34] Singularity advocates suggest that sometime in the next 50 years it will be possible to meld the human and the machine, either through modelling human intelligence in a way that allows the 'uploading' of consciousness to machines or through integrating machines with bodies through nanoscale engineering, to allow humans to move to a 'post-human' or 'trans-human' phase.

Such a future vision, while highly contested and far from widely accepted as either achievable or desirable, does bring into sharp focus the question of what we would want to protect and preserve about our current way of 'being human' and what we might want to change. Would such developments, in fact, matter? We have after all come to terms with living in profoundly different information and networked societies compared to only 100 years ago. Or would such developments fundamentally undermine our sense of selves, our sense of humanity, our sense of the preciousness of life?

Such future visions also expose the limited boundaries of many contemporary discussions of the implications of socio-technical change for education: if the children entering school today might conceivably (in some visions) come to live, work and play in a trans-human era before the end of this century, then fretting about whether they can drive a spreadsheet or not may be the least of our worries.

Counter-measures

Socio-technical development does not usually happen in smooth and predictable trajectories. It hits barriers, it experiences sudden changes, and it also meets resistance. One particular site of resistance may be around the model of the individual that is presumed in the move toward ubiquitous computing and toward the seemingly inexorable merging of identity with digital networks. In particular, there are understandable anxieties about the integration of human and machine. As Cascio wryly observes:

> in a world of ongoing technological acceleration, today's cutting-edge brain implant would be tomorrow's obsolete junk – and good luck if the protocols change or you're on the wrong side of a 'format war' (anyone want a Betamax implant?). And then there's the question of stability: Would you want a chip in your head made by the same folks that made your cell phone, or your PC?[35]

Already today, for example, we are seeing the development of a backlash against participation in social networks amongst certain groups.[36] One online service, the 'suicide machine', sets out to remove you and your connections from all of your social networks. Its rationale explicitly contrasts online communications with face-to-face encounters, as this transcript of the explanatory video shows:

> hi there. I used to be just like you, always online, chatting, poking, things were OK, but I was really missing something, I was missing my family, my kids growing up, my wife, I didn't even have time to cook dinner for them, and then something great happened. I discovered the Web 2.0 Suicide machine and things were about to change … my internet life is dying but my real life is starting, I'm going to go and have fun with them now [shot of him walking in park with his children]. Isn't time precious these days. … online experience is absolutely no substitute for real time experience, all the images, YouTube links and tweets, leave us feeling empty. Get your life back.... sign out forever… suicidemachine.org it's your life, your choice.

At the same time, just as digital technologies saturate working lives, the craving for disconnected 'nature' seems to continue. Look at any commuter train carriage and the screen savers on laptops show images of seaside scenes, forests, hills, children, gardens. Activity holidays teaching survival skills and adventure holidays offering 'real' unmediated experiences continue to be popular. Discourses of anxiety surrounding our interactions with computers and other media proliferate, particularly around children.[37] Some internet commentators are arguing that constant connectivity and rapid information flows are 'making us stoopid' and taking us away from the practices of sustained reading and reflection.[38] Whether such responses are more than wishful thinking for escape from the ways of working that such technologies have facilitated, or something far more profound that expresses a deep commitment to alternative ways of being human and of thinking, however, is hard to tell.

There are specific areas of resistance to these augmentations of the self around which social movements are organizing. First, in the field of civil liberties; secondly, in debates around (dis)ability.

The potential for building information about the individual, in the context of the socio-technical developments I have already discussed, is enormous. Online activities, physical location and movements, interactions with information resources and with people online, physical and emotional responses to events, can be captured already. With the emergence of ubiquitous computing, sensors and advanced data mining techniques in the near future, the rest may be easily accessible, searchable and usable. Such ongoing ambient data collection provides a number of challenges to contemporary conceptions of privacy.

There is already growing resistance to the rise in ambient surveillance and to the growth of 'surveillance as entertainment' approaches such as Operation Border Star (where constant video streams of the US/Mexico border can be watched by anyone)[39] or Internet Eyes (where CCTV footage is made public in real time so that observers can report incidents to the police).[40] As each of us builds an ever larger digital footprint, through online exchanges for work or pleasure, through using online facilities to manage or store our archives of pictures, videos and files, our digital history also becomes both richer and potentially more useful. We can use our digital footprints as personal life records; we can, for example, more easily search, recollect and draw upon what might previously have been scattered across disparate areas of our lives, from childhood friends at school to holiday photographs taken last year. These digital footprints, however, also provide a massive data set for others to access to both tailor services to us, and also to make predictions about our likely future needs and interests. Such data can also be aggregated to generate massive and powerful datasets that can be used in a predictive capacity about particular groups. Consider how today, for example, postcodes are used as a basis for prediction of everything from consumption to educational performance.

At the same time, the capacity to augment or 'correct' the body also raises profound questions about the sorts of embodied experiences we value. The body, after all, is our first and most abiding interface, it filters our perceptions and experiences of the world. If we begin to change that interface, to correct its flaws, to enhance its capacities, we change our means of interacting with the world, our way of 'knowing' it. Our cultures are also shaped by our bodies. Our sense of beauty, our means of expressing intimacy, our numerical systems are all informed by the way in which our bodies interact with the world. People who have different senses and who inhabit different bodies, therefore, experience different ways of living in, knowing and making sense of the world.

This is why some in the deaf community, for example, are ambivalent about prosthetics such as cochlear implants.[41] To get rid of deafness is seen by some deaf people as equivalent to the process of losing a language, a culture, a way of being in the world. As we manipulate, correct and augment our bodies for necessity, for pleasure, for competitive advantage, we potentially change not only our bodies but our cultures and our identities. And should our augmentations tend in the direction of uniformity and conformity, we may lose some of the complexity and diversity of human experience. The experience of the deaf community, and their debates today, may extend to many more of us as the arena for intervention in the body extends more widely.

Diversity and interdependence

These concerns and the growing social movements who voice them suggest that there will need to be political and democratic debate about these future developments. Such debate will lead to different regulatory settlements in different jurisdictions, and to different cultural and legislative responses to the use of data, augmentation and enhancement. This means that the science fiction fantasies of a universally uniform human future comprising fields of marching drones or the disappearance of all humans inside 'the Borg'[42] remains, fortunately, highly unlikely. Instead, as today, socio-technical changes are more likely to offer messy and complex ways of being human.

Over time we may see some people living in communities designed to promote much longer lives, surfing medical waves to keep going that little bit longer, but resisting integration with machine intelligence (those people who today radically restrict calories and reject any use of chemicals might be candidates for this way of living). Other people may become known for their brilliant orchestration of multiple machine intelligences, for their web-like connectivity with each other (the Twitter fanatics could be candidates for this approach). Some individuals may decide to focus on enhancing their own cognition through investment in brain imaging, cosmetic pharmacology, meditation (would the MENSA crowd like this sort of approach?). Others may decide to go it alone, heading away from the machines and the enhancement and the prosthetics and living outside these networks (perhaps some in the more radical wing of environmental movements might take this approach). And then there are those who will be seeking the Singularity, the merging of mind and machine (and they are already pretty easy to identify).

Individuals may mix and match, may move in and out of different ways of being. Different institutions may require or promote certain acceptable ways of being human (as they do already). As different regulatory regimes and cultural priorities develop, some characteristics may come to be equated with different national characters and cultures. Some ways of being will gain more status than others. Over the long term, the significant unanswered question is whether these different ways of being will be able to live, learn and love alongside each other, or whether they will become the start of radically divergent trajectories for being human.

These developments also present more immediate challenges to educators. Over the next 5–10 years it is likely to become commonplace for some children, parents and teachers in wealthy countries to have access to massively powerful computing devices as personal tools; for them to expect constant connectivity to information, people and resources through the digital landscape overlaying the physical environments of the school and the city; for the digital tools they are connected with to be taking on increasingly 'intelligent' functions in managing their information resources; for children to be able to capture on an ongoing basis all of their experiences and to recall these on demand. Other children in these settings will be regularly using medication to manage behaviour or enhance attention.

What does this mean for education? It means that when we design our school of the future, we need to recognize that the people in the school will be mobilizing, in their lives outside it, a range of digital, biological and pharmacological resources in highly diverse ways that are patterned by economic and material resources, by cultures, by regulatory regimes and personal preferences. As different cultures and families respond to new socio-technical capabilities in different ways, depending upon their values and material resources, children will bring highly diverse resources into the school. Some children may bring into the educational arena the capacity to draw on massive informational resources through digital networks; others may bring the capacity to concentrate, attend and analyse rapidly through cognitive enhancement; others may through choice or circumstance be reliant solely upon their wits. Some children will have easy access to all resources, others will not. Importantly, some of these augmentations will have the function of empowering and extending children's agency, others may be administered to limit and control them, and these different patterns may play out along lines of wealth, ethnicity and gender.

Diversity, as it is today, will be the default setting outside the school. The question is how the future school will respond to such diversity. Today, although formal education exacerbates rather than reduces economic disadvantage in most Western countries,[43] it still remains theoretically possible for children from highly divergent economic and social backgrounds to be educated together in the same space and to claim that educational aspirations are attainable by all. Over the next two decades, as cognitive, biological and technical enhancement continue to develop, the stakes of the debate about how education responds to diversity and to inequality outside the school will be even higher.

Will our forms of assessment continue to be designed for the autonomous individual working alone or for the child plus specific enhancements, tools and access to social and information networks? Should we attempt to educate all children together despite their different resources and will that still be possible? Should we attempt to ensure that all children enter educational spaces with a common benchmark of resources (and if so, who decides what these should be)? Should we decide to educate children separately according to the tools and capacities they bring with them and so develop, for example, pharmacologically enhanced streams, digitally connected streams, 'disconnected' streams? Should we mobilize genetic and pharmacological tools to enhance cognition at all costs? Should education become a site that is subject to a pharmacological arms race for enhancement? Our answers to all of these questions will shape expectations of socio-technical diversity.

In the light of these possibilities, I would argue that if the significant diversity in socio-technical practices is not to radically amplify educational inequalities, we need to rethink the dominant mental model of the child that underpins many assumptions about education. Instead of maintaining the myth that education is a set of relationships between autonomous individuals, we need instead to recognize children as being connected to a unique constellation of networks of people, tools, information and processes. We need to see children not as clearly defined and bounded by biology, but as intimately embedded in and interconnected with their tools, their environment and their social networks.

This networked child requires educational processes to help her explore the different networks and resources that she is already connected with, to explore the networks that others have access to, and to understand how best to develop and use these networks and tools. This process would be directed not at attaining an enlightenment model of rational autonomy but towards what we could call instead a 'principled interdependence' with the people and machines with whom she is connected. Principled interdependence implies a recognition of the extent to which we are dependent upon other people, wider institutions, environment and tools to be able to act in the world; and of the extent to which our own actions therefore also have implications for other people and for their agency in turn.[45]

The educational encounter, under these circumstances, becomes not only an encounter between human beings, between adult and child, between teacher and taught, with the aim of enhancing the capacity of the student to attain autonomy. It is also an encounter which has as its purpose the opening up of and reflection upon the nature of the resources – human, cultural and technological – that can be brought to bear upon the educational project. In so doing, educational encounters are oriented towards understanding the actors and networks that are already or potentially available as resources to draw upon – the data the child has access to, the peers the student regularly talks with, the experiences they have had, the tools that are available, the specialist communities they have been participating in. The educational encounter between networked individuals becomes one of understanding how best these resources can be mobilized, and where they need to be extended to attain greater understanding or purchase upon an inquiry.

In this context, the role of the school is to make visible the rich and diverse experiences that students bring into school, to show how the differences between children can be used as a basis for building all children's capacity to create, mobilize and build powerful resource networks, and to make visible the sorts of network resource that others have access to and that are needed for building particular future trajectories.[46] In this context, the school becomes a democratic space designed to enable those with different resources to talk, learn from and work with one another. Today, as students enter schools with an increasingly diverse range of socio-technical resources, as they and teachers have access to a growing pharmacy of cognitive enhancements or pharmacological controls on behaviour, the need to work towards the creation of an educational encounter that makes visible these diverse resources and works actively to overcome the inequalities and injustices that they may cause, is increasingly urgent.

Chapter 4

Collective, embodied and dangerous knowledge

Changing socio-technical practices necessarily alter the resources we have for learning, and for the last 30 years it has been around the uptake and design of learning technologies that a significant debate about education's capacity to adapt to 'the future' has been conducted. From the 1980s to the present day, harnessing technology to create better learning environments has been a useful political strategy for adapting to socio-technical change, and has served as an important symbol of what is usually called 'Modernizing Education for the Twenty-first Century'. This approach, however, tends to see the relationship of education to socio-technical change as a technical and specialized issue, concerned with the mechanics and methods of learning rather than affecting the wider goals of education.

Changing socio-technical practices, however, also change *what* it is that we might need to know. They raise questions about whether the knowledge that was once highly prized remains so – indeed, an unsettling of confidence in traditional knowledge and experience underpins the unsettling of the intergenerational relationships I discussed earlier. They raise questions about the sorts of skill and competency we might need as we choose different ways of being human. They raise questions, in other words, about *curriculum* as well as pedagogy, about educational philosophy as well as efficiency.

The question that socio-technical change poses to education, then, is not merely one of exploring how we can harness technology to our existing educational objectives. Instead, it requires that we ask whether our educational *goals* might change if new socio-technical practices are emerging, whether new capabilities are being developed to cope with these changes and whether new risks and opportunities in turn may arise.

Collective intelligence

One of the questions that researchers and educators are currently struggling with, is how educational goals might change as a result of a new landscape of practices for gathering, sharing and collating information. The range and type of tools that individuals have available for casually capturing and sharing information are, as

I've already discussed, increasing rapidly. The average 'smartphone', for example, is a device that can take photographs, record notes, snip information from the Web, record voices and messages, create videos, capture our location and our physical movements, and all in a device as small and portable as a wallet.

Easy access to such production and recording tools has underpinned the development of services that allow people to archive and share this information with others, which has in turn stimulated the demand to capture more and more data about daily lives. Take Facebook, for example; it can be considered both as a platform and as an invitation. It is a platform for those who are already capturing information about their lives – in other words, it acts as a digital photo album for families, an archive of clips and resources for groups and so forth. But it is also a practice that models ways of producing and repurposing and sharing data. It makes visible the possibility that you might share information about what places you are visiting, what games you've been playing and books you've been reading, or that you might tell people you are attending a particular event. Similarly, Wikipedia acts as a platform and an invitation; it is a resource for sharing knowledge, yes, but it is also a space for modelling how that knowledge might be shared and for encouraging others to do so. In this way, these practices not only reproduce the existing processes of capturing and sharing information, but actively fuel the production and sharing of more and different forms of information.

As well as this proliferation in our own intentional data production, our physical environment is also becoming an increasingly effective collector of data. Indeed, it is increasingly child's play: children's toys are augmented with sensors and memories that allow them to record how they have been put together; cuddly toys are embedded with voice recorders, speakers and accelerometers to allow them to respond to children's interactions.[1] Digital identities are being embedded by retailers, service providers and manufacturers into everyday household objects. Supermarket groceries come with barcodes attached; our wallets have a load of plastic cards that carry our digital financial identities. This move is taking us toward what has been called 'the internet of things' – in other words, the attribution of a digital identity and a digital record to every physical object. These hybrid digital-physical objects become important not only in themselves, but in the records that they carry of their histories. Just as a 16-year-old might worry less about losing his phone than his sim card, so the actual artefacts may come to take on less importance than the rich history that is associated with them. And this history, once stored not in physical artefacts like a sim card but on the Web, begins to have a life beyond the physical artefact. The digital record becomes the important thing, the physical instantiation of it merely a temporary feature that can be changed over time.[2]

The melding of digital and physical landscape, as with the development of social networking services, has the potential to act as a platform and an invitation. The digital landscape of a city can be used simply as a map of services and systems that are already there, a digital layer that helps you navigate the visible environment. More interesting, though, the digital landscape of a city is also an invitation to generate new, competing and conflicting accounts of these spaces. It can be used to make visible forgotten histories or magical alternatives.

Bristol, for example, the city that I sometimes live in, has become a testing ground for designing the digital city. Overlaying its streets and squares, for example, are multiple different 'cities' designed by researchers, artists and developers. Walking into a square in town one day, you could find researchers and developers offering you the chance to 'walk around' the riot that happened there in 1831. As you attach your headphones, you are thrust into the middle of the battle, hearing shouts from desperate mothers and commands from military officers. In another area of the city, during the annual IgFest, you can join in mass collaborative games that allow you as a family to hunt out and find the monsters that are 'living' in the trees and undergrowth of the city's parks. Wandering south of the river and through the city streets near the old tobacco factory, with the right mobile devices you can now hear the rich histories of the older residents' experiences there over the last 100 years.[3]

Just as we now take it for granted that we can upload an image to the internet for sharing with others, there is significant effort being dedicated to creating accessible tools to allow anyone to upload a digital record to a physical location, to allow anyone to digitally 'tag' the city with their ideas, experiences or an alternative reality. In these conditions, day-to-day life in big cities already means the ambient production of massive amounts of digital data and may increasingly mean the creative production of myriad parallel digital landscapes.[4]

The scale at which we are able to capture life and present it as digital information is also expanding massively. We are gathering massive amounts of data about our planet, our solar system, our universe – from the thousands of satellites constantly circulating and cluttering up the lower atmosphere, to the deep ocean probes mapping the ocean floor, to the Large Hadron Collider generating historical records of the origins of matter, to the electron microscopes producing images of atoms.[5] The number-crunching abilities of computers are enabling us to open up new scales of exploration that multiply the sources of data available to us about our world, and such data can be recorded and shared infinitely courtesy of the internet and the Web. And as the data is shared, it stimulates the production of analysis and synthesis of the data and of new inquiries, generating a 'cornucopia of the commons' in which more value, more information and more data is produced as more people use the data, and in turn, the demand for more data increases as its potential uses are identified.[6]

This flourishing in the capacity to gather information, and the creation of platforms to share and encourage the production of information, has led to many grand claims about the future.[7] The sheer scale and complexity of the information that can be gathered and linked together via the Web has led some to claim that we are entering a period in which it becomes possible to talk about a 'global brain' that can be harnessed to tackle the collective global problems of the coming decades.[8] And we can see that the response to pandemics such as SARS or bird flu, for example, did indeed involve the collective and rapid sharing of intelligence and data around the international scientific community.

The Web can also be used to choreograph the combined activities of thousands of people, distributed across time and space, around specific shared problems or tasks, offering the possibility of a form of 'collective intelligence'.[9] The NASA clickworker project, for example, sees thousands of volunteers scanning images of Mars to identify craters and producing results (when combined) comparable with their in-house PhDs.[10] Claims that such connectivity will lead to a breakthrough in collective consciousness need to be treated with caution, of course, not least because history is littered with technologically determinist future visions that proclaim the imminent arrival of universal peace on the back of a new technology;[11] but also, more importantly, because such claims risk obscuring the wealth of human experience that is not yet subject to digitization and which may play an equally important role in human survival and resilience over the coming century, from the knowledge that is built up between couples over a lifetime to the unknown medical benefits of plants in threatened rainforests.

Nonetheless, this digital information landscape does unsettle important assumptions about how we value information and produce knowledge. In one respect, for example, it destabilizes assumptions about who is able to produce valuable knowledge because it makes it easier for anyone to find a space in which their specialized expertise and interest can find a home and a welcoming audience (there will always be a forum concerned with your interest in that model of aeroplane, that obscure '60s spy series, that particular medieval artist). The digitization of information also makes it available in a form that allows it to be easily searched for and used by people who have interests and intentions that may be entirely different from the intentions of the people who generated the information in the first place, thus widening the scope of the potential application of any data.[12] That spreadsheet on crime statistics, for example, suddenly becomes potentially powerful when combined with that data on school investment or income patterns. Those everyday holiday snaps become helpful when trying to map out patterns of historical change over time. Those photos of a toddler become meaningful when they're located as part of a family's social network. What counts as valuable information is not determined by its source but by its capacity to be used in particular contexts. We can think of the Web as a space in which the contingent value of information is amplified. What 'counts' as valuable knowledge in this environment is answered not with a list of important information but with the questions – Who for? When? In what contexts? And for what purposes? In this context, as the philosopher Pierre Levy argues, 'no one knows everything, everyone knows something, all knowledge resides in humanity'.[13]

Technologists and broadcasters, educators and researchers are today struggling with questions of what these shifts towards a new form of 'collective intelligence' might mean for questions of expertise and authority, for our trust in and the quality of information. We are trying to work out how we might begin to manage and to mobilize these massive information resources and to understand what sorts of new capability we might need to flourish in these contexts.

Stewarding the knowledge commons

Such visions of the potential of collective intelligence bring with them a responsibility to steward the systems and spaces through which they can be built. The protection of the Web as a diverse public resource is dependent upon it surviving as a shared 'knowledge commons', to which we can all contribute and from which we can all take according to our needs. It is dependent upon the internet remaining a place that folk educators, universities, beginning banjo players and sock knitters can draw upon to get started and share ideas, and a place where they can easily make available their knowledge and link up with others with shared interests. Such a vision of the future, however, will require defending. It will not come about without concerted efforts, as the rich history of analysis of common resources shows. There are risks to this public resource: risks of enclosure, of pollution, of lack of investment, that threaten to create a profoundly different educational landscape.

For example, there are risks of enclosure of previously shared and collective information resources by private interests. In the digital landscape, such fears greeted the news of Rupert Murdoch's purchase of MySpace or Google's purchase of YouTube for example. The concern was that sites that had previously been seen as spaces of free expression and exchange of ideas would become sites where fees would have to be paid to participate and where the nature of the exchange would be restricted. The reliance of these spaces upon 'free' exchange of ideas for their very success, and the vocal concerns of many participants, however, means that to date such fears have not materialized.

The vision of a global collective intelligence is also built upon socio-technical systems that are subject to material and legal risks. One of the most important resources in the digital knowledge commons is code, the code that allows the production and reproduction of ways of sharing, linking, annotating and aggregating information; the building blocks, in other words, upon which the knowledge commons is produced. Early in the history of computing, it became clear to some programmers and developers that the very openness of the processes of programming that allowed rapid sharing of ideas and development of new approaches, could lead to risks of enclosure. Publicly funded production of code, for example, could, by making only minor modifications, be subject to copyright law, potentially limiting the subsequent use and circulation of that code. As a strategy for prevention of such enclosure, the early programmers developed a new 'Copy-left' process, whereby ownership of the code was claimed, but encoded into the copyright was the requirement for the code to be publicly available, shareable and modifiable in perpetuity.[14] Arising from this are operating systems such as Linux and web browsers like Firefox, all based upon the open sharing of code. Such 'Copy-left' systems potentially act as a challenge to enclosure practices and have been copied in Creative Commons licences. These allow the producers of other artefacts – such as reports and publications – to make available their work without fear that it may subsequently be enclosed by private interests.

Code, however, can also act as a means of enclosing other information by encoding rules about levels and types of access to information. This might mean, for example, that instead of buying a book, which you can then pretty much do anything with, the code that you use to download the book would control the ways in which you were then able to access it – how many times you could read it, whether you could use segments from it elsewhere and so forth.[15] Such forms of enclosure are already visible in the privatization of academic journals and the massive increases in costs that this has led to for access to publicly funded research information.[16] With intellectual property rights coded into products, the potential to control access in perpetuity increases. Despite this, there are growing movements to disrupt attempts to control circulation of information; the recent trend in Japan for self-digitization of books, for example, suggests a counter-trend to continue the long line of file-sharing activities in other cultural areas.

The internet is also a material network, built of cables and computers, and therefore vulnerable to enclosure via these material elements. Who owns the root computers, for example, matters – should they all be based in one country or distributed globally? What link should there be between the cables that deliver the Web and the web content itself? The principle of net neutrality that has to date separated the cable companies from the content provided via these cables is not guaranteed in perpetuity, opening up a potential situation in which the selection of a broadband provider also brings with it the selection of the type of content that there is easy access to and the sorts of space it is possible to participate in.[17] The loss of net neutrality opens up the possibility of a 'fast-speed' sophisticated private Web, and an under-invested and maintained public access Web.

Pollution also constitutes a significant risk to the future of the internet as a knowledge commons. The openness of the commons, the potential for it to be seen as a site which no one tends and the low barriers to access, all make it easier for material to be both neglected and degraded. The interdependence of participants in networks and the opening up of network participation to diverse social actors generates risks of over-communication and pollution, of disease and contagion. Where biological metaphors proliferate to describe how networks function, so too do they proliferate to describe the 'viruses' that are seen to threaten their very underpinnings. Recent malware, like Kneberbot for example, has been responsible for stealing personal data from nearly 2500 corporate and government networks around the world. The infiltration of national information networks has become a familiar part of international disputes, with countries allegedly launching 'cyber attacks' on national information infrastructure.[18] When combined with the rising tide of spam, such pollution risks destroying the knowledge commons and increasing the risks to individuals of participating in such space; the public knowledge commons becomes, like a neglected park, a site to be avoided – a site that, then, is open to the risk of enclosure through privatization.

Another risk to the knowledge commons is the risk of the invisibility of the labour that goes into the production of knowledge and information. The creation of free educational resources in online environments, for example, is supported by the offline institutions and structures of universities, schools and colleges, and the salaries and information resources that such institutions provide. The provision of 'free' education resources in online spaces should not therefore be equated with the idea that the production of such resources is itself without cost. A risk to the knowledge commons might therefore be the assumption that because knowledge resources are currently available free online, no further investment is needed in the institutions and people dedicated to tending and updating them.[19]

Similarly, there is only limited investment in and attention to archiving. At present, our understanding of what might constitute robust and appropriate archiving practices is only just developing.[20] This brings risks. Increasingly, we are reliant upon search engines to index and recall information; when these engines no longer index a particular publication, however, it can become invisible and unfindable. Governments also are making available massive amounts of data at the present time and have been running websites as archives of policy, research and data. Governments, however, change, and there is no guarantee that public data will continue to be available, putting at risk both the services designed upon that data and the reliability of the Web as a public record.[21] New ground rules for updating, managing and searching such archives will need to be established if we are not to enter the world of the endlessly rewritable historical archive of 1984. At present the UK's National Archives, while making over 300 million documents accessible online, still only saves 5 per cent of government records in its collection, is still dependent upon parliament for its funding and is encouraged to seek commercial applications for its work, rather than being resourced by the sort of endowment that would guarantee its long-term independence.[22] The recent donation of the Twitter archive for public, non-commercial use to the Library of Congress provides an interesting example of how commercial and public bodies might begin to develop new rules of engagement for archiving practices.[23]

The development of the knowledge commons also requires the development of more everyday practices to allow us to assess the quality of the information resources being shared. Traditional gatekeepers of quality – the established publishing houses, the established broadcaster, the established newspaper or journal – may be destabilized, and a new environment emerges in which information can be published by anyone, risking pollution or irrelevance of the resources in the commons. We may see the rise of new mega-gatekeepers: Facebook or Google as new custodians of the knowledge landscape. Alternatively, indicators of quality may be built around social groups rather than institutional benchmarking; you choose your friends and colleagues carefully, and you trust them to act as your filters. As an extension of this, new metrics are emerging that attempt to calculate the value of individual contributions to social networks, and of their impact and relevance in that space. Reputation currencies (still at the level of very early experiment) such as the Whuffie, for example, calculate contributions to social networks along the lines of: public endorsement; level of influence;

influence amongst respected other members; and specific content of contributions.[24] Such an approach begins to monetize reputation and contribution in a way that sees social networks not as altruistic collaborative efforts, but as individualized competitive networks for the production of knowledge. Less contentiously, sites such as eBay and Amazon have been successfully using reputation indicators for years, based on feedback from customers.

There are, therefore, both serious and foreseeable obstacles to be overcome over the coming years if these knowledge commons are to fulfil their promise. Because they are foreseeable, however, they are not insurmountable. They require us to learn the lessons from the long history of previous commons – from marine fisheries to public parks – and to develop a new form of governance that can protect the potential of the knowledge commons to act as a democratic resource for collective intelligence.[25]

Thinking with the body

The ways in which information is represented are also undergoing some interesting changes. Already, the Web has become a space in which text and audio collide with photography and film, cartoon and game. For at least the last two decades, we've known that 'literacy' can no longer be thought about simply as the ability to read and write text.[26] Instead, the capacity to participate in these information spaces also requires complex multi-modal literacies, allowing the reading, critique and production of sophisticated audio-visual texts.[27] Such environments, however, do not breach the boundary between 'object' and 'representation'. We are still, when we're reading websites, watching YouTube clips or manipulating avatars in games, working with representations that only minimally involve acting on the physical world or one's own body.

As new haptic and tangible technologies are developing, this is changing, and the body is increasingly being seen as a new form of interface. Five-year-olds and grandparents are familiar with popular commercial applications like the Wii, which use movements of the body as a means of interacting with digital environments. As devices like accelerometers, motion sensors, compasses and other sensors are built into the objects we use, the capacity to interact with the digital information landscape through gesture and other senses is enhanced.[28] At the same time, haptic technologies, which offer physical feedback as the body moves around and through a virtual 3D representation, use touch as a mode of interaction with information. Sarah Baille's famous 'haptic cow', for example, allows trainee vets to insert their hand into a virtual-reality cow and to 'feel' computer-generated virtual objects representing the uterus, ovaries, pelvis and abdominal structures, while the teacher observes their movements on a separate monitor.[29] These interfaces also, importantly, open up the potential for groups, working with each other but in different places, to collaborate through touch on shared representations, allowing them to work together in the same way as if they were moving building blocks around in the same room.[30]

As we combine new visual interfaces with bio-sensors and haptic technologies over the next few years, we may come to find new ways of living with data flows. Can we imagine 'feeling' our way through an information landscape rather than reading or seeing our way through it? As we get to areas of interest perhaps the experience gets more sticky and resistant, as we move through areas of little concern perhaps we experience a flying sensation?

There are other ways in which the digital and physical are being reintegrated. Today, 3D printers that allow you to create a physical prototype of any 3D design and to embed electronics within the prototype usually cost thousands of pounds and tend to be available as a shared resource to students and colleges. As computing costs continue to decrease, the capacity for every school or every local corner shop to have a 3D printer increases (in the same way as local shops had photocopiers or fax machines).[31] The development of tools such as the Rep Rap, however, promises to leapfrog such a development. This device is a low-cost 3D printing machine that allows you to print most of the components required to create another 3D printing machine.[32] In other words, as its creators say, it is 'self-replicating'. If we add to this possibility the development of new materials[33] that overcome some of the environmental costs of the current materials used for 3D printers (often plastic and cellulose), such machines offer the possibility of low-cost, just-in-time localized production (and recycling) of products. With these devices, the capacity to create rapid prototypes becomes possible – in fact, it becomes nearly domesticated. The idea of the home prototyping kit – putting the capacity to create complex animatronic devices in the hands of every hobbyist or child – is not so far away.[34] Already, today, we are seeing the development of community prototyping and development hubs that begin to show what democratic modelling processes might look like. The MIT Fablab, for example, comprises resources that allow community groups, small developers, school groups and others to rapidly design and build their own tools to meet their particular needs and interests.

What these changes imply is that, just as we take for granted that we should be able to convey our ideas easily in writing, so *we may soon take for granted the idea that we have easily accessible tools that allow us to convey our ideas fluently in models, both virtual and material.* If we are able to develop the capacities and new 'literacies' needed to use these tools, the processes of production of potentially complex artefacts become everyday activity, open to communities and children as well as industry and business, as a way of making ideas a reality. Modelling therefore becomes a powerful tool for knowing and for sharing knowledge.

Such developments are already well established and in train, with implications within the next decade. When we look towards the second half of the century, however, towards the broad field of nanoscale engineering, the potential for modelling and experimentation as a form of knowledge production massively increases. Some commentators, for example, imagine tabletop nanofactories, in which nanorobots can be programmed to build, learn from and rebuild hundreds of thousands of new models or materials, working at the scale of DNA or the molecular level.[35] As the genome is published for a whole range of living things – from viruses to rabbits – the capacity for democratizing the industrial-scale modelling and production of life is massively expanded, with consequences we are far from certain of at the present time.[36]

The resurrection of modelling and the development of tangible and haptic interfaces potentially bridges the divide between the academic and vocational knowledges, between knowing 'that' and knowing 'how', between reflection and action. The integration of digital and physical, of representations with objects, requires a re-integration of the strategies we use for thinking and making. They allow for the translation of ideas into realities, and of physical models into revised theories. The ivory tower and the studio can be reconnected in rapid cycles of testing and development.[37]

From filtering to integration

The proliferation of digital information brings an important problem of how to filter and manage the information landscape. A range of different approaches is being explored. Some, like the 'sixth sense' prototype being developed at MIT, for example, are designed around the creation of a personal 'interface' for the world. This device aims to allow the user rapid access to the most pertinent information for that person for that time, place and situation.[38] Among many other things, it reads barcodes and pulls up production history and ingredients (what some have called an 'interface for capitalism'). More contentiously, it allows the individual to project clouds of words onto people they meet, showing key themes derived from that person's online searchable identity (from their blogs, newspaper reports and any other records that are searchable). While this prototype, at the time of writing, is still held together, like any good prototype, with bits of tape and optimism, it provides an insight into the sorts of filtering device and tool we may have at our disposal within the next decade. The question that these devices raise is, on what basis will that filtering take place?

One approach being explored depends on conscious setting of filters and priorities by yourself and your friends and colleagues. It is a bottom-up approach that sees groups acting as first filters on the massive data stream in which they are participating. Small online groups, for example, can serve as effective filters to manage the information flow by tagging information that they have produced with terms that have shared meaning, or pointing others to information that is relevant.[39] As groups form around a shared interest, they can serve to focus attention on information and resources from the wider information flow that are particularly relevant for that group.[40] While we've always relied on workplace and communities to filter our information, being careful about whom your tech systems 'think' your friends are may be increasingly important to manage if this approach becomes widely accepted.

Another approach is also premised upon studying people's behaviours and producing results on the basis of aggregated choices, but with much less conscious attention on the part of people participating to the implications of their decisions. Every time we search the Web, for example, we are already relying on systems that filter the world of information based upon other people's choices and actions. We get our search results not because Google has simply matched our search term to the words that appear in the ranked websites, but because the search engine has looked at hundreds of thousands of other sites and users' links from and to those sites, and from this has inferred what we (the users of the Web) think is most likely to match the words that we enter when we're searching. The search engines are using us, our actions and our choices, to map out what sort of knowledge is likely to link with what sort of questions. When searching, therefore, we are searching through and with an archive of ideas, assumptions and connections that already exist in our online cultures. In some ways, such tools have made thinking with others so banal and so invisible that much of the time we don't realize that we are doing it.

This intuitive and invisible ease of use of socio-technical systems is a design goal for some sectors of the technology industry. Significant effort is being put into making our interactions with socio-technical systems intuitive and, ideally, invisible.[41] When I scan my travel card, for example, I am not encouraged to think about the nature of that interaction with a network. As I phone my gas company to pay my bill, I'm greeted by name, I'm talked to colloquially and thanked, all in an attempt to obscure (not usually successfully) that I am interacting with a computer rather than a person. We are being encouraged not to pay attention to the way we are interacting with computers and to get on with our lives instead, while the systems we are using connect us to each other, gather data and filter our information landscape on our behalf.

We are already used to getting our machines to filter, analyse and manage information that is just too vast and too complex for us. It's not just our search engines; instead, problems such as how to program our traffic systems, manage our baggage at airports, send information through the internet, are being tackled by machines in ways that we could not attempt, as they require massive data processing power.[42] When applied to information filtering, as with our search engines, we can't simply think of our interaction with these systems as a process of 'using' them. Instead they are playing an active role in shaping and managing our interactions. We are not the rational, detached users of such information systems. Rather, we are integrated with them, we collaborate with them and we have devolved to them a whole range of functions that previously we had taken for granted as part of our own responsibilities. The incremental 'offloading' of various cognitive functions to interconnected systems sees the gradual diffusion of cognition across and with the machines that we live with.[43]

Working with digital networks, however, means working with tools that 'think' and 'learn' differently from ourselves.[44] While the great white hope of artificial intelligence seems still to be some way off delivering what it promised, the use of computing to model the problem-solving behaviours of other species, such as ants, has led to new forms of machine intelligence. Such machine intelligence, for example, involves programming software to follow very simple rules which, when combined, lead to highly sophisticated evolutionary techniques where the software evolves on the basis of results.

The critical issue here is that unlike the robot butler of 1950s futures' fantasies, who is simply instructed to do things, this software is not told precisely what to do, but given a set of rules that will allow it to *work out* what to do. This software is built on principles of bottom-up, emergent behaviour as a problem-solving strategy. And this works because the machines can iterate rapidly through cycles of trial and error, through generations of progressively refined responses, to generate solutions.

Working with these technologies does not merely mean 'using' networks that act as a platform or a neutral stage for our advanced human intelligence. Instead, *we are working and integrated with networks that are employing different ways from us of solving problems and 'thinking' about things. The global collective intelligence we are developing, then, is not just human, it is also machine.* Whether human or machine intelligence poses the greatest risk, however, is up for some debate.

Dealing with dangerous knowledge

The socio-technical practices emerging from the use of complex computing systems raise some concern amongst those who are familiar with them. Of particular concern are the interconnected networks of socio-technical systems, so-called systems of systems. These systems of systems underpin a range of critical health, finance and government information systems, many of which were never designed to work with each other, many of which have been programmed to be self-managing and self-repairing. There is increasing concern that we do not have the strategies and processes in place to think through what it means to depend upon and work with these systems. As Dave Cliff, Professor of Computing and head of one of the largest projects on large-scale complex systems in Europe, observes:

> As the number of interacting components that determine the overall behaviour of such systems increase, so the prospect of accurately predicting the system-level behaviour becomes ever more difficult. Technically, these are complex systems, which is a shorthand way of saying that there are mathematical non-linearities (tipping points) in the responses of the components, and in the interaction between the components, which compound across the system in such a way that even if you know everything about all the components and all their interactions, it may not be possible even in principle to accurately predict the system-level behaviour. This is particularly worrying because it implies that there may be types of failure which can occur that we simply do not know about until an instance of that type of failure actually does occur. And, it is in the nature of complex systems that in certain circumstances the effects of the failure or malfunction of one

or two components can interact and ripple out, causing disruption across the entire system/System of Systems, or even collapse of the entire system/System of Systems.[45]

With such complex systems, it is not only possible that we don't fully understand how they work, but we may not be able to even know that they are not working until they fail spectacularly.[46]

The devolution of responsibility to machines, however, doesn't only raise questions about whether we know how to manage and control the resulting systems. Instead, moral and ethical questions are also raised about what we should and should not offload to non-human actors.

Domestic applications for robotics, for example, are currently restricted to smart fridges relying on barcodes to judge expiry dates or dumb-bots that constantly mow the lawn. As families age and there are increasing demands for care for the elderly,[47] we may be offered the choice of whether we wish to devolve responsibility for some aspects of caring in the home to automated and intelligent systems. Telemedicine and 'intelligent homes' are areas of significant investment and marketing, and promote themselves as able to monitor and meet the needs of the elderly without demands on family members. We are already seeing the emergence of systems that allow remote diagnosis and the development of assistive technologies to help people manage the long-term illnesses often associated with longer life (such as Alzheimer's, diabetes and cancer). The 'caring' home, for example, is already today equipped with audible reminders for medicine, pill dispensers, remote control of devices, pressure pads and lighting controls, infra-red sensors to control water temperature, and video monitoring.

In this way, the home is being re-imagined as an outpost of the hospital and the hospice, and the human relationships of domestic care are being medicalized and devolved to technical systems.[48] These domestic medical technologies have particular implications for women's role and identity, as women continue to bear much of the responsibility for caring. In the USA, for example, there are 30–38 million informal carers, and two-thirds of the non-institutionalized elderly rely on help from family, primarily wives and daughters.[49]

Military applications of quasi-autonomous systems are also advancing. Remote aerial drones today allow 'pilots' sitting in one country to kill people in another, and then return home of an evening for dinner with the family. News reports of such events talk about 'drone attacks' as though no human agency is involved. The US military has published a report suggesting that over the longer term, humans would restrict their role to monitoring robot soldiers' decisions in the field rather than actually controlling them.[50]

The emergence of the capacity to model and manipulate biological matter has also been identified as a cause for a debate about responsibility and ethics, and about the limits of desirable knowledge. In 2005, for example, *Science* magazine published the genome for the 1918 flu virus. This prompted the following response by Bill Joy (former chief scientist for Sun Microsystems) and Ray

Kurzweil (internationally recognized futurist and chief proponent of the Singularity Theory) – neither of them, it should be noted, known for being Luddites:

> This is extremely foolish. The genome is essentially the design of a weapon of mass destruction. No responsible scientist would advocate publishing precise designs for an atomic bomb, and in two ways revealing the sequence for the flu virus is even more dangerous. First, it would be easier to create and release this highly destructive virus from the genetic data than it would be to build and detonate an atomic bomb given only its design, as you don't need rare raw materials like plutonium or enriched uranium. Synthesizing the virus from scratch would be difficult but far from impossible. An easier approach would be to modify a conventional flu virus with the eight unique and now published genes of the 1918 killer virus. Second, releases of the virus would be far worse than an atomic bomb. Analyses have shown that the detonation of an atomic bomb in an American city could kill as many as one million people. Release of a highly communicable and deadly biological virus could kill tens of millions, with some estimates in the hundreds of millions.[51]

The rapid development of tools that allow us to manipulate life in radically new ways, the devolution of responsibility for global socio-technical networks to self-managing, emergent systems mean that for the first time humanity is facing a high risk of catastrophic disaster over the coming century. While we have faced risks before, we have the resources now to effectively eradicate humanity, possibly through accident or the unintended consequences of small decisions, or through the unexpected shift in a complex system, in a way that is unprecedented in human history.

Martin Rees, President of the Royal Society and Astronomer Royal, and therefore a man with a sense of perspective, argues that unless we learn rapidly how to handle this knowledge, this may be the last human century.[52] At the very least, these developments raise profound questions about responsibility for the consequences of our use of quasi-intelligent technologies. Learning to live with intelligent systems will require a debate not only about risk and reliability, but a much wider discussion about the sort of future relationships of care, gender, ethics and responsibility that we want to characterize the societies that we live in.

Discernment, responsibility and multiliteracy

What do we need to know to live well in these futures? What curriculum will ensure that we thrive in such contexts?

There cannot, of course, be one answer, one final meta-curriculum 'to rule them all' that will provide us with the reassurance that we completely, and definitively, know what we need to know for our future wellbeing. And indeed, who would want one? A monocultural education, like a monoculture in ecology, would be a highly risky strategy, a single bet on a particular future that, if it fails to pay off, leaves us stranded with little to draw upon. A monocultural curriculum would also overlook the significant strength of our emerging collective intelligence, namely, that all knowledge has the potential to find its use somewhere, the challenge lies in finding the right community or context.

Rather than a list of prescribed content knowledge or learning outcomes, this collective, embodied, intuitive, human-machine collaborating and potentially dangerous knowledge landscape suggests that we will need to ensure, at the very least, that our students develop three attributes: discernment, multiliteracy and responsibility.

Discernment

Discernment is about the ability to judge not only the traditional qualities of information – trustworthiness, reliability and so forth – but, more importantly, to judge the relationship of information to other information, to your own goals and interests, and to the contexts in which it is used. In other words, discernment is the attribute we need when we realise that the main problem we face in a rich digital landscape is not primarily a 'filtering' problem but a 'relational' problem, a problem of judging value against context.

This means that there won't be universal laws about what counts as valuable information and that critical questions we may need to learn to ask will be: 'what am I interested in?' 'what am I working on?' 'what matters to me?' This does not imply narcissism, simply a recognition that a strong sense of identity and purpose is needed to allow relational judgements to be made about the value of information. Reciprocally, this recognition also brings with it attention to the ways in which information is judged by others, and to the rules by which different knowledge or information is admitted as valuable in different contexts.

An education for discernment, then, is concerned with supporting students to explore and to make visible the relationship between individuals, contexts and information. When the filtering problem is understood as a relational problem, discernment helps the individual explore what knowledge counts, for whom, in what contexts. In so doing, the individual can better map the uneven contours of 'collective intelligence' and better understand the different forms of judgement that are in place to police the boundaries of different communities. As Michael Young reminds us, after all, not all knowledge is judged equal and not all knowledge is admitted as valuable by all communities.[53] A concern for equity in education in these new knowledge contexts implies developing the capacity of all students not only to 'decode' information environments, but to create their own identities within them and to understand the criteria that will be operating if they seek to play a role in different knowledge communities – whether in politics, in friendship networks or in high stakes research communities. Fostering discernment is one means by which this can be achieved.

Multiliteracy

The proliferating modalities of the digital landscape, encompassing audio, visual, text based, embodied, haptic, musical and gestural modes of communication require fluency in multiple literacies. To be 'literate' in this environment, is to be able to model, to experiment, to visualize, to verbalize, to write and to film (among many other things). The 'literate' student, worker or citizen will need to reconnect the mind and the body, to move fluently between working in sight or sound, simulation or storytelling.

A full education for multiliteracy, however, will need to break out of its ghetto in 'English', 'Communications' and 'Media studies' and build bridges with Computer Science and Biology. If we seek to equip students to engage with the processes by which knowledge is produced, by which ideas are represented, by which information is circulated and encoded, it will not be enough to continue to be concerned only with representation. Educators will need to engage with the materials by which representations are produced, with the ways in which the hardware and software, the networks and biology of our modes of communication also serve to structure our possibilities for representation, modelling and comprehension.

Responsibility

An education that nurtures responsibility nurtures an acknowledgement of the limits of our understanding of our tools, systems and networks.[54] It encourages an exploration of unintended consequences, tipping points, complex systems. It encourages an examination of the potential impacts on other people of the ways in which we manage, circulate and control the information flows central to our networks. An education for responsibility means, therefore, seeing our developing socio-technical knowledge as the product of choices and intentions rather than as a disembodied inevitable and unstoppable force.

Such an education would usefully manifest itself in a reflection upon the school as a data, information and knowledge producing entity. What choices does the school make about how its information resources are sourced, circulated and stewarded? What are the implications of such choices for different students, for their communities? How might the school become, in turn, a knowledge commons that is stewarded and tended by students? In asking these questions, the school has the potential to become a prefigurative space for living ethically and responsibility in our new knowledge environments.

An education system that nurtured these three attributes would not guarantee a trouble-free path towards the future. It would, however, begin to equip our students to participate in society's conversations about that future.

Chapter 5

Mind the gaps

The next two decades raise interesting questions about relationships between adults and children, about relationships between humans and machines, about the ways in which we manage the challenge of radical diversity and information surplus. The debate about the implications of socio-technical change over the coming decades therefore cannot be squeezed into the narrowly instrumental economic debate that has dominated public rhetoric about 'equipping schools for the twenty-first century' to produce 'tomorrow's workforce'. Clearly, there is both more to education and more to the potential contours of social and technological change over the coming decades, than that.

Notwithstanding this broader canvas, however, if we have learned anything from the last few years it is that the economic landscape is also a site of profound (not to say turbulent) change that is critically important for our personal lives, family lives and public services.[1] What's more, work is an important component of wellbeing and a critically important means of building social and economic capital.[2] It is therefore important to explore some of the highly conflicting visions of economic futures that are emerging from contemporary analyses of the relationship between technological and economic change.

In mapping these competing visions of economic futures it becomes clear that the public rhetoric of universal wellbeing in a global knowledge economy is a highly optimistic and increasingly implausible account of the future. The challenge for education and for educators, therefore, is to examine what resources we have at hand and what resources emerging socio-technical developments may offer, to build an alternative, robust and attainable vision of the future that will be sustainable and fair for *all* the students in our communities.

Disaggregating institutions

In 2006 IBM ran a 150,000-person, 104-country, 3-day 'Innovation Jam'. This event was designed to harness the knowledge, expertise and insights of IBM employees and partners to generate new ideas and strategic possibilities for the organization. It invested £10 million in proposals emerging from the event and generated ten new divisions.[3]

IBM's innovation jam is a now famous example of what's become known as 'crowd sourcing', a model of ideas generation and decision-making facilitated by digital technologies to draw large numbers of people into the processes of solving problems, identifying new opportunities or deciding strategies.[4] Companies like IBM may run such crowd-sourcing activities on a spectacular one-off basis. Alternatively, they may embed them as part of their day-to-day working practices (like companies such as Google or Gore who assign employees '10 per cent time' to explore their own ideas, passions and interests).[5] The assumption (and the evidence) being that over the long run, such undirected work will lead to the creation of new products for the business. Whether spectacular or embedded, crowd sourcing is seen as a form of 'edge thinking' that recognizes that hierarchical decision-making processes have significant drawbacks when it comes to scanning the environment for ideas and opportunities. Opening up space for all employees to generate ideas and identify potential opportunities, this approach argues, will allow institutions to be more responsive to rapidly changing environments or customer demands.[6]

This concept of radically democratized creativity acting as a driver for generating economic value has underpinned many accounts of the future of western economies in the context of socio-technical change. These accounts suggest that knowledge and creativity are the new natural resources that have to be tapped by nations, businesses and individuals to ensure economic competitiveness and survival at a time when manufacturing industries will drain to low-income countries.[7] As a consequence, we see a range of industries and organizations engaged in a rapacious search for ideas that, when combined with the capacity of digital technologies to facilitate social networks, has begun to change organizational structures.

In the scientific arena, for example, 'Grand Challenges' are posed in areas where new breakthroughs are needed, and scientists from around the world are encouraged to compete to come up with solutions. The InnoCentive model, developed and spun off by pharmaceutical giant Eli Lilley, is designed to allow scientists to receive recognition and reward by solving problems posed by major corporations. In this model, companies such as Boeing, Proctor & Gamble and others pose their most challenging R&D problems online and anyone registered on the site is free to post their theories or answers (you don't have to be a formally qualified scientist to participate). If responses meet the technical requirements for the challenge (specified up-front), respondents are rewarded with anything between $10k and $1m.[8] The major corporations get to tap into a massively broad base of R&D expertise without keeping it permanently employed; the successful respondents get financial reward, reputation and peer recognition.[9]

Crowd sourcing as a way of drawing on amateurs and volunteers in order to achieve institutional goals has a long history. Shows such as *Crimewatch* in the UK or *America's Most Wanted* in the USA are examples of processes that harness the massive distributed knowledge of the broadcast audience to solve crimes. Arguably, crowd sourcing has much older roots. The eighteenth century, for example, saw a famous competition for a method to calculate longitude at sea. This competition, prompted by numerous sea disasters, led ultimately to the development of the first accurate and reliable chronometers, bringing with them the modern era of synchronous time. More recently, the UK government has again turned to crowd sourcing to tackle a major problem, this time asking for examples of areas where budget savings should be made in response to the deficit (although, interestingly, not asking for examples of areas where budgets should be protected or taxes raised). In these cases, participation is seen as something intrinsically valuable in itself. You are not labouring for institutions and governments, these sites suggest, you are making a social contribution.[10]

The search for ideas is also leading to changing relationships between consumers and producers. The unique or 'leading' consumer, for example, is increasingly held up as a source of ideas and inspiration (think about street fashion blogs for example).[11] At the same time, it is now possible for cash-rich consumers to personalize the products they purchase; drinks consumers can change the images used on bottles, trainer buyers can have them made in the colours and with the stitching that they want. Each affluent individual can create something 'unique' in a world of mass production, as a signifier of taste and distinction.[12] The consumer is playing a role as co-producer of the products and services they buy and bespoke, mass customization is a growing expectation, with the customer playing the role of 'customizer'.[13]

Some businesses are intensifying this process by offering the opportunity not merely to 'customize' individual products, but to get involved in designing them in the first place. As Daren Brabham describes, the Threadless T-shirt company has built a highly successful business on the principle of opening up the design process to 'amateur' designers and consumers. Anyone can post their design for a T-shirt to the 'community' website and participants in that community all rate the designs, flagging up whether they would buy the design or not. The company chooses the most highly rated designs and manufactures them, and the successful designers receive £2000. In similar initiatives, consumers have been invited to create new applications for mobile phones, advertisements for cars, new political posters.[14]

The reconceptualization of the consumer as originator of ideas and services[15] is another way of looking at the growth of social networking applications over the last five years. The economic model here is one in which content is created by users but can be exchanged for economic value by the owners of the services. Facebook, MySpace, Flickr, Del.icio.us are all businesses based around enabling people to create spaces and share information of personal value to their users that can then be used to 'deliver' users' attention to advertisers. Taken one step further, online games worlds and virtual worlds are increasingly being reconfigured as highly sophisticated platforms that allow their players to create a whole range of other services and goods for other participants. These participants are co-creating the environment with the owners of the business. Such co-creation is in evidence in the fanfiction and other fan communities, where participants take the cultural product and use it to create new cultural goods in the form of more stories, costumes, events, expertise, groups and fan products. Similarly, across fields as diverse as consumer protection, music and government information we are seeing the remixing and 'mash-up' of diverse outputs to create new products. And as the boundaries between the organization and its consumers and employees blur, so too do the boundaries around 'the product'. Nothing is finished, nothing is complete, nothing cannot be modified. There is always a possibility for the consumer/producer to contribute and take action, to reshape the product in pursuit of personalization or improvement.

Some 'consumers' are beginning to generate an income from such activities – there are those in virtual and games worlds able to make a profit from the artefacts they create for and in these spaces; there are those winning competitions with their designs and their technical solutions; there are those able to build new services on the back of the core platform.[16] New businesses are also being established that rely on people selling their hobbies or their 'spare' time. iStockphoto, for example, is an online photo bank where amateur photographers attaining a basic level of expertise can post a photograph for potential commercial use; if the image is selected, the photographer gains a share of the proceeds.[17] Other sites monetize people's spare time: the Mechanical Turk from Amazon, for example, farms out tiny micro tasks for individuals, often image identification, that can be done in spare time and which are rewarded with micropayments.[18] In the same vein, but requiring a modicum of training and more substantial time commitments, a new model of 'call centre' is developing where people can sign up to become telesales people 'from the comfort of their own home'.[19]

These new models of working are not clustered only in the creative, cultural and hi-tech sectors, they are beginning to impact fields as conservative as law, as industrial as car manufacturing, as sensitive as healthcare. For businesses and organizations, what these processes do is turn the business from an institution with clear boundaries into a hazy cloud where the consumers and co-producers and regulators and commentators outnumber the 'core' organization, and where the boundaries between employees or consultants, volunteers or players, consumers or contractors are blurred. Surrounding each industry and each product, now, is a corona of other industries built upon the core and generating massive revenues from the contributions and commitment of people who would previously be known as 'consumers', but whose consumption looks increasingly like a form of production.[20] Motivation for work is highly diverse and uneven in these contexts, with some contributing to goals for the greater good, others for the pleasure of participation, others for wages, others for reputation enhancement, others for something to do in their spare time.[21]

In the optimistic analysis of these working practices, it seems that the early promises of a new knowledge economy to radically democratize demands for creativity is being fulfilled. Successful participation in crowd-sourcing activities can lower some barriers to entry to institutions and offer a range of rewards to participants, not only in the form of financial return but in the development of recognition and peer respect that can later be translated into employment or further paid work. This form of work, however, also requires significant personal investment and new capacities. Managing an online reputation becomes a personal 'branding' project, and the individual is responsible for nurturing and developing their own creativity, for keeping their expertise up to date and for scouring the landscape for opportunities to contribute their ideas.

These moves towards the disaggregation of the organization, however, raise difficult questions about how employment rights might be re-imagined in these circumstances.[22] Working practices in which outsourcing is replaced by crowd sourcing, in which temporary working affiliations are developed alongside a smaller core business, are leading to the casualization of employment in many sectors. The rise of the amateur producer, for example, while empowering for those amateurs, poses risks for professionals. Work is being lost to trained professionals not from international competition but by engaging amateurs and users in the economy.

Such changing working practices, particularly in the highly unregulated media industry where they are combined with a narrative in which 'passionate creatives' are understood to work for love as well as for reward, have led to the rise of what Andrew Ross has called 'sacrificial cost–longer hours in pursuit of the satisfying finish, price discounts in return for aesthetic recognition, self-exploitation in response to the gift of autonomy, and dispensability in exchange for flexibility'.[23] The erosion of the boundaries between work and play also opens up the opportunity for the exploitation of domestic life and family time, as digital technologies are used to extend the workplace across time and space.[24] At the same time, some of these models could be seen as the privatization of leisure, the enclosure of passionate fandom or human friendship (via social networks) as a resource for generating income. Such developments raise questions about how to protect the spaces beyond the formal economy that may in fact act as the wellsprings of the creativity that is held at such a high contemporary premium.

Developing 'creative capital' in these contexts requires more, then, than simply nurturing individual creative capacity and imagination. It requires the development of the strategic tools that will allow individuals to identify employment and build a reputation. It requires the development of the capacity to build allegiances and networks in unstable employment conditions, and to develop the capacity to negotiate fair rewards for employment. It requires the capacity to identify new niches and opportunities, and to constantly maintain and update expertise. Developing such creative capital will require a lot of hard work and significant resources of social and economic capital to provide protection during lean times.

Radical polarization

In 2006 Wu Qidi, then Vice Minister of Education for the People's Republic of China, made a speech to an international conference convened to discuss the development of the creative industries in China. In this speech Wu Qidi argued that the creative industries would be playing a major role in enhancing China's international competitiveness and raising the added value of its goods and services. China, like the USA and the EU, was keen not to be seen as the low-wage, low-quality sweatshop of the world. Instead, they wanted to see products produced that were *created* in China, as well as 'made' in China. In rhetoric familiar from the speeches of western politicians, Wu Qidi argued:

> The real wealth of humankind is ideas, knowledge, and creativity – which come from human minds. With the development of the knowledge economy this becomes more evident. Therefore, in order to vigorously promote the knowledge economy we should not only develop new technologies but should energetically develop creative industries. In saying that the resource of creative industries is talented personnel, the fostering of creative talents is key to the development of creative industries.[25]

Since that time, China has invested significantly in developing its own 'creative class', and its cultural creative industries[26] are breathlessly reported as developing apace in the eastern cities of Beijing, Shanghai and Shenzhen, with growth rates reportedly exceeding those of other industries.[27] The same desire to move from production to creation is repeated in a range of other countries. Countries such as South Korea, Singapore, India and Brazil are investing in education, research and innovation to ensure that they are able to generate the high-value jobs that have driven innovation in scientific, technological, manufacturing and media sectors.[28] Now, creative industries from computer games to bio-tech are developing around the world and some countries, such as South Korea, are taking the lead in fields such as game and multimedia design.

The idea that the USA and Europe will be able to ensure economic success by dominating the field of 'knowledge work' and outsourcing manufacturing to low-wage countries, therefore, is becoming increasingly untenable. There is no 'natural' European or US monopoly on creative talent.

Such developments open up to global competition areas of the labour market that had previously been reasonably protected: designers, inventors, researchers and professionals across a range of industries now find themselves in competition with their peers, working for less, across the globe. The idea that there is only so much 'creative' knowledge work to go round is naïve (such activity can also breed new opportunities and activities) and the idea that investment in human creativity, research and innovation is only of competitive economic value also overlooks its potential to enhance the quality of life for everyone.[29] Nonetheless, the development of international competition for high-skills work in a climate of neoliberal free market economics undermines confidence in assumptions about a high-skills, high-wage future.

An important series of studies of major multinational corporations provides insights into the potential future trajectories of such competition.[30] The increasing availability of highly educated creative professionals around the globe, these studies suggest, means that corporations are now beginning to say that they are free to choose 'where to think' when they make decisions about where to locate their headquarters. They are developing global recruitment strategies, looking to universities all around the world for their recruitment. Such a situation of increased competition amongst international workers for high-value jobs ushers in the potential for a global trajectory towards high-skills, low-wage economies, where return on educational investment does not guarantee security and reward (although it should be recognized that it is still essential to avoid dispossession and exclusion).

At the same time, these studies show how working practices in these corporations are also becoming characterized by a form of 'Digital Taylorism' in which previously creative and autonomous work is transformed into a set of software prescripts and packages that can be used to guide workers, regardless of where they are and, increasingly, regardless of their education. We might look to changes in the banking industry to see the implications of such practices. Consider, for example, the changing role of the local business manager in a bank: he is increasingly required to have strong affective and communication skills to build relationships with valued customers, but his freedom to make decisions, respond to local need, creatively invent new solutions to problems or identify opportunities, has been radically curtailed. At the same time, a small but highly autonomous group in central office are able to generate radically new sets of products and services, script these and circulate them around the world as prescriptions for practice.

Based on the observation of a range of multinational corporations, these studies by Phil Brown, Hugh Lauder and David Ashton suggest that the combination of Digital Taylorism and the investment in education and innovation in countries around the world mean that these multinational companies are beginning to make a distinction between a global 'talent' pool and the rest. This global 'talent' is seen as a small group of people, increasingly fought over by businesses, invested in and nurtured, and able to work anywhere around the world. They are contrasted with a second tier of workers, 'the rest', who are still required to demonstrate high-level communication, team-working and personal efficacy skills, but whose autonomy is radically curtailed.

These practices lead to a highly polarized workforce, as Brown and colleagues conclude:

> Those defined as 'top talent' enjoy the benefits of corporate largesse, while the majority find themselves in a positional struggle to reap a return on their investments in higher education, in terms of salaries, pensions, career prospects and quality of working life. This reflects a trend towards 'winner-takes-all' markets. People with similar qualifications in the same occupations, organisations and countries are experiencing increasing polarisation in their career prospects, intensifying the positional competition within the middle classes.[31]

The trajectory towards polarization is echoed by other labour market analyses that see a growth in higher-level managerial and professional jobs, a hollowing out of middle tier occupations and a growth in what are often poorly-paid jobs in areas such as caring, personal service, retail and tourism roles.[32] The gap between a large body of poorly paid labour and a small body of elite global talent seems ever larger.

A number of other factors also intensify this trajectory towards polarization. Geography and mobility, for example, play an important role in making it harder to move up the 'employment ladder'. Cities are increasingly acting as magnets for industry and higher-wage employment.[33] Cities also, however, bring prohibitive housing and transport costs for many. Geography matters most for those with the poorer skills who are less likely to search for and be able to take up jobs over a wide area; if you don't have access to the means of travel, you cannot make the most of jobs being set up a long way away from your home.[34] At the same time, lower-wage entry-level employment is being outsourced to remote suburbs or other countries, making it harder for those with the fewest resources to position themselves where the work they could take on can be found.[35] Geography and gender also intersect. Those with caring responsibilities, often women, may find it harder to compete for jobs if they require travel or relocation. Place also matters in other ways: 'global talent', for example, requires citizenship of a country that is internationally accepted and from which immigration is allowed to the majority of countries in order to guarantee mobility.[36] Without legal citizenship and nominal allegiance to a country, movement between countries is dangerous and precarious. At the same time, countries are policing their borders, building their walls against unwanted citizens, increasingly testing those who enter for their allegiance to the idea of the nation. Geography also shapes access to digital technologies. Rural areas without access to high-speed broadband, for example, are increasingly excluded from participation in certain industries, fuelling even more the drive to employment in cities.

Higher education policy is also sharply contributing to polarization. Research monies are increasingly invested in a smaller set of international super research universities. As a result, the proportion of students who are exposed to opportunities to participate in a rich research-based education necessary for entry into the world of 'top talent' is being restricted. This production of a new university elite is emerging just at the time when the opportunity to access higher education is supposedly being opened up to many more people.[37]

What narratives of the future can reasonably be built upon such contemporary signals about work in these contexts? *The prevailing analysis of these trends points to a highly polarized future.* In this future a large pool of low-wage labour is trapped in an enlarged low-skilled jobs sector, with few opportunities to move out of such work and, when they do, their progress can be small in terms of earnings and short-lived.[38] The middle classes are trapped in high-skills, low-wage competition in increasingly casualized employment in disaggregated institutions. And a small pool of global talent is able to live and work across national boundaries and claim significant rewards. In this future, a significant group of people also fall outside the formal labour market, as both surplus to and ill-equipped for contemporary requirements.[39]

Such a polarization would make it harder for social mobility, let alone social equality, as the occupational ladders that would have provided opportunities for progression are broken by the scale of the gap between 'talent' and 'the rest', and by the increasing insecurity of those in 'the middle' protecting their position.

Such a vision of the future makes claims that investment in education will necessarily lead to secure futures look increasingly implausible. Not only for the large group of children who have long been excluded from the market, but for a much wider group of middle class children and families who will be increasingly insecure in their employment. Low-wage employment, and unemployment in this context, become not a problem of aspiration but a 'demand-side' problem.[40]

Such radical inequalities and increased employment competition and instability have the capacity to erode the social contract, as the poorest people are resented for their perceived 'security' on benefits, while the remainder seek to maintain their work in an increasingly insecure and risky environment.[41] The costs for society of any further erosion of the social contract would be severe. Charles Murray's vision of a 'custodial democracy'[42] and Naomi Klein's analysis of the emergence of neo-liberal 'green zones' around the world,[43] for example, describe trajectories towards segregation, penalization and criminalization of the poorest. Investment in education, fair employment and working rights would be undermined.

Giroux and other commentators argue that this narrative of the future is already visible in contemporary conditions:

> entire populations are now seen as disposable, marking a dangerous moment for the promise of a global democracy. The discourse of liberty, equality and freedom that emerged with modernity seems to have lost even its residual value as the central project of democracy.[44]

Indeed, in 2009 the income gap was at its widest since the 1960s, with 2.9 million children in the UK in poverty.[45]

The costs of intensifying such a polarization would not be borne only by the poorest. Life in the middle would be unpleasant. Ensuring competitive advantage in disaggregated institutions and unstable employment would eat into domestic life, erode family relationships and encourage exploitation of the pharmaceutical and prosthetic augmentations described earlier, as a means of 'keeping up' or 'getting ahead'. For those 'at the top' life in the green zones of the world would be increasingly circumscribed by the need for investment in security and would necessitate a retreat from public life.

Such highly unequal societies are forecast to provide little in the way of positive benefits for anyone. From fields as diverse as economics to child welfare, we are beginning to see the growth of a robust evidence base for the argument that unequal societies are less successful societies. Richard Wilkinson and Kate Pickett, for example, have drawn on sociology, evolutionary psychology and medical statistics to make a persuasive argument that increased relative inequality within nations leads to worsening indicators of a whole range of social ills such as mental illness, murder rates, obesity, crime and violence, life expectancy, rates of imprisonment, and drug use. In other words, the more unequal a society, the more the costs for everyone living in it, and the greater the cost to the state of dealing with these issues.[46] Such criticisms also originate from other sources, who point out the economic cost of failing to tackle rampant social inequalities. The New Economics Foundation and Action for Children, for example, argue that there will be costs of £41 trillion over the next 20 years if the UK fails to address causes of crime, drug abuse and family breakdown.[47] Others point out that the acceptance of massive economic inequality in society fails to acknowledge its psychological costs – such as the one in five UK adults living in debt to try to 'keep up' with their peers, or the third of British families with depression or chronic anxiety.[48]

Such are the futures emerging from a trajectory in which intensified international and intra-national competition for high-status, high-value knowledge economy jobs obscures the wider consideration of the continued demand for ordinary jobs able to pay a living wage for everyone.

Breakdown: the twenty-first-century canyon

There are other commentators, however, who argue that even this forecast of a highly polarized global economy is implausible. It is premised, they argue, upon unsustainable economic growth models that overlook the extent to which the global digital economy is dependent upon limited resources of materials, a stable climate and currently unquantified human relationships of care and stewardship.

The growth models that underpin a global economy are, for example, premised upon continued access to sufficient cheap oil and energy to sustain international transportation of goods and food, a prospect that is increasingly in doubt given the critical uncertainties about how rapid or gradual the decline in oil will be.[49] Alternative energy sources are not expected with confidence to be able to compensate for the decline in the near future; many of them also bring competition for land that will be needed for food production and some bring environmental risks of their own.[50] The global knowledge economy is also premised upon continued access to mineral resources (needed for making digital technologies), that are finite, are already in high demand, are subject to strict controls on supply by nation states and are sometimes only accessible by supporting highly dubious political regimes.[51] The global knowledge economy is also premised upon access to the very basics of life: clean water, reliable food supply and shelter. These are threatened by increased global demand and by inadequate infrastructure investment for adaptation to climate disruption in many of the countries that are currently the manufacturing centres of the globe. The underpinning resources needed to maintain and sustain the material infrastructure of the global digital economy are under threat.[52]

There is also an economic critique of both unchecked market economics and the expectation of continued growth upon which it is premised. These accounts argue that continued growth is dependent upon 'accumulation by dispossession',[53] namely, the exploitation and enclosure for private profit of resources that were previously considered inalienable common or public goods. There are risks in enclosing such goods, as David Bollier argues:

> because market theory postulates that 'wealth' is created when private property rights and prices are assigned to resources, it often has trouble respecting the actual value of inalienable resources. Economists tend to regard market activity and growth as inherently good, when in fact it is often a force for eroding valuable nonmarket resources such as family time, social life and ecosystems.[54]

This erosion of non-market resources can be seen as a potential cause for economic failure, because the formal 'wealth-creating' economy is dependent upon precisely those public non-market resources for its functioning. Neva Goodwin calls these non-market resources the 'core' economy, the non-monetary economy of care, contribution and support. This includes the currently unquantified cost of child-rearing, of caring for the elderly, of maintaining and stewarding neighbourhoods. All of these are currently not built into the calculations of the formal economy. Yet without this core economy, the formal economy cannot function. Without this core economy, the costs to business of breakdown and disarray are unsustainable.[55] A model of growth that relies on the erosion of the core economy resources of time, family and human relationships is, in these accounts, unsustainable.

On the basis of these and other analyses, one leading international think tank[56] has explored a set of divergent future pathways for the coming century in a search for strategic alternatives. One of the pathways they present describes the implications of failing to challenge the trajectory towards increased polarization and environmental degradation. This pathway envisages a transition from contemporary society to a period of profound social upheaval and disruption caused by the interplay between population growth, population ageing, energy and resource constraints, conflict, climate disruptions and technological change. These disruptions, they argue, may lead to global breakdown, characterized by pervasive conflict and crisis; or a fortress world scenario, in which a form of global apartheid exists, with elites in protected enclaves surrounded by an impoverished majority. The following, taken from the GSG group's 'Fortress world' narrative, gives an indication of how such a pathway might unfold:

> As the level of poverty increases and the gulf between rich and poor widens, development aid continues to decline. The remnants of the institutional capacity and moral commitment to global welfare are lost. Meanwhile, environmental conditions deteriorate. Multiple stresses – pollution, climate change, ecosystem degradation – interact and amplify the crisis. Disputes over scarce water resources feed conflict in regions with shared river basins. Environmental degradation, food insecurity and emergent diseases foster a vast health crisis.

Tantalized by media images of opulence and dreams of affluence, the excluded billions grow restive. Many seek emigration to affluent centers by any means necessary. Criminal activity thrives in the anarchic conditions, with some powerful global syndicates able to field fearsome fighting units in their battle against international policing activities. A new kind of militant – educated, excluded and angry – fans the flames of discontent. The poison of social polarization deepens. Terrorism resurges, escalating from waves of suicide attacks at popular gatherings and on symbols of globalism, to use of biological and nuclear weapons.

In this atmosphere of deepening social and environmental crisis, conflict feeds off old ethnic, religious and nationalist tensions. Poor countries begin to fragment as civil order collapses and various forms of criminal anarchy fill the vacuum. Even some of the more prosperous nations feel the sting as infrastructure decays and technology fails. The global economy sputters and international institutions weaken, while the bite of climate change and environmental devastation grows fiercer. The affluent minority fears it too will be engulfed by rampant migration, violence and disease. The global crisis spins out of control.

The forces of global order take action. International military, corporate, and governance bodies, supported by the most powerful national governments, form the self-styled Alliance for Global Salvation. Using a revamped United Nations as their platform, a state of planetary emergency is declared. A campaign of overwhelming force, rough justice and draconian police measures sweeps through hot spots of conflict and discontent. With as-needed military and reconstruction support from the Alliance, local forces, nearly everywhere are able to subdue resistance and impose stability backed by international peacekeeping units.

A system of global dualism – some call it a Fortress World, others Planetary Apartheid – emerges from the crisis. The separate spheres of the haves and have-nots, the included and excluded, are codified in asymmetrical and authoritarian legal and institutional frameworks. The affluent live in protected enclaves in rich nations and in strongholds in poor nations – bubbles of privilege amidst oceans of misery. In the police state outside the fortress, the majority is mired in poverty and denied basic freedoms. The authorities use high-tech surveillance and old-fashioned brutality to control social unrest and migration, and to protect valued environmental resources. The elite have halted barbarism at their gates and enforced a kind of environmental management and uneasy stability.[57]

These analyses suggest a need to rebalance discussions about the implications of socio-technical change for the future economy. They suggest that our future economic strategies should not only rely upon knowledge and service industries, dependent upon global economic production and cheap manufacturing. Instead, we need to look at how to build the industries that will underpin adaptation to changing environmental conditions; we need to invest in the agricultural production and research that will allow us to feed a growing population in a depleted environment; we need to develop a new infrastructure that will support families and societies to care well and to reward care for our elderly and our children; and we need economic activity that builds the resilience of local communities and that enhances social solidarity rather than polarization. This is not an argument for a return to unthinking localism; the problems of food and water supply and of carbon reduction are, after all, global and unlikely to be addressed by disconnected local activity. Global digital networks also provide important resources for social movements. Instead, it is an argument to reintroduce the material conditions necessary for our continued existence and the human and environmental conditions required for wellbeing into our narratives of future economic activity. It is an argument to re-integrate materiality into our narratives of socio-technical futures.

Building living futures

The vision of global breakdown and planetary apartheid, while plausible, is not inevitable. Instead, organizations such as the Tellus Institute who produced the Global Scenarios, along with other researchers, activists, politicians and economists around the world, are seeking to build more hopeful alternatives.[58]

One of the foundations for building alternatives is an attempt to rethink what might lead to real wellbeing if economic wealth is seen as an unhelpful indicator of future sustainability and security. Increasingly, there is a new common sense emerging as a body of research begins to show that wellbeing beyond a basic level of income depends not on more money, but upon lasting relationships, good health, exercise, education, good relationships with children, community, friends, faith and sex.[59] This approach does not imply that you can simply 'think' yourself happy (as some of the derivative self-help books would have you believe); rather it seeks to reposition money as only one part of the many factors that make up a good life and only one of the measures of wellbeing.[60] It seeks to address what Robert Kennedy described in 1968 as the failure of accounting systems to account for what makes life worthwhile:

> The Gross National Product counts air pollution and cigarette advertising, and ... the destruction of the redwood and the loss of our natural wonder in chaotic sprawl .... Yet [it] does not allow for the health of our children, the quality of their education, or the joy of their play ... the beauty of our poetry or the strength of our marriages ... it measures everything, in short, except that which makes life worthwhile.[61]

This perspective is being appropriated, at least rhetorically, in policy and industry circles. As the personal and public costs of the desperate and unprincipled scramble for profit and easy credit that underpinned the economic meltdown of the last couple of years have become visible, politicians and businesses are seeking to position the search for profit in its wider context. Consider, for example, the views of Adair Turner, head of the UK Financial Services Authority:

> If you spend your time thinking that the most important objective of public policy is to get growth up from 1.9 percent to 2 percent and even better 2.1

percent we're pursuing a sort of false god there. We're pursuing it first of all because if we accept that, we will do things to the climate that will be harmful, but also because all the evidence shows that beyond the sort of standard of living which Britain has now achieved, extra growth does not automatically translate into human welfare and happiness.[62]

These ideas are being picked up in the 'conscious capitalism' movements that seek to recognize that the responsibility of business is not merely to its shareholders, but also to the communities and ecosystems within which it works. Such ideas also underpin commitments to work–life balance and to 'corporate social responsibility'. This rhetoric opens up the possibility of holding policymakers and businesses to account against their stated values. These ideas are also beginning to underpin educational programmes designed to educate the next generation of business leaders.[63]

Beyond rhetoric, new ways of measuring value, new economic practices and new experiments in sustainable living are being explored. National governments are being encouraged to introduce new accountability systems that include in economic value an assessment also of the costs to the 'core economy' and the environment in production processes. Legislation such as the European Union's Waste Electrical and Electronic Equipment Directive, for example, requires manufacturers of electric and electronic goods to be legally responsible for their products throughout their life cycle, embedding the principle of 'polluter pays' into the economic principles of the sector. In contrast to the technocratic solutions of the European Union, Bhutan is exploring the possibility of measuring not GDP, but Gross Domestic Happiness as a benchmark for government success. The New Economic Foundation has developed a mechanism for national accounts of wellbeing that can be used to assess personal and social wellbeing at a national level, offering a practical and achievable alternative to GDP as a measure of a country's 'wealth'.[64] Such ideas are becoming increasingly mainstream; in November 2010, for example, the UK coalition government followed the 2008 example set by Nicolas Sarkozy in France by announcing its intention to develop a national index of wellbeing.

The idea that countries and people are irretrievably locked into competitive relations with each other is also being questioned by new economic analyses. These foreground the relationships between cities' participation in knowledge industries and their industrial and agricultural roots. These roots, as economist Saskia Sassen has demonstrated, serve to give different cities distinctive sets of expertise and skills. Such distinctiveness means that cities can see themselves not necessarily as global competitors, but as potential allies in the process of negotiating with global business; there is a basis for cities to work together rather than compete with each other.[65]

Other analysts have demonstrated how even the most impoverished communities have (in aggregate) significant financial resources and that their unmet retail demands could be seen as a basis for significantly improving urban neighbourhoods by bringing in investment, providing training and creating jobs for local people.

Alongside these we are seeing the emergence of living wage movements that seek to ensure that work is repaid with the financial reward sufficient for dignity and family wellbeing. In some cities, businesses that do not adhere to this goal are not rewarded with any public contracts.[66]

There are some indications also of a generational change in attitudes to work, with more young people reporting that they work to live, rather than live to work,[67] placing work in a subordinate position to the rest of life. Other reasons for work are also becoming visible,[68] in particular in networks such as open source communities. Participants in these networks may be hobbyists who have full-time jobs already, but who enjoy working on the particular challenges presented, seek to participate in the networks of exchange and ideas that surround the challenges, and enjoy and benefit from the collaborative learning that develops in tackling problems.[69] Arguably, one of the benefits of participation in these sorts of community is simply gaining the right to participate in these networks, of being inside rather than outside, of benefiting from the enhanced speed of communication about problems, ideas, opportunities that are circulating quickly within this network as compared with being outside it. Participation can also confer other benefits as the networks help to confer legitimacy on ideas that circulate within them and to de-legitimize those ideas that remain outside.[70] These networks make visible the other benefits to work, beyond the monetary.

Organizations that seek to create benefit for members and value to the community rather than shareholder profit are gaining strength in the wake of dissatisfaction with traditional financial services and industry ownership models. Social and co-operative enterprise is growing rapidly around the world.[71] The co-operative movement, for example, has a turnover of £28 billion and includes such famous household names as the retail giant John Lewis. In the UK social enterprise is estimated to have a combined turnover of £24 billion a year.[72] In the USA, co-operative projects are playing a big role in developing sustainable energy infrastructure: one co-operative community wind project costs £360 million and powers 38,000 homes, for example, while other smaller-scale businesses are owned by farmers and community members and provide the power needs of their local towns.[73] Micro-finance and Village Bank systems are also being used to build solidarity across different communities and to empower grassroots community-beneficial enterprise.[74] Such social enterprises are also beginning to colonize neglected areas of cities and to bring new economic life and activity to the buildings and infrastructure left behind in the collapse of manufacturing activity. Tempelhof airport in Berlin, for example, once the largest building in the world apart from the Pentagon, is now being taken over by social enterprise, community and grass-roots businesses.[75] This is a non-trivial movement that is beginning to locate care for its workers and responsibility for community and ecosystem at the heart of viable businesses.

Efforts to develop local economies that are less reliant on global transportation systems and that promote low-carbon living are developing. The import replacement model advocated by Jane Jacobs, for example, which seeks to produce with local goods and local labour those products which are currently being imported, both seeks to avoid the offshoring of exploitation just as it seeks to promote sustainable, robust and vital regional economies.[76] The Transition Towns movement and Dark Mountain projects are seeking to model new approaches to local economies that are fit for post-oil contexts by building long-term strategies for food, energy, transport, employment and health policies that are not dependent upon fossil fuels. Perhaps most subversively, they seek to argue that happiness is not dependent wholly upon our current surfeit of material goods and that it may be possible to live a good life without them.[77]

These developments are being matched by calls for political and democratic reform, and by the search for new strategies to ensure accountability and good governance. New democratic economic decision-making processes, such as collaborative budgeting practices that enable citizens to achieve power over significant economic decisions at local levels, are being developed.[78] And local activities are being linked together to form international networks such as the World Social Forum, established in 2001 to act as a competitor to the Global Economic Forum held each year in Davos. In these processes the capacity of digital networks to bring many more people into decision-making are being exploited.

These developments constitute new knowledge about the relationship between economics and ecosystems, constitute new viable models for economic structures that sustain human wellbeing, and constitute new democratic practices to ensure that the formal economy is located within its wider ecological and human context. They are by no means 'finished' economic and social models, but they map out what might be strategic waypoints towards the building of equitable and sustainable futures.

Education intervening in economic futures

In the introduction to this book I said that I wanted to ask whether the orthodox future of an ever-expanding global knowledge economy is sufficiently rich or robust to act as a basis for redesigning education systems today. I hope that my discussions in this chapter, and in the previous chapters, make clear that it is not.

As I have already discussed, the orthodox future does not prepare us for the choices we may have to make about how and whether we wish to augment our intelligence and play with our identities. It provides us with no guidance for building intergenerational relationships of care and no basis for ethical debate about the socio-technical systems we are beginning to build. It does not equip us to protect our emerging knowledge resources nor prepare us to exploit them. And in the area in which it claims most authority to speak – its economic imagination – it assumes a magical solution to the self-evident problems of energy scarcity, climate warming and global inequalities, while assuming that other social structures such as international financial systems and cultures of competition are too robust to change. In short, the orthodox future we are using as a basis for designing our education systems at present is a myopic, largely implausible and highly selective vision of the future.

If education continues to allow its assumptions about the future to be dominated by this vision of a global knowledge economy, and to see its role as preparing students to take up their assigned places within it, there are real risks. *The risks are that schools will be preparing students for a future of radical inequality that offers desirable futures for only a small elite and sustainable futures for no one.*

If this is not to be the case, we need to put aside our fingers-crossed optimism that things will work out, and our pessimistic cynicism that things cannot get better, and begin to work out how schools can act as sites to intervene in these futures. We need to work out how schools can act as resources for their students to imagine and build alternative futures that offer real hope of viable and sustainable ways of living.

First, the school needs to act as a public space for students, teachers and communities to participate in a conversation about the sorts of future that are in development. It needs to become a place where people can come together and examine what the trajectories for their communities and their children might be. It needs to build the capacity of individuals and communities to critique, challenge and contest the visions of the future they are presented with and to advocate for better alternatives. It needs to be a place where schools and communities talk together about how they can in concert nudge these trajectories in the direction of more sustainable and equitable futures.[79]

Secondly, the school needs to set aside the illusion that it is a purely academic 'non-economic zone'. It needs to recognize that large numbers of young people, far from being non-economic beings, are already involved in some form of work. They are already active consumer/producers and need tools to think about and reflect upon that activity.[80] It also needs to examine how the school itself can become an engine for sustainable economic development in its own area of influence. It needs to examine its own purchasing and employment practices and explore whether these can be reconfigured to promote sustainable and equitable economic activity in its own community.[81] The school, most importantly, needs to open up to its students the possibility of intervening in and shaping their own working futures, whether this means making informed decisions about educational and career trajectories based upon robust labour market information, giving students the opportunity to set up their own social enterprises or participate in real crowd-sourcing, or equipping students with the knowledge and understanding needed to create the 'green' or caring industries that can drive new economic trajectories. In these ways, schools can act today as powerful resources for intervening in socio-economic futures.

Over the longer term the school needs to rewrite its relationship with the future. It needs to see itself not as preparing students for futures designed elsewhere, but as equipping students to critically examine the stories about the future they are being sold, and to build their capacity to create futures that they, and their communities, might want to inhabit. The school needs to become a laboratory for building sustainable economic and social futures.

Chapter 6

Networks, collectives and crowds

As I start to write this chapter I am aware of a bigger conversation going on around me. Scrolling down the screen of my phone are short messages and exchanges from about a hundred colleagues, friends and strangers. As the messages flow down the screen, I see today's patterns of debate, advice, gossip and outrage forming. There are the gentle aftershocks from last night's discussion about education policy still bubbling with final comments or last-minute suggestions for follow-up;[1] there is a new strand of comment coalescing around the government's decision to use Facebook to encourage public sector workers to make suggestions for cuts; there are calls to sign petitions, send messages, provide help, give advice; there are suggestions of books, conferences, gigs, events and websites. There is a broiling, bubbling world of anger, excitement, generosity and exchange. And there are bad puns, dodgy jokes and spam.

Twitter is just one of the many 'networked publics'[2] in which people are beginning to participate in conversations about their futures. These new public spaces are beginning to play a role in the election of presidents and the support of opposition regimes, in the development of local civic society and the spreading of gossip. And in these spaces, new forms of democratic engagement are developing that are very different from the models of representative democracy that we have come to be familiar with over the last two centuries.

Such spaces create the impression of an open public sphere and hold out the possibility of collective agency at a time when such capacities are being eroded in the real world. Whether such a possibility is fully realized or not, whether such a space can come to involve more than a small percentage of the population, and whether the screams of anger and shoots of optimism that are expressed here will effect change in the physical world in which harm, injustice and violence is done to people and ecosystems, however, remains uncertain.

These emerging networked publics and the related tools to support accountability, social movement building and democracy that are developing today are important developments for schools to consider for three reasons. First, these spaces constitute a new site for citizenship. Therefore, schools need to ensure that all their students have access to the resources and to the competencies to allow them to participate in such spaces. To fail to do so is to fail to equip students for contemporary democratic practice. Secondly, such tools offer new resources to enable schools themselves to effect change; they offer resources for movement building, opinion shaping, accountability and representation that would equip schools and their communities to advocate for themselves. If schools are to act as powerful advocates for their communities, knowing how and when to manipulate such resources will be important. Finally, schools themselves are places in which students learn what it means to 'do democracy'. The ways in which new technologies are used in the school to silence or to empower, to control or to engage, has the potential not only to structure the quality of public space in schools, but to shape student expectations about how democratic practice and civic engagement should play out in the socio-technical spaces of the twenty-first century.

New public spaces

At a time when our real world public spaces are being increasingly enclosed by private ownership (the shift from the marketplace to the mall)[3] and when many young people's access to public space is being limited to traversal by car between sanctioned pockets of 'safety',[4] the social spaces of the online world are becoming increasingly important sites for the development of social and civic identities. danah boyd, Christine Greenhow, Julia Davies, Guy Merchant, Mimi Ito, Henry Jenkins and many others have all made visible how participation in online communities constitutes participation in new public spaces. These spaces, whether 'hanging around' at the edges of eBay, shouting abuse in 4Chan, gossiping in Facebook or playing games in World of Warcraft, are spaces where participants work out what it means to engage with others, to explore and develop identities through encounters with others, to negotiate shared values and rules of collective behaviour. Online spaces are becoming increasingly important places where we can explore what it means to live with other people.

These spaces allow for new forms of self-representation and new ways of telling stories about ourselves and our lives. We can represent ourselves through our choice of photos, images, links and friends. We can create alter-egos, 'avatars', to represent us in games worlds and in virtual spaces such as Second Life. These self-representations can be faithful reproductions of ourselves or radically different animal, mechanical or fantasy projections of our imagination. Through virtual worlds or online games worlds, millions of people are becoming used to designing and operating digital characters as representations of themselves in online spaces. The figures are surprisingly high – in 2008 there were already over 350 million avatars (more than the population of the USA). And just as young people's access to public space has declined, their participation in online space and in virtual worlds has massively expanded. Forecasts are that by 2011 50 per cent of all children in countries with accessible broadband will be creating avatars and participating in virtual worlds.[5] Already today, as Victoria Carrington and Jackie Marsh argue, 'a new generation is growing up in an era and culture where it is normal social practice to design and deploy an avatar (or many) in a range of online worlds'.

Such identities can be inhabited playfully, fleetingly, as temporary explorations of alternative possibilities of the self, changed as frequently as a hairstyle or a mode of dress. Alternatively, such identities in games worlds or virtual worlds can be sustained and developed over years and can represent significant emotional investment.[6] Guild leaders in the massively multiplayer online games worlds, for example, can feel themselves as responsible for their guilds, their success and the people within them as any manager of a national sports team (or more). These identities are far from trivial; they are also sites of significant and serious investment of time and money. That they are sites of such investment is evidenced by the emergence of 'goldfarming' sweatshops, where workers are paid to play games for hours on end to gain in-game rewards (game money or artefacts) that can then be sold to other players for a profit online.[7] As such spaces are appropriated for work, some commentators have suggested that the capacity they offer to produce new representations of ourselves will see us all increasingly 'dressing' ourselves as middle-class, middle-aged white men in suits.[8] The current predilection for fairy wings and gothic accessories in Second Life and other similar persistent online worlds, however, might suggest the opposite.

The online space is also providing a new arena for testing out familiar off-line rituals and tools of civic participation. Social network spaces teem with voting systems and rankings, with discussions about whether people should be allowed in or kept out of online communities because of their unacceptable behaviour. Second Life, for example, has witnessed tax riots; World of Warcraft has seen gamers (subsequently banned from the game) organize demonstrations;[9] and Wikipedia is involved in a seemingly endless formal discussion about the different levels of authority that can be claimed by bureaucrats or newbies.[10] In many of these spaces, the boundaries between commercial and the civic are increasingly blurred; 'civic' leadership in online spaces, for example, may be combined with a role as brand advocate and evangelist, while voting and feedback systems designed to enhance the community are also functioning as a means of harvesting commercially useful information.[11]

Social networking sites or online interest groups, massively multiplayer online games or fansites, all have the potential to act as 'first publics'[12] for those who are new to participation in public, whether young or old. They have the capacity to serve as places in which people can begin to test out their public voice and ideas, they can explore what it means to 'speak' in a more public domain. They offer a new scale for activity that mediates between the personal world and the public sphere.

These spaces need therefore to be understood as important resources for practising democracy; they are, in danah boyd's terms, new 'networked publics' that are growing increasingly important. They are emerging just as traditional resources for identity formation, such as the workplace, the family, the faith group or the local community, may also be becoming less stable and more complex.[13]

Such developments imply that we need to recognize that the public spaces of the coming century will not only be the physical spaces of our cities and our schools, but the fantastic spaces of our games worlds, the new commercial spaces of online malls and the hybrid sites of our social networks. We need to learn what it means to nurture democratic practices in these spaces, just as we do in the day-to-day lives offline. And if we want to effect social and economic change we need to explore what social activism might mean in these spaces, just as we need to reinvigorate such activism in the public spaces of our city streets.[14]

Potential tools for social change

The contemporary digital landscape offers a set of powerful tools for real world action in the hands of expert user-activists. These range from tools that allow citizens to hold the powerful to account, to strategies that enable the creation of new forms of economic exchange. All of these are critical if we are seeking to support our students to intervene in and improve the quality of the public conversation about the sorts of future they will inhabit.

Citizen journalism

The rise of a body of citizen journalists, able to gather information and circulate it widely outside the restrictions of the traditional broadcast media, is seen by many cultural scholars as offering the potential to reshape the quality of public debate. Now that 'the people' are equipped with cameras in their phones, oppression and corruption, it is suggested, will be harder to sustain. Howard Rheingold, for example, reports that in the USA investigative bloggers helped to uncover information about and break the story of covert surveillance of students and citizens.[15] In the UK, the death of an innocent bystander after being pushed over by a policeman during riots was captured on mobile phone and prompted the subsequent investigation and scandal. Citizen journalism has supported the production of alternative accounts of contemporary events: webzines in Korea were responsible for tipping the balance in presidential elections.[16] The news-site Indymedia came into being out of the need of anti-globalization protesters to share information, news and updates about their demonstrations against the WTO at Seattle. Similar needs for self-organization and communication led to new media spaces to support the anti-Iraq War movements in 2003, and the Copenhagen Climate Summit in 2009.[17] The rise of citizen journalism and user-generated content has been called the rise of the 'fifth estate': a distributed public commons producing its own complex, contradictory and powerful accounts of the world.[18]

Traditional broadcast media, however, still remain an important mechanism for directing and focusing public attention. A co-evolution of broadcast and online is developing in which they are dependent upon and shape each other. Broadcast events such as election debates can act as a focal point for bringing people together for online comment and discussion. At the same time, the social media space and citizen journalism can surface information and ideas that feed the broadcast news; they can also act as a site for correcting and augmenting broadcast content.[19] Such developments, as Jenkins argues, may lead to a mixed media landscape:

> Ultimately, our media future could depend on the kind of uneasy truce that gets brokered between commercial media and collective intelligence. Imagine a world where there are two kinds of media power: one comes through media concentration, where any message gains authority simply by being broadcast on network television; the other comes through collective intelligence, where a message gains visibility only if it is deemed relevant to a loose network of diverse publics. Broadcasting will place issues on the national agenda and define core values. Grassroots media will reframe those issues for different publics and ensure that everyone has a chance to be heard. Innovation will occur on the fringes; consolidation in the mainstream. But that makes it all sound a little too orderly, since in our transitional moment, the power relations between these forces are being fought over amid much namecalling and acrimony.[20]

Such a mixed media landscape may lead to new forms of public debate in which broadcast media are routinely augmented with calls for action and mobilization of the 'fifth estate'.

Projects such as the BBC 'ICAN' and Channel4's 'Battlefront' have specifically begun to mobilize young people's social networking activities as a resource for building social action and information sharing in a manner that diverges radically from the 'objective informing' principles familiar from the twentieth century.[21]

Making information legible

The second important tool for social change is the growing capacity to collate, analyse and represent vast amounts of information in ways that allow it to be more easily visualized and interrogated.

The Open Data City/Open Government movement is growing across the world. This movement sees information as a public utility and requires local governments to make their data publicly available in machine readable forms in order to allow anyone to reuse that information for their own purposes. The consequence of this is that this data becomes available for developers, programmers and activists to analyse and to produce new representations of the world. This might see some developers creating programs that would allow easy comparison of air pollution results with public transport routes with childhood asthma. This might mean developing programs that would allow the visualization of economic spending decisions against the special interests declared by local politicians. This might mean mapping crime statistics against education results against private sector investment. Such capacity for combining data carries risks – what stereotypes and assumptions will inform which datasets should be combined? It also brings opportunities for citizen-programmers and developers to collaborate in building new mental maps of cities that can be accessible on mobile phones or websites for anyone to interrogate with only limited technical skills. The huge potential of such facility is visible in the Worldmapper website, which uses data from governments around the world to create clear visualizations and comparisons of trends from education, to investment, to mortality.[22]

As citizens are increasingly able to annotate their cities – either intentionally by leaving digital records and comments about different places, or implicitly through the data trails they produce as they walk around a city – even more data becomes available for analysis. The invisible city is made visible, and being made visible, it can be analysed to provide new accounts of contemporary circumstances.[23] Such analysis is being used as the foundation for developing public policy, for enabling citizens to act as informed participants in negotiating planning, health and educational decisions, for equipping community groups with the information needed to initiate change. Indeed, public space in cities from San Francisco to Berlin to Tokyo are being uncovered, reclaimed, pluralized and transformed as groups use open data, digital mapping and collective intelligence tools to make visible alternative possible futures for city spaces.[24] The ability to collate data, to generalize beyond the particular experience and to do so on an ongoing basis, opens up the potential for the creation of powerful knowledge about the conditions that structure our lived experiences.

New models of accountability

Personalized, mobile and networked devices combined with infinitely cheap data storage also begin to open up new accountability, scrutiny and reporting practices. It becomes cheap and easy to capture information (videos, photographs, documentary records, speeches, people's physical location, noise levels, chemical make-up). It becomes cheap and easy to circulate that information (through blogs, wikis, YouTube and social networks). It also becomes cheap and easy to review that information (as it is saved and recorded for comparison at a later date if the archiving systems are in place). These practices open up new ways of holding those in power to account. Public statements of intent can be reviewed years later, inconsistencies in position and hypocrisies more easily exposed, as the mass of public data can be easily searched and drawn up for later analysis. Statements can be tested against reality. Citizens can use these new tools to demand new standards of accountability, reciprocity and collaboration.[25]

Such techniques of accountability can challenge old power relationships and underpin new ones. Sites like RateMyTeachers, for example, allow students to post comments about their teachers and their experience of education in a public forum. This has been resisted by a number of teaching unions in the UK, who see this as opening up the profession to unjustified attack and see it as a new frontline in an increasingly hostile relationship between teachers and students.[26] Councils like Lewisham in London, in contrast, have harnessed these new tools as a way of involving citizens in civic activity: the LoveLewisham site, for example, allows anyone to post photographs of problems in their local area, and the council uses this to alert them to issues; they then post their response to the problem online. These tools are providing the basis for a new language to describe citizen–government relationships, as one UK Minister argued:

> The time for a one-way stream of communication from Government to the people has gone. The way we interact is now much more complex – it's not even just two-way with the customer providing feedback – it is a multi-layered web of mutual support, customer led service development, and a completely new view of Government as enabler not controller.[27]

Aggregating individual actions

Many commentators argue that the real power of social media tools for social change is that they allow people to easily coordinate actions and work together. Clay Shirky argues that such ease of coordination through social media acts as an outlet for a human instinct for generosity.[28] He points to Facebook campaigns that have enabled women to come together to reclaim their right to participate freely in public spaces in India in the face of religious sexism. He points to patients' groups where individuals freely share their personal data in order to enhance scientific understanding about their conditions. He points to carpooling schemes in Canada where relationships of trust have been built up to allow people to create new transport systems.

While it is clear that it isn't the technical systems themselves that 'make' these social movements happen, they do offer the potential to aggregate the small and seemingly inconsequential actions of hundreds of thousands of individuals. The PledgeBank site is probably the clearest example of the capacity we now have to easily mobilize collective action at a micro-scale. The site is simply a space where an individual can commit to taking an action (writing to an MP, knitting a sock for charity, cleaning up a city street) if a certain number of others also sign up to commit to such an action. This isn't thousands of individuals committing their lives to revolution, but it is, as Shirky calls it, hundreds of thousands of individuals committing their 'cognitive surplus', their underused time and energy, to civic action.

The power of individuals working together can be harnessed, through these mechanisms, without requiring such collaboration to be simultaneous, geographically co-located or institutionally structured. Social media lower the threshold for action and participation, they enable individuals to aggregate their actions and amplify the impact of any one choice, and they support the intelligent co-ordination of activity – reducing duplication of effort, encouraging shared activity around shared agendas or objectives. As such, they offer a new form of political organizing, organized around campaigns and specific achievable goals rather than the grand narratives of political and institutional affiliation.

Bypassing traditional institutions

Democratic educators Ivan Illich and Paulo Freire suggested in the 1960s that individuals and communities might be well served by the creation of structures that would allow individuals to find 'peers' from and with whom they might learn rather than relying on their education being mediated via institutions such as the church and school.[29] The development of networked digital technologies to enable people to self-organize fluidly outside traditional institutions is particularly in evidence in relation to the development of new funding models for social organizations. Kiva, for example, is an organization that allows individuals to bypass the traditional mediating role of banks. This microfinance website allows individuals to lend small sums of money to other specific named individuals across the world, many in developing countries. As of 2009, Kiva had facilitated over $100m in loans.[30]

Such an approach is premised upon the idea that individuals can help each other, that individuals have skills, expertise, ideas and resources, and that the challenge in initiating social change is not one of overcoming deficits in aspiration and capacity, but in building systems that allow people to connect with each other without having to rely on what are seen as overly conservative mediating institutions.

Tools for decision-making and legislating

New strategies for consensus-based decision-making are also evolving where creative digital tools are being picked up by social activist communities. Formats such as Open Space, BarCamp and Unconference events see participants develop their own agenda on the day, self-organize into groups who are able to work together, and share ideas openly and freely.[31] In these events, everyone is expected to participate, everyone is expected to listen. New tools for deliberative decision-making are being developed that overcome the weaknesses of majority voting and instead support participants to share their ideas whatever their 'status' in the group, and encourage others to build upon and develop these.[32]

Such exchanges can be combined with resources such as Fablabs, where communities have access to programming and rapid prototyping tools that allow ideas to be turned rapidly into usable products to demonstrate what the next steps for action might be, or to showcase alternatives. In Arjun Appadurai's 'democratic research' approach, for example, communities build powerful prototypes of small-scale interventions that make a big difference, and these are used as a basis for changing policy decisions.[33]

A participatory design approach is also beginning to be applied to the processes of governing: 'Wiki' government, for example, is being used to allow citizens to analyse, comment upon and redraft legislation, while participatory budgeting tools enable citizens to comment upon and make suggestions for public expenditure and taxation. Such processes have the potential to erode the distinctions inherent in representative democracy between government and governed, between those with the right to act and those who are acted upon.

As we enter the second decade of the twenty-first century, then, there are new resources for building social movements, pooling resources and holding people to account. There are new public spaces in which to create allegiances and identities. There are new mechanisms for decision-making, designing new policies and collaborating to achieve them. For educators seeking to support students and communities to participate in society's conversations about the future, these are potentially powerful new tools.

False democracies

And yet, there are risks in the more celebratory accounts of the potential of our new digital tools to generate positive social change over the next two decades, not least because there still remain profound economic, educational and cultural barriers to participation in these practices. In 2010 the UK was far from a society of universal internet access and use: 9 million adults in the UK had never accessed the internet; only 73 per cent of households had internet access and fewer had broadband. This access was patterned according to socio-economic status and education, with nearly 95 per cent of adults under 70 with a degree or equivalent having internet access compared with 52 per cent of those with no formal qualifications. In the USA, 74 per cent of adults had internet access at home, with even more extreme differences in access depending upon education; only 39 per cent of those without a high school diploma were accessing the internet. Access to these spaces is also premised, in the large majority of cases, upon the ability to read and write in order to make your voice heard; and access to literacy is patterned by educational, social and financial capital.[34]

When we look at figures for active participation in digital spaces, we also find that only a limited percentage of people are currently involved in the sorts of active production that capture headlines about new forms of digital citizenship – uploading images, videos, blogging and commenting.[35] Even amongst young people, who are commonly seen to be spearheading the development of online social networks, such rich participation is far from common and the indications are that it is those who are already socially active and engaged offline who are most effectively making their voices heard.[36] The democracy that these digital tools offer at present, therefore, does not overcome the long-standing failure of public space to engage the voices of the poorest and most vulnerable in society. Moreover, the tools that can be harnessed to share information and build allegiances by social activists and campaigners can also be used by those who would suppress opposition and democratic debate. Already there is evidence of social networking tools and recording devices being used in a retaliatory fashion by governments, to gain forewarning about protests and to document who is participating, in ways that lead, subsequently, to further constraints and surveillance.[37]

The quality of participation in networked publics and therefore their capacity to promote meaningful social change is also contested. The ease with which individuals can ally themselves to a cause, and the limited commitment required from such a process, may turn political engagement into a form of lifestyle accessory. Group allegiances and social concerns can become garnishes added to online profiles as part of what Willets calls the 'compulsory individuality' of digital cultures, 'where the freedom to express oneself becomes a requirement, which then allows identities to be managed and regulated'.[38] Participation in online discussions can become participation in an echo chamber as views are reflected back, validated and amplified by friendship networks. Twenty-four-hour social media may provide spaces for feedback and citizen journalism, but they also fuel a demand for novelty and a retreat from a politics of explanation and responsibility. In this political culture, a shorthand politics emerges in which an individual's character comes to stand for his position, and scandal politics focused on the destruction of character and reputation are born.[39]

In place of sustained and committed civic engagement, digital spaces can encourage instant reactions and rapid responses. Such engagement is only surplus time and energy. It cannot be mistaken for the sorts of difficult commitment of resource and energy that, for example, some religious groups might require, demanding a tenth of your income and a significant investment of your time.[40] It also cannot be equated with the difficult business of learning to live with and confront difference required from participation in the lived reality of a local community.

A perception of citizenship as the activity to which we dedicate our 'surplus' energy and attention also risks, as Alex Steffen has argued in his critique of the transition town movement, that we do not contribute the best of ourselves and our expertise to tackling the urgent problems that face us today. His critique of transition town movements, for example, talks about:

> 'surplus powerlessness' disguised as practicality. All over the world, groups of people with graduate degrees, affluence, decades of work experience, varieties of advanced training and technological capacities beyond the imagining of our great-grandparents are coming together, looking into the face of apocalypse ... and deciding to start a seed exchange or a kids clothing swap.[41]

People do these things, understandably, precisely because they are easy, they are a place to start. The question is whether such early steps will lead to more sustained and profound change. Jean Anyon argues that engagement is built upon the experience of participation in social movements, perhaps implying that any form of participation in social action is a good starting point. Andy Hargreaves's study of processes of educational change suggests, however, that an addiction to quick tips, rapid changes and fast results can militate against long-term change. As he argues, 'successful short-term strategies ... seem to serve less like levers to longer term transformation than lids upon it'.[42]

Some observers of emerging youth participation in civic activities now suggest that the divide between the traditional worlds of representative democracy and the emerging spaces of online social engagement may be widening. W Lance

Bennett, for example, argues that there is a divide emerging between different forms of citizenship identity. On the one hand he argues that there are still 'dutiful citizens' (usually older people) who maintain a traditional citizenship and democratic identity oriented around the rituals of voting, government-centred activities and reading 'the news'. On the other, he sees the emergence of a new generation of 'actualizing citizens', younger people who are motivated less by a sense of obligation to government than by a sense of individual purpose; who see voting as less meaningful than other personally defined acts such as consumption, volunteering or activism; who mistrust the media and politicians; and who prefer loose networks of action to civil society organizations or political parties.

And yet, such a divide may be only temporary, as the networks of traditional representative democracy increasingly harness the capacities of online digital cultures to build their support. John Prescott, former UK Deputy Prime Minister, is a surprisingly committed tweeter; the UK government is building alliances with Facebook; while the Obama election of 2009 demonstrated how far the traditional powers of financial and educational capital can be enhanced by articulating it with the digital networks of communication power.[43] Reciprocally, those campaigners who harnessed the power of digital networks over the last decade to mobilize massive global demonstrations are increasingly confronted by the failure of some of these campaigns (against the invasion of Iraq, in support of climate change legislation for example) to lead to real and pervasive change. Given such failure, the appeal of returning to and gaining a foothold within traditional representative democratic structures may be increasing, and the need to invest in systematic face-to-face community organizing and social movement building may become more apparent.[44]

The critical choice in modes of civic engagement over the coming years may not therefore be between 'traditional' and 'digital' media, which are likely to increasingly sustain and feed off each other. Instead, there may be a choice between civic engagement as a cultural accessory cultivated to maintain an *impression* of agency (whether through voting for a political party or signing up to a Facebook group) or civic engagement conceived of as an embodied and lived commitment to sustained dialogue.[45]

Democratic futures?

Radically divergent futures are offered by these choices. One future offers a trajectory of 'fast citizenship' in which digital technologies are used to ensure that everyone 'has their say'. In this future, mass referenda calling for instant responses are the default mechanism of government and superficial change is achieved through the efficient mobilization of flash mobs who coalesce around temporary campaigns either virtually or physically. Public debate engages and responds to each new development, collates the information, forms an opinion and rapidly moves on. Such fast citizenship would be a numbers game, equating citizenship with quantifiable choice-making, hyper-democracy in action.

Governance structures built around fast citizenship models pose potentially serious equity risks, as they are premised upon the assumption that all citizens can and will equally participate in digital engagement activities;[46] even while the very people who are involved in such debates may be those who have always historically been advantaged by access to economic, educational and social capital. Who counts as 'the people' for the purposes of online civic engagement, and what responsibilities are encumbent upon the state to ensure that all are enabled to participate, therefore become urgent questions if the conversation about the future is not to automatically exclude many people from participation.[47]

A second trajectory is a 'slow citizenship' future. In this future, citizens, civil society and governments might tackle the substantial challenge of exploring how the tools of digital cultures might be used to enhance a sustained commitment to the lived communities, local neighbourhoods and social relationships through which we all live and depend. Slow citizenship would require commitment not only to making your own voice heard, but also to building tools for others to be heard and to creating spaces for listening and exchange. Slow citizenship would require a commitment to developing the protocols of communication that allow and encourage us to talk across difference, and to learn from and with diversity. As Castells argues:

> A process of material construction of the culture of the network society is under way. ... It is the process by which conscious social actors of multiple origins bring their resources and beliefs to others, expecting in return to receive the same, and even more: the sharing of a diverse world, thus ending the ancestral fear of the other.[48]

Slow citizenship would not seek to retreat from the discomforts and constraints of the physical world into the instant gratification of action in the virtual world, but to address the lived problems and opportunities that are being presented to communities by socio-technical change. Slow citizenship would seek to create space to explore and live with the new (and old) forms of diverse identity that our new socio-technical tools might offer. Slow citizenship would create a space for old and young to talk together, share expertise and insight across generations and build common responses to shared problems. Slow citizenship would create a conversation about the socio-technical structures we are building, and our responsibilities within them and to each other. Slow citizenship would seek to reconnect the digital and the physical, to build bridges between the city street and the virtual world, and to explore how these can enhance each other.

Where the arch-symbol of fast citizenship might be the online referendum delivered to your mobile phone and responded to with a tap of the thumb, the defining symbol of slow citizenship might be a digitally augmented corner cafe. This cafe is first and foremost a site for conversation, conviviality, collation of memories and sharing of aspirations at a local level. It is also, however, a site for recording memories, expertise, ideas and aspirations – it allows the past and the future to come together, providing a repository of memory that helps guide the future. It is also a meeting point, a place where problems can be posed and answers offered, where new allegiances can be built. And it is a space that connects the local and the global, creating connections between different communities and their expertise, insight and ideas around the world.[49]

Schools building a quality conversation about the future

Schools are places where people learn to 'do democracy', where their expectations are shaped about their own voice and rights, about their entitlement to speak and their obligations to listen and act.[50] Schools are also public spaces that act as gateways to democracy, they are powerful institutions for social change in their own right, and they can provide a platform and a resource for people to shape their local democratic landscape and as a resource for mobilizing their communities.

In the light of these observations it is instructive to note that over the last ten years UK schools have seen a gradual increase in surveillance technologies (both CCTV and biometrics) and in the use of data primarily for purposes of audit and performance management. In teaching and learning practices, while personal portfolios owned and shared by students have been slow to take off and social networks have been banned in many schools for fear of disruptive behaviour, rapid voting technology is being enthusiastically promoted by educators to assess student comprehension (or manage attention). Such taken-for-granted patterns of technological appropriation and resistance make visible the ways in which many schools are currently constructing public space and digital democracy.

Rather than promoting relationships of control and cultures of fast citizenship, a school that truly sought to enable its students to participate in the new public spaces of the twenty-first century would need to take a different approach. It would ensure that its socio-technical practices were oriented towards democracy rather than dictatorship, towards creating spaces for dialogue and debate rather than for 'expressing a preference', and towards building long-lasting human relationships of care and interdependence rather than fickle expressions of transient support. The democratic school in the twenty-first century would be a space in which the political basis of socio-technical development is made visible and subject to scrutiny. The school that sought seriously to support its communities to participate in a conversation about the future, in other words, would need to build the capabilities and conditions for slow citizenship that are adequate to the serious challenges of contemporary socio-technical change.

This would mean creating schools committed to building human relationships, committed to allowing the people involved in a school to come to know each other well and build trusting relationships. Fielding & Moss's proposal for a 'Common School', deeply connected with its local community and premised upon smaller school sizes, provides one template for this approach.[51] Slow citizenship in schools that is cognizant of socio-technical change would also mean equipping students to reflect upon the nature of the public conversation developing in online spaces and to explore what democracy, citizenship and politics looks like in these spaces. It would mean creating opportunities to use social software, to participate in online communities, to harness tools for citizen journalism, and to create new accounts of neighbourhoods using open data. Slow citizenship in schools would also mean locating the school as itself a public space. This means harnessing technologies in ways that are respectful of human rights of students and staff.

It means, finally, seeing the school as an important public space for local democracy. It is a space that can provide access to the resources needed for its community to come together and discuss its problems. It is a space that can act as a focus around which communities can organize to advocate for the change they need for sustainable futures.

Chapter 7

A future-building school

Beyond 'future-proofing'

The myth that has dominated discussions of the relationship between education and the future over the last two decades suggests that there is only one question about socio-technical change that the 'future-proof' school needs to address: namely, how successfully will the school equip young people to compete in the global economy of tomorrow?

Such a question, however, is clearly inadequate as a basis for thinking about the roles that we urgently need education to play in helping us to equip young people for the full range of potential socio-technical futures that are latent in contemporary developments. It is premised upon a vision of the future that can be seen as increasingly implausible and undesirable, and it fails to address the other more profound challenges that socio-technical change may present us.

Rather than working simply to service this impoverished future narrative, we need education institutions that can help us to work out what intelligence and wisdom mean in an age of digital and cognitive augmentation. We need education institutions that can teach us how to create, draw upon and steward collective knowledge resources. We need educational institutions that can build intergenerational solidarity in a time of unsettled relationships between generations. We need educational institutions that help us to figure out how to deal with our new and dangerous knowledge. We need educational institutions that act as midwives to sustainable economic practices that strengthen rather than hollow out local communities across the globe. We need educational institutions that are capable of nurturing the capacity for democracy and debate that will allow us to ensure that social and political justice are at the heart of the socio-technical futures we are building.

If we persist in restricting our discussions of socio-technical futures to unsustainable visions of a global competitive economy, we will have failed in the one commitment that we make to young people when we ask them to spend years of their lives in schools, namely the promise that we make to prepare them for the future.

Today, growing concern that our orthodox vision of the future is no longer robust has led many educators to retreat into uncertainty and to take refuge in a commitment to flexibility, adaptability and openness to change. Such a commitment is in evidence everywhere in education: schools are built with folding walls, multi-purpose spaces, multiple wall sockets; curricula are designed to nurture infinitely flexible students, able to adapt and respond to whatever comes about. Such adaptability, we say while keeping our fingers crossed, should allow us and them to cope whatever happens.

Such a retreat into flexibility, while understandable, is nonetheless politically inadequate if we wish to avoid the worst excesses of economic polarization and social and environmental breakdown promised in some trajectories. A commitment to adaptability to socio-technical change without a vision of a better alternative future to work towards provides no basis for optimism, no resources for the imagination, and no impetus for change.

It is also premised upon the mistaken assumption that the future is a product not of our combined actions and intentions, but of some unknowable force entirely beyond us. The future, however, as Barbara Adam and Chris Groves remind us, is being produced out of the materials of the past and the present.[1] It is being shaped by the decisions of our politicians, our industrialists and our civic leaders. It is being produced from biological and environmental processes already in train. It is being shaped by the aspirations and anxieties of our popular culture. It is being built by our research, our scientific inventions, our businesses and our creative dreams. It is being created by the millions of decisions each of us makes every day. The future is not some place 'out there' beyond our reach; rather, it is an imaginative, material and political set of processes already in development in which it is both possible and ethical to seek to intervene.

Instead of simply retreating into uncertainty about an unknowable and out-of-control future, therefore, schools have both a responsibility and an opportunity to intervene. They have a responsibility to try to tip the balance of socio-technical change in the direction of sustainable, equitable and positive futures for their communities.

Schools are, after all, critically important institutions in their local communities. They are one of the last remaining universal public services; they are of intimate concern to parents who will often move mountains for their children; they are staffed in the main by people who have a commitment to and concern for the public good; they are deeply connected with the lived economic, social and cultural experiences of their communities; and they have powerful intellectual and material resources to support communities to improve their capacity to act in and on the world. Schools are one of the key mediating institutions that play a critical role in building and mobilizing community social capital.[2]

Schools also have the capacity to act as prefigurative spaces, as environments in which communities can model today how they might want to live with each other in future. The sorts of choice that schools make about their use of technology, for example, their attitude towards surveillance, towards technological and cognitive diversity, their use of data, the platforms they provide for encounters between different generations, the opportunities they create for participating in networked publics or democratic decision-making – all serve to model different ways of living and responding to socio-technical change.

In and of themselves, therefore, schools have the potential to influence how socio-technical change plays out in communities by shaping how well-equipped communities are to lead and resist change, and how far communities can harness socio-technical developments for their own ends. They are also important sites in which it is possible to model alternative socio-technical futures.

Rather than envisaging a 'future-proof' school that tries to insure itself against socio-technical change, therefore, we have the opportunity to create future-*building* schools that actively support their communities to tip the balance of socio-technical change in favour of fair, sustainable and democratic futures. Such schools would recognize their role as prefigurative spaces for building socio-technical futures. And such schools would see themselves as places where students, educators and the wider community can come together to participate in a conversation about the future.

What then might be the attributes of such a school?

A public space at the heart of its community

The future-building school acts as a powerful platform within the community for creating a conversation about the future. It brings together students, parents, grandparents, community organizations and staff to ask what sorts of future are in development for the school's community, and to examine what alternative futures for their students and their neighbourhoods they might seek to create. In order to build the conditions for slow citizenship that allow dialogue across difference and that build relationships across generations, the future-building school sets up new governance arrangements that allow communities to participate in a sustained conversation about the relationship between education and community. It harnesses the resources of citizen journalism, social networks and open data to build powerful knowledge to support the decision-making of the community, and equips all the members of the school community to access and use such tools. Through all of these activities, the future-building school recognizes that it has the capacity to mobilize communities for change in its local area, and to influence the trajectory of political, economic and technological change.[3]

A commitment to interdependence

The future-building school recognizes that power and agency is not the property of an individual or an institution alone. Instead, the capacity to effect change in the world is achieved through the networks, partnerships, relationships and systems with which the individual or institution is connected. Reciprocally, such interdependence also brings with it a responsibility for relationships of care with the people and environments that make up those wider networks.

As an institution, the future-building school therefore sees itself as part of a much wider network of people and institutions and draws upon them in all of its activities. It builds common cause with those people in other civic organizations and social movements who are also seeking to build a democratic debate about the future, and in doing so the school learns 'about the power of public constituencies, about the power of an inflamed, informed community' to effect change that often seems beyond the capacity of the educational institution alone.[4]

It also draws on the wider educational ecosystem that can be harnessed to support educational goals. The school itself is no longer conceived of as a bounded institution into which only certain people can enter by virtue of their age or professional qualification. Instead it is better thought of as a mobilizing resource that harnesses and amplifies the potential of a community and a country to educate its young people. Reciprocally, the school pays close attention to the responsibilities it has to those wider networks, to maintaining their health and vitality and to building their capacity. The school itself is seen as a powerful engine for local change through the decisions it takes about issues such as purchasing and employment that have implications for the communities that it serves.

The principle of interdependence also underpins a rethink of the individuals at the heart of the educational enterprise. It sustains a commitment to recognizing and valuing diversity and to ensuring that such diversity does not equate to inequality and unfairness. Students, teachers, parents and other educators involved in the processes of teaching and learning are understood to be intimately connected to networks of other people, technologies and knowledge resources. The quality of the individual's socio-technical networks is understood to be a critical component in their capacity to act and to effect change. Understanding, building and mobilizing these networks therefore becomes an important educational endeavour through curriculum and assessment processes. Reciprocally, the principle of interdependence requires a sensitive and ethical engagement with the implications of individual actions for the wider networks and systems of which the individual is a part.

A laboratory for building social futures

The future-building school is, most importantly, concerned with building the capacity of its students and communities to imagine and build alternative futures. It sees itself as a critical counterpoint to discourses of both despair and delusion. It shows how visions of the future can be subject to democratic debate, inquiry and contestation by all members of the community. It shows how socio-technical practices can be authored, designed and adapted democratically. It shows how socio-technical change emerges from political and economic projects and how allegiances and partnerships can be built to resist and promote particular trajectories. In these ways, the school becomes a laboratory for exploring and building more sustainable and equitable futures.

The future-building school acts as a laboratory for designing and modelling new solutions and new strategies. Students, teachers and community partners collaborate to research and experiment with new ideas. The school is equipped with the people, tools and partnerships that allow it to support its students and communities to act in the world, to set problems and solve them, to extend their curiosity and to act upon it. The laboratories and ateliers, the 3D printers and rapid replicators, the computing infrastructure, all are set up to act as resources for creating and testing prototypes and products and services that can be locally produced. The school's audio-visual, design, communication and creative resources are able to act as hyperlocal media tools to engage in public debate. The school meeting rooms are places for local democracy and for partnership with local communities and international partners. The orchestras and music rooms are places for public performance and community engagement. The libraries, laboratories and information resources are capable of supporting serious research. The timetable and partnerships allow students to act in and work across multiple social settings, and to test out new forms of collaboration. Partnerships with local universities, local democratic organizations, cultural institutions and the wider educational ecosystem allow the school to access resources they need to build powerful projects and precedents for socio-technical change. And the school itself is seen as an important site of social, economic and democratic practice.

Towards the future-building school

A future-building school is a school that takes seriously its responsibility to equip its students for the future. It recognizes that the old measures of future success – the accumulation of certificates, exams, positions on league tables – are no longer adequate to the task of driving a school's contribution to its students' and its community's future wellbeing. Instead, it takes on the more exciting, albeit more challenging, task of creating a meaningful debate with students and communities about the futures that are in development and the futures that they might want. It sets itself up as a partner for its students and its communities in generating visions of viable alternative futures and as a resource to develop and build them.

In so doing, a future-building school refuses to be lulled by the fairytales about endless growth and universal wealth in a future knowledge economy. At the same time, it refuses to accept the cynical pessimism that assumes the inevitability of a future of radical inequality, positional competition and intergenerational conflict.

A future-building school is a space through which students and communities can rethink their assumptions about what is possible and what is impossible.

How might these characteristics of public space, interdependence and experimentation play out in the lived realities of schools? They seem, after all, a long way from the highly individualized and institutionally competitive schools of today. The next chapter is a utopian vision of what a future-building school of 2035 might look like. I present it as a tool for opening up the possibilities for what education might become over the next 20 years and as a resource for imagining a lived alternative. If we cannot even begin to make clear what our ideal futures might look like, after all, it will be very difficult to make them happen.

This vision of the future-building school of 2035, therefore, seeks to describe just what such a school might feel like, who might work there, how it might be arranged, what sorts of teaching and learning might be going on, what games students might be playing, what difficulties it might face. It is not intended to be a pipe dream, but a plausible utopia, a viable alternative that we might aim for as we think about how best education might change to create equitable, sustainable and *desirable* futures. It is built on the foundations of existing practices in schools who are already trying to make these changes. It is built on a conservative assumption about the sorts of technological resource we will have available to us in 25 years' time. It is built, in other words, with an 'educated optimism'[6] about how we, as societies, could respond to the socio-technical developments, environmental challenges and economic disruptions that face us in the next two decades. Most importantly, it is based upon the conviction that schools have the capacity to act as powerful rallying points for rebuilding civil society and intergenerational solidarity if they can imagine a new role for themselves as a resource for building social futures.

The future-building school of 2035

Front-of-house

The school, when you first walk up to it with your child at your side, looks both familiar to and different from the schools of your own childhood. There are small groups of children playing around outside, clusters of adults talking, and staff welcoming visitors. You note, however, that there is a real mix of ages here, from some very young primary-age children like your own still holding their parents' hands, to teenagers intently playing some sort of game in a corner, to what look like a couple of centenarians sitting and talking purposefully together at a table outside a coffee bar. Indeed, when you look round, you realize the courtyard you are standing in feels more like a public square or a city market than a school. It has this feel not only because all human life seems to be there, but because around the edges of the courtyard are workshops and businesses, and a cafe spilling out onto groups of chairs and tables where people are talking, working and playing.

The space that you can see has a number of features that you have been familiar with for many years now. The roofs and many of the walls are greened, growing produce, you guess, for the cafe. The solar panels and turbines are getting on a bit – you assume they're moving over to biomass now – but they are still clearly doing their job, as the beautiful mural on one wall of the school is glowing and oscillating slowly, taking on strange tree-like shapes one minute and fractal shapes the next. The rainwater and grey water capture systems are working well and watering the vegetable plots next to the bike racks and the tramway. All of this you've come to expect since the carbon rationing and city-greening of the mid-teens got going, and many of these features you see in your own apartment building.

Next to you, your daughter is playing with her school bracelet and comparing it with yours, fidgeting and laughing as they both light up with different colours in proximity to each other and start exchanging information. Around you, you can see the children and adults who've chosen bracelets for their school access devices and wonder what colours theirs will glow when they encounter your daughter's and what sorts of information they've decided theirs will share or seek. You have a look round to see that others have chosen badges or necklaces instead;

all are glowing faintly or brightly depending upon their activity status, some are being used to project images onto tables, walls and floors around them.

You walk around the courtyard, looking into the offices and spaces that give off it. One door gives on to the offices of the local housing association, another to the local co-operative and credit union, a third to a small business start-up; another door gives onto a large common room where some people are sitting and chatting and another group are arranging chairs for a meeting and uploading new notices to the walls. Next to this room there is a library and what looks like a local media company, producing e-books, e-zines and hyperlocal TV. There are a few empty units looking onto the courtyard; signs on the doors suggest you should contact the enterprise office if you have ideas for a social enterprise that could use that space. One whole side of the courtyard is given over to a museum, and teenagers and the curator are at work here bringing in new artefacts to display, setting up a simulation and talking about upcoming exhibitions of the projects that they have been working on together. There is a counter that divides the room down the centre and provides a barrier between the space giving onto the courtyard and the public display space facing onto the city street.

All of these areas, the courtyard, the common room, the social enterprises and the museum, are the semi-public 'front-of-house' spaces of the school. They are the public areas where everyone affiliated to the school is welcome to come to hang out, spend time, meet people. And there are many, many people affiliated to the school. First, there are the primary and junior children, up to 180 of them at any one time, aged between 4 and 13 years old, who spend most of their days in or being cared for by the school. Then there are the seniors, aged between 14 and 19, who spend around half of their time in the school and half of their time in off-site activities; there are around 120 of them. These young people form, with their core staff, the heart of the school's community. Finally there are the adults affiliated with the school, up to 1400 of them at any one time. All of the children's adult family members are entitled to be affiliated to the school (although they may be affiliated to more than one, as some adults like to keep their 'home' school affiliation throughout life, as well as taking on their children's); so too are local residents. There is also a special set of affiliated adults who elect or are chosen to be part of that school community freely rather than by residency or family links. All of the adults too spend some of their time (usually around five days a year, although for some it is much longer) in the learning activities of the school. All in all, these different groups use the front-of-house space of the school at different times of the day and night as a meeting space, a talking space and a working space.

The front-of-house space of the school is where community organizations, political parties, trade unions, student organizations, local businesses, start-up co-operatives, parents' groups, housing associations, research organizations and others find space to work and are able to come together. It is a place of exchange and encounter. It is the place you go to when you don't know what to do, when you need advice, when you want to find another way to tackle a problem that's facing you, your family or your neighbourhood. It is the place the community goes to when it needs a strategy to adapt to change or when it wants to find a new direction. It is the place where the collective wisdom of the individuals in that community can be made available as resources for that community, and where other knowledge, insight and advice can be sought beyond it. It is the place you go to when you are bored, looking for a challenge, wanting to be surprised.

Resource mapping

Your daughter's mentor comes up to greet you and takes you through the door in the back wall of the courtyard that divides the front-of-house 'public' spaces from the backstage areas of the school. Here too there is another courtyard, and around this on several floors are tiered the workshops, labs, studios and study spaces of the institution that, although still called a school out of habit, increasingly looks very different from the schools of the past. The ground floor of the courtyard gives onto rooms where the primary children are now settling into their home rooms with their friends and meeting with their mentors to talk about plans for the week and the next few months.

Although half of the children's time is scheduled in advance with master classes, tutorials or group learning programmes, one-fifth of their time, even from the youngest age, is dedicated to working on their own projects. The remainder is dedicated to collaborative and community projects where children seek out areas they want to work on together – whether this is exploring a new form of material that has just been developed in one of the labs upstairs, or in solving the problems of a particular group of local residents. Conversations with mentors at the beginning of each week allow the children to discuss their progress and their plans and to manage the different demands of projects and learning programmes. In these conversations, each child's resource map comes into play. This rich map of their experiences, progress, interests and aspirations, as well as the resources that they have to draw upon at home, in the community and in their family, acts as a basis for identifying both where additional support might be needed and where the child and their family may have particular strengths and interests to share with collaborators or the wider school.

In a small quiet room off the courtyard overlooking the garden outside, you sit with your daughter and her mentor and begin to talk about your own resource maps. You've been building your maps for years, consciously or unconsciously, gathering information about where you've been, what you've been doing, things you have learned, ideas you've had. There are your own school records, qualifications, employment histories. There are recordings of the music you love and the music you've played, the films you've watched and the films you've created, the museums you've been to, the cities you've lived in, the voluntary work you've done and the care you've given. There are snippets of insight into your working life, the tools you use there, the insights and experience you've developed. You've also, in the last few years, been capturing all sorts of ambient data about your bodies: where you've been, what you've eaten, your heart activity, your circulation, your absorption of particulates from the atmosphere, your genome. There are also other people in your maps; this includes your own parents and their parents, all of whom, in their sixties and eighties, will play some role in your daughter's care and education; and your wider networks of friends and colleagues. There are the social networks you are part of for leisure, work, hobbies and pleasure. In the past, these different elements of your life might have been kept in diaries and notebooks left on shelves, or in photo albums, on your mobile phone or on computer hard drives and in social networks, anywhere you've left fragments of yourself. Now it is possible to link them all together and draw them up on demand.

On the white table between you, all three of you gradually begin to display your resource maps. These maps are not simple geographical maps, but timelines, stories, events and experiences represented visually. Each person's map is unique – there is an individual story to tell for each person; but each map can also be translated into a form that allows it to be compared for similarities and differences with another person or with a wider community. And there is no definitive 'map' for each person; instead there are multiple, overlaid maps – of history, family, biology, of friendships, of interests, of employment, of finance, of material resources – maps can constantly be developed, maps can be combined. The person is constantly changing. But the maps can also be used when needed to rapidly communicate particular areas of ourselves to others, or as a basis for understanding the resources and experiences we have to offer when we meet new people such as teachers, employers or fellow community members.

The maps are, at heart, a mechanism to support listening to and respecting each other and everything that the other person brings to the encounter. They are the foundation for the commitment to principled interdependence that underpins the philosophy of the school, as they show how much each person's identity is built upon and through their interactions with and support from others. Should children arrive in the school as refugees or without parents and with no maps of their own, the first task of the mentor and the child is to sit down and get to know each other well enough to begin to create maps that the child is confident and happy to build upon. Building the map is the basis for all learning and for the mutual encounter.

The conversation now with the mentor is the beginning of a long conversation about how much of your own and your child's history and story you want to make visible and known to the school, both so that you can work out what you need from the school and so that reciprocally, you can understand how best you might contribute to the school and its community. Your map, importantly, is your own, and sharing it with others is an act of trust and negotiation. The lessons of the mid teens earlier in the century showed just how many problems were posed by this information being held centrally rather than by the individual. There are those who are still, however, wary of building and sharing their maps. These people continue to lobby against the practice and refuse to participate in map sharing. As a rule, schools simply take the principles of mapping and carry on the conversation verbally with these parents and children, rather than using digital tools. But it still remains a subject of real contention.

Sharing maps for most people, however, is thought to bring immense benefits; it allows your mentor to understand you much better, to work well with you to understand how your history can allow you to contribute to the school and the community, and to explore with you what you may want to learn to allow you to flourish. For your daughter, sharing the map is the beginning of building her curriculum, of exploring with her where she might want to develop and of working with her to open up new areas. The map will also be the beginning of her conversations with her friends and partners in the school; it will allow her to find others with interests she shares and to look for others who have knowledge and experiences that she needs. The map also provides a basis for talking through and evaluating whether different forms of cognitive or prosthetic enhancement might or might not be desirable and for exploring different routes towards the same goals. Students can also look at the maps of other individuals and groups to help them make decisions, and explore different ways of building the map that would create the conditions for the same achievements; seeing the time and investment, resources, materials and areas of knowledge and personal development needed to achieve certain goals.

For the mentor, as well as providing the insight necessary to understand what each member of the school community needs, the maps also suggest areas for shared activity, play and collaboration. The data underpinning the maps that each person decides to make available to the school can be collated and compared, analysed and explored to look for larger patterns and problems that the school community may begin to work on.

The shared maps also become the basis for understanding and making visible the wider resources of the school; in a time of community crisis, it becomes easy to find the people who have the expertise and resources to help – the engineers and carers, the artists and the organizers who might help to overcome whatever problem is at hand. On a day-to-day basis the maps provide the insight into the resources that are available in the community to help with student projects, or to run the masterclasses and studios that are such a feature of school life. In exchange, these folk educators know that they too will be able to turn to the school as a source of insight and learning and support when they need it. Without this wider body of resources to support the school, it is well known that the school simply could not function as it does, as it would have to rely only on the expertise of the staff in the school to work. Although familiar in the past, the idea that a 'school' would be made up only of staff and students seems, today, strangely impoverished. Instead, responsibility for making the school a rich and powerful community resource is dispersed across 1400 adults, all of whom have a stake in how it works and understand how they might contribute to it.

Your daughter, mentor and you agree together some of the basic principles of how she will share her map, and some of the areas for development that you would encourage over the next term. This discussion will, of course, be repeated again and again over the years, growing richer as you all come to know one another better. The mentor, after all, may be a lifelong companion for you both, unless you disagree with each other or want to get a different perspective.

The museum

Following this conversation, you begin your tour of the school with the mentor at your side, providing a running commentary and introduction to its key features. First, you walk back through the museum. The mentor explains that the museum is one of the most important parts of the school as it is a place for capturing and building a shared history. Each museum in each school is different: some reflect the industrial histories of the area, others a particular event and its causes, others specialize in a particular field from botany to nuclear engineering. The purpose of the museum is central to the work of a future-building school, the mentor argues, because the museum makes visible that the world hasn't always and won't always be like it is today. The museum, says the mentor with a hint of melodrama, releases us from 'the tyranny of the present'. It is a space where the other possible futures that might have emerged are made visible, where the uncertainty and contingency of each discovery is made apparent, where the struggles people had to go through for each scientific breakthrough, each piece of legislation, each new work of art, are presented. History, these museums show, is not a simple progression of inevitable change, but a site of debate, contestation and choice.

These museums show how things have been different in the past, they provide a record and a collective memory of other ways of doing things, they provide a resource for confronting new situations. They are a commitment to remembering and nurturing different ways of living in the world. The museum 'exhibits' are often objects that are annotated with different historical accounts. Produced by the students either with new research that challenges them, or with greater discussion of the period, the exhibits often have alternative history simulations attached to them, crafted beautifully by the students, showing how a different decision at a key moment might have led to a different trajectory for social change. Some of the most annotated artefacts are those associated with the great war of 2020 that many children have a fascination for – surely it would have been easy to avoid this, they argue. Each annotation, each alternative simulation becomes part of the museum's own resources, accessible not only by the school community but by the wider world. One corner of each museum in every school is also dedicated to the 'museum of uninteresting objects', which is wholly curated by the primary children, who are challenged to bring in an object that is of absolutely no interest at all;[1] objects don't usually last long, the mentor says, as the school's members are usually pretty quick to point out something of interest in everything. This part of the museum, again, says the mentor, is important in encouraging students to look at things differently, to make the familiar strange, which is a core component of the future-building school.

The common room

The mentor then walks you round to the school common room. This is a strange old space: populated by a lot of very comfortable-looking chairs, it seems to be a place just for relaxing and talking. As you watch, however, the room begins to fill up and the walls begin to light up with lots of squares with people or avatars in them. This room, the mentor whispers now, is the most important space in the school. It is the common room, the place where we come together to make decisions, govern the school and ensure accountability. It is in this place that the community comes together once a year, virtually or physically, to decide how the school should be managed and judged. There are, of course, the familiar criteria that remain constant: the education, sustainability, health and wellbeing of the community, for example. This is also the place where, in the annual meeting, the school determines whether the national government is doing what is needed to protect the public education landscape, whether the expected infrastructure of personal technical devices and national information systems, including the requisite laws for protection against enclosure and pollution of the knowledge commons, is in place. This is a particularly important annual review, as without this underpinning legislative and technical infrastructure the school cannot function effectively. Should there be failings here, schools act together as a powerful lobbying force at national level. Each year there are also goals that the community sets itself as it assigns budgets and priorities, and this progress is reviewed again the following year. The common room is also the place where issues of ownership of data, issues of misconduct and any other education-related problems are addressed through deliberation by a panel of school community members. The discussion can get heated, and not everyone enjoys the public manner in which problems are aired. There are disagreements about whether such 'reasonable' debate is sufficient to tackle some of the issues raised. There is some disagreement about how these discussions should be managed and whether there is, after all, a chance to opt out of them.

Today, though, there is a discussion about an issue of importance to many in the local community – the new proposals to build another tram route through the town, and where such an important resource will be allocated. Entering from the front-of-house courtyard are people old and young, including many of those from the offices around the courtyard and the media company. Entering from backstage are a group of teenagers and some local councillors. All around the room on the walls there are the images of those who are joining the conversation remotely, now just having conversations with each other or those in the room. Gradually, things quieten down and one of the school staff, the community coordinator, takes to the stage to get things started. He begins by inviting a group of students to make their presentation about the likely environmental impact of the new tramway, and another group to talk about the economic benefits and costs.

These students make impressive presentations, using all the rich data about the local community that they have available through mash-ups between the school maps and the publicly available data sets. The local councillors and businessmen also make their statements and reports, and after a while the discussion gets going, focusing particularly on how the funding for the tramway might be allocated and what would have to be lost instead. A preliminary set of points is collectively agreed for a next round of discussion.

Your daughter, who had at first been cowed by the number of people present, then distracted by the flickering lights of the people participating from the wall screens, has begun to get restless. You all leave, heading out for the daylight while the debate carries on.

This sort of meeting, says the mentor, is a fairly regular occurrence. Most of the time the common room is used as the space for school governance, where all the members of the school meet once a week to talk through any problems or issues that have come up; but frequently, local government or social enterprise will approach the school with a particular proposal and seek to work with the school and its community to research and decide on the appropriate decision. 'We had a really important set of discussions around the question of changes to the living wage over the last few weeks, for example, where school members did a lot of work looking at the options. Some of the younger students were also pretty vocal in that discussion; they were able to show what it was like living in very low income households and the impact of this on their education. That got a lot of the teachers and adults pretty fired up and involved in the debate. Our maths specialist was also delighted, as it gave a really good real-life example for him to work on with the students.

'Of course, it's difficult to make sure that it isn't just the really vocal pushy people who get to have a say in these settings, or those who've just got lots of time on their hands. It is always something we have to keep an eye on and work on,' admits the mentor, 'and those people working two jobs to earn a living can find it very difficult to participate. But because the school knows its adult members so well, and because it really is a place for real accountability, there is more of a sense than in the old days that people can see real benefits of getting involved when it's about issues that matter to them. And then again, we've also got a lot better at learning how to manage these sorts of discussion and manage them more quickly. The virtual participation also helps; it means the old barriers of transport costs for participation have been overcome as well. But you're right, we do have to keep an eye on it and work hard to ensure this doesn't just become another talking shop for those with more time and energy.'

The digital layer

As you talk, you've walked out of the courtyard, into the gardens and past the planetarium in the tree house, where you're interested to see some children are working with a local researcher; apparently, according to the note outside, they are trying to map a new area of the universe. The mentor suggests you switch your viewer on to allow you to see the digital landscape of the school. You do so and realize that everywhere there are data and annotations. Around one tree there are hundreds of memories left by former students, stories of what they did there, what they'd felt there, who they'd known there. On another wall there is a memorial to the community members who died in the great resource wars of 2020. On the green roof, there is data about plant species and moisture levels. Overlying the school entrance there is the list of the people in the school grounds at the present time, the experiments that are currently running and that school members are participating in; you can zoom in to that list and begin to see the data scrolling through the screen, along with early interpretations by the teams involved.

Such a rich visual environment can be overwhelming, so you switch your viewer just to the single view that provides basic information about what each area of the school grounds is intended for, who is there now and who can access that space, and you begin to record that information to share later with your child and with your parents, who will want to know all about it. You note that the school grounds are being used intensively for energy and food production as well as for play and for learning. Schools these days, you know, have to be able to be much more self-sufficient, as energy supplies are still a little shaky and food costs are still very high.

The futures game

Finally, you head backstage again to the primary area, where you say goodbye to your daughter who is, by now, itching to join in with the game she's been watching the children play around the grounds and in the classrooms. And indeed, you too are intrigued by this game. You know only that you and your daughter had spent the day before making a set of cards with pictures on them, but you weren't quite sure what this was for.

This is the futures game, says the mentor, and it's an important part of building foresight and reflection in the school community. It was first invented by a group of academics in the 2000s[2] as a way of making visible the openness of the future, but it became an underground craze online. Each card is unique and the meaning of each card changes every time the game is played, although there are some familiar stories that come up again and again. Cards can be given to you by friends or other players, or you can make your own. It is played as follows: each player is dealt three cards; these cards have three different pictures on them. The task at that point is to interpret these pictures in any way you wish, to create a story about a possible future that might emerge as these three forces combine: a picture of a wave might stand for a story about drinking water, could stand for rising sea levels, could mean the popularity of the seaside and surfing – it means whatever you want it to mean in the story; a picture of a cup cake with bright green icing might be a story about a birthday party, about food additives, about comfort or about obesity. The trick is to decide what your three cards stand for and weave them together in a plausible story.

After that first round you get dealt another card, and you have to figure out how to fit that into the first story – what changes, what stays the same. And another round provides the same challenge. After these three rounds you are left with a story of a rich future world that you have created from the strange juxtapositions of these different random factors. The next task is to create a plausible explanation for how that future came about and to look around you at the world today for evidence that might support it. While some play this game on their own just to pass the time, others play it competitively, with players judging the 'best', 'most likely', 'most gory' or 'most beautiful' story, depending on taste. The game is usually just played for fun, with much of the pleasure for some children being in the creation of their futures cards, as they can spend hours making images and editing them until they convey something distinctive.

The cards also have a digital life; they are able to record which cards they are partnered with and the stories that are told around them. The stories, therefore, can be listened to again and again, and the best can become narratives of the future that are drawn on for ideas, inspirations or warnings. Some games generate new suggestions for projects, as people become concerned about a particular trajectory that might emerge or a new possibility opens up. Great games players are listened to and watched with real pleasure as they demonstrate how new stories can be woven out of familiar old cards. These cards can become valuable in themselves, as they accrete to them a huge number of stories and ideas. Each card carries with it its own history. But new cards are particularly prized, because they open up new possibilities to meet with these old favourites. New players and old players together make for particularly rich future worlds. You wonder to yourself as you walk past the groups of children playing the game, what cards you too might create to let you play the game with your daughter.

The staff

'Now,' says the mentor, pulling up a set of photographs on the viewer, 'I want to just introduce you to the core team here at the school. There are, of course, the mentors like me, whose primary role is a combination of personal care and co-direction with the students of their learning programmes. Each mentor works with a group of students who are associated with them, unless there are requests on either side, throughout their school career and often beyond if adults stay affiliated with their home school. All mentors also have areas of special interest, whether in biotech or music, in literature or mathematics, that are often called upon for masterclasses, but their specialist role in the school is that of co-ordinating the student learning. The mentor helps the students identify the areas that might form the basis for collaborative projects, helps them to form the groups they will work with, and supports them to figure out how best to merge their individual resource maps in the pursuit of that project and identify the other skills, understanding or people that they may need in order to fulfil that project. The mentor will take on several students each year and will be working with young people across the age range at any one time, so they are able to support students to build teams across the age ranges. The mentors are specialists in resource-map reading, in identifying where individual and group maps might be best extended and enriched depending on the children's interests and experiences, and in identifying others whose knowledge or experience might be a useful resource to draw upon for a number of children. The mentor is then able to approach the librarian for help in identifying other communities or resources beyond the school for support with these areas, or to invite known people, whether adult affiliates or others, into the school to run masterclasses or programmes of study.

'Alongside the mentors are the specialists. These are familiar from the teachers of the past, as they tend to be subject specialists. They are different in a number of ways, however, not least because their disciplinary expertise is kept absolutely up to date through their frequent interactions and placements in full-time practice (in labs, museums, universities, businesses), but they are also specialists in learning sciences, and therefore expert in developing students' conceptual understanding. Much educational research is initiated by specialists in schools and supported by university research specialists. The specialists provide introductory programmes of study for the younger children in key areas, and later they pull together bespoke activities to support the electives that the students need for their projects. The specialists also collaborate closely with other institutions and are responsible for setting up further courses or work experience for students at universities or other organizations once they need more expert tuition and development. The specialists are also responsible for contributing to the school's intellectual resources and for assessing the health of the school's knowledge commons in their specialist areas. Of course, we can't have specialists in every area we might want, but we are able to draw on the resources of other schools to help us if we run short.

'Other important members of the school are those who are now running the social enterprises that contribute to the school's finances and community viability. The cafe, for example, was set up by a group of adults and students several years ago, as a non-profit-making organization dedicated to serving good food to students and visiting adults. It is now an important site for developing students' understanding of energy and food resources, which is pretty important as we're still, like everyone else, trying to deal with the problems of food and energy scarcity. So too the garden shop has become a thriving local resource, selling surplus produce and a range of horticultural supplies and services. Similarly, the housing associations, credit unions and other community groups who occupy the courtyard spaces are both regular partners for the schools in the projects that they run, and sites for the development of community leadership capacity amongst the students. A team of expert technicians supports the maintenance of the laboratories and workshops; this team is usually made up both of students and staff, depending on levels of expertise and interest. New services and tools are constantly being developed by these teams, as students and staff have a friendly rivalry with other local schools and seek to outdo them with the services they are able to offer, although they all contribute to the shared pool of knowledge when they come up with new work-arounds or make new devices. The technicians are also expert recyclers, able to repurpose machines for different uses, and great at extracting materials from old devices for reuse.

'And around this core team is the corona of affiliated adult members of the school. Many members will provide an annual masterclass, on everything from gardening, to experiences of migration, to nuclear engineering or permaculture. These masterclasses are open to all members of the community and streamed live for everyone to be able to participate. Adults volunteer or are invited to give masterclasses and they are supported carefully to be able to do so, should they feel less than confident, by the community co-ordinator and her team. The community co-ordinator's role is to steward and ensure the vitality of the adult affiliated members. Other adult members may play a longer-term role as a team member for a community project, working alongside the students towards a particular goal that they may have an interest in. Because such an involvement can be time-consuming, it is not expected on a regular basis or from everybody. Instead, the mentors and the student groups will carefully identify the most appropriate candidates from everyone in the school map, and invite them along for a discussion about that commitment beforehand. All of the adult affiliate members are free to sign up for the masterclasses and electives that are running in the school, and for those people who for any number of reasons might find such participation difficult, the community co-ordinator's role is to try to work with them to overcome the difficulties they may be facing.

'Why do these adults take part? They do so for selfish reasons – being part of the school helps them in the long run, it gives them access to resources and people and advice and help. Some adults in the community have had real trouble finding jobs; being part of the school community and contributing helps them to build their confidence and at the same time helps them to gain new skills, while the students benefit from having more adults around to encourage them and to collaborate with them. There is another group who are in fairly unstable employment, that comes and goes or that only involves a few hours a week. These people often have high-quality skills and understanding that they can offer, and they are also keen to spend time with other people – working at home on your own can be pretty isolating. Other adults get involved because they know participation helps their own children or because they enjoy the social interaction with other parents. Some adults, particularly those much older partially retired people, participate because they get a lot out of it; contributing to others' learning maintains their sense of status and pride, as well as a feeling of wellbeing. For others, running masterclasses or participating in projects is valuable in and of itself, as the visiting educators are able to become part of their students' projects and learn from them. Some of the visiting educators become quite well known both in their own specialism and across the school system, and are invited to speak elsewhere. These educators may become affiliated with other schools where there are shortages in their area; they may also be invited to become part of national and international distinguished educator networks, where they are invited to centres of excellence to learn about new developments. Distinguished educators in the arts and sciences are often, for example, invited to join study visits to internationally famous theatres or R&D labs to participate in early-stage projects.

'The corona around the school is therefore constantly changing and developing, carefully stewarded by the community co-ordinators, whose responsibility is to support all adult members of the school, to understand their needs and support requirements as well as the contributions that they can make. Often, the community co-ordinators will be encouraging partnerships and relationships between adults who can support each other as well as between adults and younger students.

'Two other very important members of the school are the Librarian and the Gamer. The Gamer is responsible for the experimentation and modelling of possible futures and is concerned particularly with developing the school's capacity to think beyond the obvious. The Gamer's world is one that includes tools for modelling highly complex simulations, theatrical costumes for role-playing different scenarios, biotech labs for rapid evolutionary engineering. The Gamer often takes a keen interest in the Future Game, and is known to archive and review all of the games that are put out into the public domain. Alongside the Gamer works the Librarian; part activist, part curator, part lawyer, part critic, the Librarian is the curator for the school's knowledge commons, responsible for the health of the collective capacity to produce and steward the strategic knowledge that the community needs to imagine and build its desired futures. The Librarian works with students and staff to promote the capacity to critique and contribute to the information landscape. Librarians are also a highly visible presence outside the school as they are usually the people responsible for harnessing the resources of the school and the community in protecting the global knowledge commons against enclosure and pollution. The Librarian cares for the school's intellectual property, and leads the process of determining whether any data and IP generated through the school's projects is capable of being harnessed for the benefit of the community and the wider public good.'

During this description of all the people working in and contributing to the school, you and the mentor have walked through the backstage courtyard, up the stairs and are now standing on the balcony that runs around the first floor. Off this balcony run a series of workshops, studios and laboratories as well as comfortable rooms for reading, talking and just hanging out. Up here there seems to be a greater mix of age groups, and a real buzz of different activities.

In one room there is a team of people aged from about 16 to 72 working on what looks like a giant digital mural like the one on the front of the school. In another there are small groups of students sitting quietly talking around a digital table; they are pulling up images and diagrams as they talk, they are eating breakfast and seem to have been there all night. In another room there is what looks like a conventional lesson going on, although the glowing images on the walls show that people outside the school are taking part and you also realize that there are two teachers. The mentor explains that one is a specialist in ancient history from the university of Shanghai who is video-conferencing in for a short masterclass, and the other is the local teacher who has been working with the university on projects and analysis with the students in the school. In another room, you look in to see no screens, no viewers and silence, as a group of students and staff sit in silence and meditate.

'We've got this sort of range of activities,' says the mentor, 'because we've changed our approach to assessment. To be honest, the resource maps provide a constant and ongoing record of everyone's progress that's much richer than it ever was in the past, and we've got good working relationships with parents – they know us and we know them – and so there's less need to have a load of exams that prove that we're doing our job well. We've also got more ambitious about the sort of assessment that counts. We know that if a child is a brilliant musician, it doesn't make sense just to test them against some sort of average score for her age. Instead, we create opportunities for her to collaborate with other musicians outside the school, and get feedback from them. It's a much richer approach; each student has a sense of where they want to progress, and also can see how they are doing in relation to their peers and in relation to the demands of the particular communities or organizations they might want to join. It makes the old end-of-year scripts circulating around the country and getting lost ritual seem a little strange.'

As you walk round the balcony, you notice a set of maps on the wall, geographical maps this time, with a series of blue, red and green dots flashing on them. 'Those,' says the mentor, 'are the off-site students who have left their school access devices on. Some of them are working on projects, others are on placements, others have gone for tuition at the university. At any time,' says the mentor, 'we'd expect about half of our senior students to be out and about in the wider community. If they need us, or we need them, though, it's easy to get hold of them.' He taps on the map and asks whether it's convenient to talk. The head and shoulders of a 16-year-old girl appear on the screen; she's standing in a city street with a team of surveyors behind her. The mentor and the student talk for a short while about the project she's working on and whether there's any further support she needs. Once they finish talking the mentor explains that this student is one of those who has decided that she'll be taking up the funding and support needed to start her own business next year. Run along co-operative lines, she is working with a small team of researchers and developing a new material that will allow the development of rapid temporary accommodation for those affected by flood conditions. She will work with university researchers over the first couple of years to develop and test it but will also be linked with the social enterprise experts in the courtyard, who will help shepherd her through the early stages of developing her business plan.

As she tells you about the range of new community organizations that the school has helped to set up, you and the mentor have walked back past the workshops and down the stairs, through the courtyard and out to the café, where the mentor now leaves you to get a quick cup of tea before you head back to work. Sitting in the café, you take a long drink and look out through the window at the busy courtyard where you can now make more sense of what is going on.

Outside, there is a group of students working with the hyperlocal media company to create a short film, probably some sort of campaign video for a project they are working on. Behind them, the community organizer's office is full, with students and adults planning the schedule for the rest of the week. Next door there are two young women creating strange digital textiles with a couple of much older ladies, who seem to be showing them how to integrate the fibre optics into the silk. Up on the roof a group of students and technicians are discussing together how the garden might be better managed, and beginning to dig up a whole patch of sedums to be replaced with a new strain grown in the school labs. Walking out of the gate are a group of around 30 children of different ages, along with a couple of mentors, heading off on an urban walk to map the local area, your own daughter amongst them.

You look down at your school bracelet and play with it gently. It comes to life and projects your map onto the table in front of you. You rapidly cycle through to the biographical layer and scan the images that you've loaded on there over the last few months during your long journey north from your old life. And as you do, you think about the stories you could share about that journey, and about your life before, and you wonder how things might be different for you, and your family, in future. And at that point, you look up at the wall of the school and know that in the glowing map up there, you and your daughter's own maps and histories are now part of it. What, you wonder, will you add to that map, what might you learn from it and how will you change it in future?

Chapter 9

Making it real

It is one thing to envisage a possible future for education, quite another to begin to build it. If we are to make the idea of a future-building school a reality, we need to know that others are also working in this direction and that there are steps to take to get there. Both of these are the case. There are already elements of a future-building school being developed by educators and researchers around the world, and there are strategic steps that school leaders, policy-makers, community organizers, researchers and technology developers can take to bring it closer to reality.

Educational futures already in development

Many schools already see the business of education not merely as preparation for a predefined and unchangeable future, but as concerned with building the capabilities of their students to question the futures they are being offered, to think for themselves about the futures that are in development and, in some cases, to work with others to create fairer and more equitable futures. These schools are exploring new collaborations with their communities and demonstrating new ways in which they can act as laboratories for experimenting with social change.[1]

There are exciting examples of how schools can foster children's capacity to act as researchers and activists with a real impact on the world. In India, the Riverside school is designed around principles that see each child as 'a protagonist', encouraging them from the earliest age to initiate meaningful projects at local and global levels. This sees children partnering with NGOs to improve their local communities, working with other local schools and mobilizing digital networks to set up international partnerships and initiatives. The school also acts as a site where specialists are brought in to provide masterclasses and provocations to encourage reflection and trigger activities. The Earthforce programme for change in the USA equips teachers and young people with tools to research environmental problems and take civic action; these include supporting schools to conduct community audits, research solutions to environmental problems, initiate new services in partnership with local authorities and evaluate their activities. Projects such as iEARN run across 130 countries, 26,000 teachers and over 2 million students to conduct international collaborative projects defined by the question 'How will this project improve the quality of life on the planet?' This programme includes hundreds of projects, including collaborative river mapping, sampling and analysis across multiple countries to provide meaningful data on water supplies and human impacts; international collaborative travelling art projects; youth summits addressing issues such as disaster relief; cross-country projects on teen identity; and many more.[2] The HighTech High School network in the USA already successfully demonstrates the potential for young people to play an active and meaningful role in their communities through projects that build real partnerships with local community organizations and social enterprises.[3]

Democratic schools take this idea in a different direction and create spaces in which young people can be involved in taking meaningful responsibility within their educational institution. In these settings, new forms of adult–child relationship are being modelled, premised upon expectations of mutual respect and, in some cases, an openness to the expertise that individuals can offer regardless of age.[4] Young people and adults have a shared stake in these schools and in most cases are jointly responsible for developing the rules by which they are managed. These institutions act as important crucibles for democratic processes. They support students to reflect upon educational and social purpose, and build the capacity to contest, debate and imagine new trajectories for social change. Michael Fielding and Peter Moss have provided a powerful rallying point for the next stage of democratic schooling with their vision of a 'Common School' that is intimately connected with its locality.[5]

Important lessons are also being learned by the Small Schools/Human Scale Education movements about how to build educational institutions that are premised upon strong human relationships. These movements are producing systematic insights into the benefits to be gained from smaller educational structures and institutions and providing practical strategies for educators and parents wishing to create human-scale education practices even within the context of contemporary industrial-sized factory schools. These small-school approaches act as a foundation for building stronger links between schools and parents, teachers and pupils, and a basis for building the human relationships and understanding that can underpin real dialogue about educational purpose for the individual and the community.[6]

A new relationship between educational institutions and economic practices is also being developed by the growing involvement of some schools in co-operative and social enterprise activity. The Co-operative Movement, for example, has schools around the world where young people are encouraged to explore and develop business models dedicated to co-operative and other common wealth principles. Critically, these schools are often run through co-operative governance models, with every member of the school community having a stake and a say in the running of the schools, and with membership forums setting agendas for the organization. The promotion of social enterprise is a taken-for-granted part of many co-operative schools in Portugal, Spain and Scandinavia, often with children involved in budgeting and financial control as well as the production of products. In the UK, there are examples of Special Needs Schools setting up successful potteries and eco-schools establishing garden centres.[7] Internationally, there is a network dedicated to increasing the availability of agricultural education in developing countries by making it financially sustainable.[8] What these institutions demonstrate is the potential for schools to act as powerful resources not merely for preparing children for participation in global economic networks, but for enabling them to build resilient local enterprises and reduce their dependence upon external economic factors.

The long-standing Reggio Emilia initiative in Italy has for many years been a resource for insight into education as a collective community responsibility. It has inspired early years and primary education around the world.[9] In the UK, the Royal Society for the Arts is developing its Area Based Curriculum, a curriculum designed with students and local communities to better allow schools to draw upon community resources from museums to local community organizations to individual and informal learning resources.[10] More recently, initiatives such as author Dave Eggers's superhero stores across the United States have begun to inspire a range of artists, community activists, parents and educators to play a role in enhancing students' learning. These stores are staffed and run by community volunteers in partnership with local schools, with a specific focus on developing student literacy. They create desirable places (the first was behind a Pirate Supplies store selling spare wooden legs, parrots and eye patches) for students to learn in, and they harness the creative and passionate skills of communities with time to give.[11]

We are also seeing universities beginning to develop creative and resilient partnerships with schools and communities. The Educational Justice Collaborative in California, for example, seeks to harness the distinct expertise of researchers, school students and community organizers to build shared knowledge resources that can document causes of, and strategies to address, educational inequalities.[12] Universities can also draw inspiration from community activists who have been building meaningful partnerships with schools for decades, such as the Logan Square Neighborhood Association in Chicago founded in the 1960s. This has developed effective initiatives to respond to issues ranging from poor school buildings, to parent literacy, to the development of mortgage programmes to encourage educators to live in the communities they teach in.[13]

The generational divide that has seen schools only as centres for children is also being challenged. Intergenerational learning projects are being promoted by advocates for older generations as critical resources for building intergenerational solidarity and improving wellbeing in older generations, as well as enhancing understanding amongst younger groups. Projects include those in Manchester where three generations of women and girls work together to build archives about suffragette and feminist knowledge. One cross-generational educational institution is being built in London that promises to embed principles of intergenerational learning into the heart of educational practice.[14]

Some schools and developers are also beginning to harness digital technologies to overcome long-standing obstacles to changing the organization of time and space in schools. Personal learning environments are being developed by researchers to help students marshal learning experiences across diverse school, informal and workplace settings.[15] New planning tools are emerging that begin to offer educators significant flexibility and freedom to respond to student interests and to reconfigure learning spaces and resources around their needs on a more responsive and ad hoc basis.[16] New timetabling tools, along with changed teaching and learning practices, have the potential to make it easier for schools to act as platforms for collaborative, cross-institutional projects and begin to shed light on how to overcome the logistical difficulties that often seem to preclude exploration of alternative practice.[17] The deliberative democracy movement also offers powerful examples of community dialogue in action and new tools to facilitate meaningful public debate across highly diverse communities.[18]

A future-building school is not, therefore, a pipe dream. It is already, and in many different ways, in production. It forms part of the diverse educational experiences of educators, communities and students around the world and it has deep historical roots, whether in the co-operative traditions dating back to northern English cities in the nineteenth century, or in the anti-colonialist movements that shaped rural education in India in the mid twentieth. This very small snapshot of some of the different approaches already in place offers an insight into the rich resources for a future-building school that we already have to draw upon.[19] They offer useful inspiration, confidence and precedents for educators and show that it is possible to design educational practice that escapes the confines of the test score and the constraints of performance management. They also begin to demonstrate ways round the long-standing difficulties of logistical and organizational inertia.

The challenge now is to bring these different elements together, to combine the view of children as actors in the world, the strong relationship with community, the humane socio-technical systems and the development of an equitable economic language. A future-building school, after all, is not just a democratic school, or a school that promotes problem-based learning, or a school that builds strong links with its local community. Nor is it simply a well-equipped school that appropriates digital technologies to offer new approaches to project work, timetabling and curriculum.

Instead, it is a school that recognizes its role as a prefigurative space for building socio-technical futures. In other words, it sees itself as a place in which students, teachers and the wider community can come together to understand how to live well and wisely with our emergent technological capabilities. It is a place that is profoundly reflective upon the questions of how our socio-technical practices shape the social, economic and cultural institutions in which we live. And it is a place that seeks to ask how these practices – whether networked democracy or nano-medicine, whether virtual call centres or the creation of new digital textiles – can be harnessed to achieve fairer, more sustainable and more democratic futures for all. It is a democratic school that neither resists technology because it mistakenly assumes it is an inevitable force for dehumanization nor uncritically accepts it as an inevitable good. Instead, it is a school that rewrites the relationship between education and socio-technical futures; it sees socio-technical change as a process that its students and communities can intervene in and which should therefore, in the school, be the focus of democratic critical experimentation with new ways of living.

To build such schools requires the wisdom, creativity and passion of educators, policy-makers, researchers and technologists, and it requires action in multiple arenas, some of which are already well under way, others requiring a little more of a kick start.

Nine conditions to enable a future-building schools

1   *Build new governance and accountability arrangements for schools*
    For schools to really begin to design educational practices that address the needs and aspirations of their communities will mean addressing the question of accountability and success measures for schools.[20] A first step towards a future-building school is therefore the development of new governance structures that embed community–school dialogue about educational purpose at the heart of the school.[21] The co-operative approach that establishes community ownership of the institution and establishes members' forums to shape school strategy, offers a raft of models for such a structure, and there are thousands of schools worldwide that demonstrate how such principles can be adapted to widely divergent local circumstances.[22] On the basis of meaningful dialogue with students, parents and communities, new discussions can begin about the value and purpose of education, and alternative measures of assessment and success can be negotiated beyond league tables and exam certificates.[23]

2   *Ensure that schools have the right to create a local curriculum*
    The future-building school requires the creation of space in the curriculum for local communities to define educational goals that will equip them to adapt to change. In some countries this is taken for granted and has a long tradition. In the UK, however, this means that the balance between local and national responsibility for curriculum design will need to be shifted. A national curriculum has some benefit in terms of creating a shared consensus around the entitlements that all students might expect from education. It also, however, has the deleterious effect of making it very difficult for educators to explore with communities and students the educational programmes that might best meet their needs, experiences and aspirations.[24] The recent Cambridge Primary Review's recommendation that schools should operate a (70:30) split between a nationally prescribed curriculum and a locally prescribed curriculum has evident merit in this context.[25] It retains the basis upon which a national debate can be held around entitlement,

and it opens up the potential for communities, students and educators to define educational needs at a local level.

3   *Build tools for mapping students' and schools' wider education ecology*
New ways of mapping the resource networks of members of a school, of the school as a whole, and of the wider community need to be developed. These are needed to allow students to reflect upon their own networks; to allow parents and community members to know where and how best they might contribute to schools; and to allow schools and the members of the school community to understand the resources that are available.[26]

In the short term, existing social networking tools can be used to build these networks. Over the longer term there is an interesting technical challenge to create easy-to-use, beautiful resource maps that allow individuals control over how much, when and where they share them with others. Creative digital artists as well as programmers with an interest in interoperability will be needed to figure out precisely how it is possible.

More than that, however, this is a social challenge that will need to overturn centuries of education being seen as a separate space from society. The organization of the school around smaller units to build deeper human relationships between teachers, parents and students; the establishment of the school as a site of intergenerational learning so that all adults can begin to participate in and contribute to the educational process, may be steps that can be taken to enrich the school's education ecology.[27]

4   *Reconnect education with housing, economic, transport and environmental policies*
Schools cannot overcome the insidious inequalities produced by wider economic and social policies on their own and the interdependence of education and these wider issues needs to be acknowledged. Housing problems, for example, are exacerbated by school selection policies. Educational attainment, reciprocally, is affected by poverty, lack of access to work, and poor and unstable housing.[28] At local and national levels, housing, transport and employment policies need to be developed with their impact on educational fairness in mind. Free transport for schoolchildren, for example, would radically increase the access of all children to cultural organizations. Affordable housing policies that supported long-term family stability would enhance educational attainment.

Schools can also take steps to build sustainable communities beyond the school walls. For example, they can initiate fair banding selection policies that will overcome the use of housing purchases as a basis for school entry.[29] They can act as responsible employers and purchasers, able to make a contribution as a large employer to a local community.

5   *Assess for competency not certification*
Changed governance arrangements and the development of a local curriculum begin to open up the possibility of schools developing more meaningful assessment arrangements that are not wholly determined by comparative test scores. At the same time, socio-technical developments will also play an

important role. Our existing assessment system was designed in an era in which it was difficult to capture and circulate information about a person. The next two decades are likely to usher in a period in which we are able to produce massive amounts of data about the individual on an ongoing basis, in which we are able to analyse that data intelligently and provide continuous feedback. In this setting, the annual ritual of exam halls and sporadic high-stakes testing, rather than constant ongoing observation and feedback on practice in the context of people and resources, will be hard to sustain.

There is a an urgent and pressing need, then, for educators, students, parents and employers to begin to talk about what a fair representation of the student might be for their own benefit, to inform their teachers, and as a means of explaining their potential and their expertise to the wider world of employers and communities.

6   *Rethink child protection policy*

The future-building school needs to build new relations of care and support between generations. This offers an opportunity to come at the question of child protection policy from a different direction. In the UK, the costs to civil liberties of seeking to scrutinize every adult who encounters a child through schools are becoming increasingly clear. At the same time, the increasing regulation of access to children by non-familial adults cannot guarantee children's safety.

It may therefore be time to explore whether the co-production models of public services that are being applied in areas such as policing and health could reasonably be used as a basis for discussions of child protection. Such a model would imply that child protection cannot be seen simply as a matter for professionals and parents but needs to be embedded in much wider relationships of care and concern within the community. Rather than seeking to prevent as many adults as possible from engaging with children, then, the strategy would seek to equip as many adults as possible with responsibility for and tools to support children. The strategy would seek to build and enhance the bonds of intergenerational care within communities and between non-familial adults and children. At the same time, children themselves would be seen as important actors in their own protection, and equipping them with the skills to recognize risk and the confidence to draw on multiple sources of support from friends, professionals, family and other adults as appropriate, would become a priority.[30]

In this revisioning of child protection strategy, the school that sought to build relationships of care and of reciprocal exchange between children and the wider adult community would be understood not as placing children at risk, but as building the social solidarity and social capital needed to help them resist potential harm. This is likely to be a highly contentious debate, but without it there is little chance of an intelligent redesign of schools over the coming decades. It should be noted that the school systems that are held up as international models of educational success, such as those in Finland, operate in a social context where children have significant amounts of social and spatial freedom, in which their rights to participate as social actors are valued and acknowledged, and where their protection has not been equated with their separation from adult society.

7 *Rethink teacher education and build a programme of public engagement with education*

The future-building school needs new sorts of educator.[31] It will require expert pedagogues, able not only to appropriate and lead debate about developments in learning sciences and learning technologies, but also to choreograph the disparate elements of the wider educational ecosystem into coherent educational experiences for learners. It will require expert mentors, able to work with students and families to think carefully about possible futures, and to build programmes of education around them. It will require new roles for librarians, supporting school members to harness and filter the information ecosystem and harnessing the intellectual property of the organization. It will require the development of school leaders with the humility, insight and knowledge needed to build common cause with wider social movements and with expertise in inspiring and leading a massively diverse body of educators, informal educators and community advisors. The school will still require subject expertise and specialists in pedagogic content knowledge – the ability to translate disciplinary understanding into the creation of effective learning environments. Such teachers may still be based in schools, others may be drawn from universities and even from industry and may share their teaching activities across multiple settings.[32]

At the same time there will be a call for a new 'public understanding of education' programme that serves to support community organizers, local government and others seeking to build bridges between education and other policy areas. This programme will also need to support the folk educators, volunteers, adult learners and others who may want to play explicit pedagogic roles in school. Programmes of teacher education will therefore need to radically diversify to meet these needs.

8 *Build school–university collaborations to democratize research*

For universities, museums or industry partners who have a vested interest in developing new knowledge, the rationale for engagement with schools as research partners is becoming clearer.[33] The value of working with 'users' of services and products in early-stage development is already widely acknowledged. As the digital tools for data capture, collation and analysis become more accessible, non-specialists such as students, schools, parents and communities can play a useful role in gathering, developing and analysing valuable knowledge. In these arrangements, museums and universities get access to new ideas in the development of programmes of research and access to a wider body of people to help conduct that research. Reciprocally, schools get access to specialist expertise and to support with ensuring the rigour and public value of the resources and ideas that they generate.[34]

9   *Develop an ethical code for the educational use of digital and bio-technologies*
The critical challenge for developers, designers and publishers working with
education is to recognize that the sorts of socio-technical practice that they
envisage for schools have the potential to act as prefigurative practices for
wider society. In this context they need to ask whether the sorts of human
relationship and interaction that they are developing for schools are the ones
that they would wish to see replicated more widely as students and
communities become habituated to them.

Over the next decade, the sorts of powerful tool we envisage students
using may extend into the fields of bio-engineering, of rapid animatronic
prototyping and material fabrication. They may offer the capacity to
document children's genetic inheritance, their brain functioning in response
to stimulus from teachers, and pharmacological tools to affect concentration,
attention and retention of information. We need to be certain that schools
cannot simply be treated as new markets like any other. The education
system, like medicine, requires an ethical code to govern the appropriation
and use of emergent technologies, and a system of sharing lessons learned
about their risks and potential around the system.

Teachers, students and communities, under these conditions, would take on new
roles as explorers and critics of new socio-technical practices. No longer simply
recipients of socio-technical futures designed for them elsewhere, the schools
would rewrite the relationship between education and socio-technical change as
one of active design, critique and engagement.

Conclusion

In the introduction to this book I said that I wanted to ask whether the orthodox
future of an ever-expanding global knowledge economy was sufficiently rich or robust
to act as a basis for redesigning education systems today. I hope that my discussion of
the stranger, more disruptive and potentially less benign future trajectories that are
latent in contemporary socio-technical change makes clear that it is not.

The orthodox future does not, for example, prepare us for the choices we may
have to make about how and whether we wish to augment our intelligence,
enhance evolution, learn across very long lifetimes, or work alongside other forms
of machine intelligence. It does not equip us to protect our emerging knowledge
resources from pollution and enclosure, nor prepare us to build and exploit them.
This orthodox future is silent about the choices we have about the relationships of
care for our elderly and our young and the systems of democracy and accountability
that we may want to build. Most importantly, the orthodox future has little other
than unfounded optimism to offer as a strategy for tackling self-evident problems
of increasing inequalities and economic dispossession, energy scarcity and climate
disruption. In short, the orthodox future we are using as a basis for designing our
education systems at present is a myopic, largely implausible and highly selective

vision of the future and is no longer 'fit for purpose' for equitable educational design and policy-making. If such a future is no longer a reliable guide for educational design, we need a new approach. And this approach has to be one in which education institutions are not seen merely as servicing a future designed elsewhere, but as institutions capable of helping all of us, young and old, to make good decisions about the futures we want and the social, technological and ecological resources we need and have available to build them. *We need schools that are resources for enabling students and communities to imagine, and to take achievable steps along the road to the building of, sustainable and equitable futures.*

Schools themselves are not secure, unchanging institutions from which to observe socio-technical change; they too are sites through which new socio-technical practices are being negotiated through the control of biometric data, the appropriation of new pharmacological regimes or the implementation of performance management systems. Beyond the school there is also a growing educational ecosystem made visible by the current structures of the Web that enables the flourishing of informal learning through digital cultures, the easy networking of folk educators, the circulation of information and educational resources. In the light of the increasing oppression of 'schooled' socio-technical cultures and the seeming flowering of a new culture of informal learning, one strand of thought suggests that we should leave behind the school and transform the homes, neighbourhoods and workplaces of our cities into a new integrated learning society.

The potential for socio-technical change to intensify radical social, economic and educational inequalities, however, means that there are very good reasons to argue the case for the school as a physical public institution and as a public educational resource. As one of the last universal public services, the school has the capacity to act as a forum for communities to come together to understand and navigate changing socio-technical contexts. As public educational institutions, schools have the capacity to ensure that communities have access to the powerful and strategic knowledge needed to drive socio-technical change. As a community institution, the school has the capacity to act as a hub for mobilizing the resources of that community and for networking and linking the community strategically to others fighting the same battles.

If they are to play these roles, however, schools need to be re-imagined as institutions that are designed for future-building not future-proofing. They need to be designed to help students and communities engage with the real choices, risks and opportunities posed by contemporary socio-technical change in their neighbourhoods, workplaces and lives. They need to be designed to help students and communities to test out, critique and develop alternative ways of living in new socio-technical contexts and to develop the capabilities they need to solve existing problems, build strategic allegiances and create stronger, more equitable and more resilient neighbourhoods. The school, as Jean Anyon argues, needs to 'join the world of communities, families and students; it must advocate for them and emerge from their urgent realities'.[35]

We need education institutions, in other words, that are premised not upon the doomed modernization that seeks to 'retool' existing institutions with new technologies, like strapping wings onto a caterpillar. Instead, we need to return to the core DNA of schools, their claim to act as a resource for helping students, communities and societies to thrive in the future, and to ask what that really means today.[36]

The future is not certain. The socio-technical developments of the next 20 years will not evolve smoothly and inevitably along one predictable trajectory. They will emerge messily and unevenly out of the aspirations, struggle and compromises between different social actors. We cannot determine the future that will unfold. We can, however, create schools that are public spaces and democratic laboratories that can play a powerful role in tipping the balance of that change in favour of sustainable futures for all of our students.

Notes

Introduction

1 Michael Young (1998) argues that debates about education are 'always, implicitly or explicitly, about alternative views of society and its future'.
2 Obama (2010)
3 Gates (2005)
4 Adams and Groves (2007)
5 Sidorkin (2009)
6 This account of the future is perhaps best exemplified in the Shift Happens slideshow (Fisch, 2000), a brilliantly compelling slideshow first made by a teacher in the USA, then picked up and promoted by policy-makers, industry and educators, including Microsoft and the head of the World Bank. The slideshow consists of a series of slides that present a set of statistics about socio-technical change to a soundtrack (in some versions) from *The Last of the Mohicans*. Seen by over 4 million people, the slides present images both of relentless and unpredictable technological change, and of inevitable economic competition. One slide, for example, reads, 'they [China] have more gifted and talented students than we have students'; another reads, 'if you took every single job in the US today and shipped it to China they would still have a labour surplus'. A compelling sequence of slides argues, 'we are currently preparing students for jobs that don't yet exist .. using technologies that haven't been invented .. in order to solve problems we don't even know are problems yet'. The slideshow finishes with the statement 'Now You Know.' The message is clear – this is the future, education needs to change to meet the needs of this economically competitive digital environment; what are you, as educators, going to do to ensure that we can compete to keep our place in the world?
7 Papert (1993)
8 O'Hara (2007)
9 In these future visions, however, education is often overlooked. Instead, where visions of educational futures emerge, the schools of *Star Trek* or the *Jetsons* are pretty similar to those of the *Flintstones*, giving the impression of education as a fixed cultural practice while all around it changes. There are some brilliant exceptions to this rule, such as the all-teaching, all-responsive 'Book' in *The Diamond Age*, the use of cloning and immersive experiences in *A Rag, a Bone and a Hank of Hair*, or the intergenerational problem-solving of *Rainbow's End*. As an educator, these can provide an interesting shock to the system. See Stephenson (1995), Fisk (1980), Vinge (2006) respectively.
10 The field of futures studies is less a field than a highly diverse network of different organizations, theoretical perspectives and methodologies that resist summarizing

in this limited space. It comprises academia, NGOs, commercial consultancy and government bodies. The following people's work has been influential in shaping the arguments in this book: Barbara Adam and Chris Groves, James Dator, Sohail Inayatullah, Richard Slaughter, David Hicks, Ivana Milojevic, Francis Hutchinson. Recent texts relating particularly to educational futures from these authors include: Dator (2008), Inayatullah (2008a), Slaughter (2004), Hicks (2008), Milojevic (2005), Hutchinson (1996), Beare and Slaughter (1993). The three-part summary in the next paragraph draws on Inayatullah's 'Futures Triangle' described in Inayatullah (2008a).

11 My reading of these perspectives is that they are in many respects a different way of coming at the age-old social sciences question about the relationship between individual agency and existing social structures. The Critical Futures perspective, upon which I draw here, takes a position that is congruent with the perspectives of Critical Social Sciences (e.g. Bhaskar 1975, Sayer 2000, Chouliaraki and Fairclough 1999) in arguing for a historical and structural analysis of the conditions of possibility of change.

12 There are, of course, radically different attitudes towards the future and how it is produced. Different religious, cultural and historical perspectives towards the future, for example, would see it differently, as a space shaped by mutual responsibilities across generations, or as determined by natural cycles, or as foreseen by prophets. Adams and Groves (2007) provide an insight into these diverse perspectives. They do conclude, however, with a call for a reconnection between action, ethics and knowledge in the handling of 'futurity' and argue that 'knowing that things could and can be different empowers us to infuse future making with concern and responsibility appropriate to our timeprint'.

13 Latour (1988), Standage (1999)

14 Grint and Woolgar (1997) and Woolgar (2002) provide useful accounts of the risks of technological determination and examples of how socio-technical practices are produced.

15 Silverstone and Hirsch (1992)

16 This argument is indebted to Williams (2006).

17 These questions have been the subject of curriculum debate since Dewey. Three provocative recent contributions to this field are Michael Fielding and Peter Moss's *Radical Education and the Common School*, Kieran Egan's *The Future of Education* (2009) and Gert Biesta's *Beyond Learning* (2006).

18 Baker (2009)

19 The BCH team included (from Futurelab) Steve Sayers, Richard Sandford, Clara Lemon, Joanne O'Hagan, Jessica Pykett, Duncan Thompson, Mary Ulicsak, Dan Sutch, Cecilia Thirlway, Lacia Ashman, Marisa Harlington, Sarah Godfrey, Graham Hopkins and (from DCSF) Doug Brown, Dominic Flitcroft and Bill Gibbon. The commissioning and analysis of evidence reviews in four key areas was led by Professor Sarah Harper, Professor Carey Jewitt, Professor Helen Haste and Professor Rob Wilson and specialist technical expertise was offered throughout by Professor Dave Cliff. A wider expert advisory group played an important role in the programme and the full list of members can be found at www. beyondcurrenthorizons.org.uk. Any errors or ommissions in this book, however, are my own.

20 These are available to view in abbreviated form at www.visionmapper.org.uk. The lengthy scenarios authored by Richard Sandford and Helen Beetham (2009) are available at www.beyondcurrenthorizons.org.uk/evidence

21 This list derives in particular from Cliff *et al.*'s 2008 paper for BCH on future socio-technical trends and upon the UNICEF (2007) analysis of the implications

of climate warming. It also draws upon a number of publications including Amos (2006), Steffen (2008), Rees (2004) and Castells (2009), which provided further generative insights into socio-technical and environmental perspectives. The final assumption is informed by Wilkinson and Pickett's *Spirit Level* (2010) and Danny Dorling's *Injustice* (2010a). My argument that these assumptions can act as a basis for optimism as well as anxiety, particularly for educators, is based on a combined reading of Jean Anyon's (2005) *Radical Possibilities* that maps out the potential for schools to act as powerful resources for social movement building, Mario Luis Small's (2009) argument that community organizations have the capacity to build social networks, and Peter Levine's (2007) argument that digital resources can be mobilized in support of building community knowledge capital.

22 Cliff *et al.* (2008)
23 Khajeh-Hosseini *et al.* (2010), Cliff *et al.* (2008)
24 Cliff *et al.* (2008)
25 Harper *et al.* (2008)
26 Daanen and Facer (2007)
27 Sefton-Green (2009), Price *et al.* (2009)
28 Carrington and Marsh (2009), Greenfield (2003)
29 Woolgar (2002)
30 Price *et al.* (2009). See www.specknet.org/. See Cliff *et al.* (2008). See also the journal *Nanomedicine*, www.futuremedicine.com/loi/nnm
31 Cliff *et al.* (2008)
32 Castells (2009)
33 Mulgan (1998)
34 Leadbeater (2008)
35 Turney (2009)
36 Blakemore and Frith (2005)
37 Rose (2001), Lee (2011)
38 Harper (2009)
39 Harper (2009)
40 Hall and Day (2009), Leggett (2005)
41 Bafilemba (2010)
42 UNICEF (2007)
43 This assumption is not necessarily borne out by contemporary political decision-making, but its alternative would be to overlook humanity's long-standing ingenuity in the face of catastrophe.
44 UNICEF (2007)
45 Wilkinson and Pickett (2010), Dorling (2010a)
46 Dorling (2010a)
47 Erik Olin Wright (2009) argues for the importance of developing viable alternative futures in his Real Utopias project, and details interesting criteria about what might constitute a viable alternative.
48 In this selective focus, I was heavily influenced by the earliest discussions in the Beyond Current Horizons Programme, where we sought to scope out our area of attention. In this project, educators, policy-makers and researchers were asked what they thought the most important issues for education were in relation to socio-technical change, and these were the broad areas that were identified.

I Is there a future for schools?

1 See Kelan and Lehnert (2009) as well as the Macarthur Foundation Series on Digital Media and Learning, for a summary of the wide range of projects in this field.

2 Ito *et al.* (2010), Stephen *et al.* (2008), Sefton-Green and Buckingham (1998), Facer *et al.* (2003), Holloway and Valentine (2003), Downes (2002), Drotner (2008)

3 Rogoff (2003) see also Hughes (2009–10) and Colley *et al.* (2003) for a discussion of patterns of learning in informal and formal settings. See also Erstad (2009) for a different take on learning lives across different locations.

4 See, for example, Hoffman (2007).

5 Sefton-Green (1998), Buckingham (2000)

6 Crook and Harrison (2008), Ito *et al.* (2008, 2010)

7 Plowman *et al.* (2008), Ito *et al.* (2010)

8 Crook and Harrison (2008), Ito *et al.* (2008)

9 See, for example, Payal Arora's (2010) analysis of the various international 'hole in the wall' learning experiments.

10 Facer *et al.* (2003), Hughes (2009–10)

11 DiSalvo *et al.* (2009), New London Group (1997)

12 Muller and Young (2009). Young (2010) argues the case for recognizing the differences between informal learning and the systematic teaching required to develop conceptual understanding in fields such as science and mathematics.

13 E.g. Claxton (2008)

14 E.g. Boseley (2007)

15 E.g. Lawes *et al.* (2007)

16 E.g. Sawyer (2009), Craft (2010)

17 Aldrich (2008)

18 For a good long-term summary of these debates, see Selwyn (2011).

19 See Oakes *et al.* (2008) for a discussion of the mistake of assuming that narrowing 'the attainment gap' is the right measure for educational fairness. See also Dorling (2010b).

20 Biesta (2007)

21 Alexander (2009)

22 Hargreaves (2003)

23 Hannam and Razzall (2007). See the [US] National Center for Educational Statistics *Digest* (2009). In the USA, the increase in the percentage of home-schooled students represents a 74 per cent relative increase over the 8-year period to 2007, to 2.9 per cent of students.

24 Woods *et al.* (2005)

25 Smeaton (2009)

26 Davidson and Goldberg (2009)

27 Borja (2005)

28 Barbour and Reeves (2009)

29 First College (www.firstcollege.co.uk/), InterHigh (www.interhigh.net/), LBGTQ (www.glbtqonlinehighschool.com/academics.html).

30 See Sohail Inayatullah (2008a)

31 Chain schools are familiar in the TEFL (Teaching English as a Foreign Language) world and operate internationally with standardized practices, as do the private schools in the GEMS network. In mainstream education there are a wide variety of types of education 'chain'. For example, the United World College chain links together schools that seek to promote international solidarity and global citizenship (www.atlanticcollege.org/). Others are private corporations working within state systems, such as the Kunskapsskolan chain of ICT-rich primary and secondary schools in the UK and Sweden (www.kunskapsskolan.se/foretaget/inenglish.4. 1d32e45f86b8ae04c7fff213.html).

32 This metaphor of the learning ecosystem and educational ecology has been explored by a number of other researchers. I first came across the idea in discussions with Patrick Dillon as part of the development of a response to instrumental ideas of

personalization. He and Loi take the idea in the direction of exploring adaptive educational systems in Loi and Dillon (2006). Rose Luckin (2010a, 2010b) has also developed a language for mapping and describing the ecology of student learning resources that is particularly relevant for those seeking to build new institutional and technological arrangements. See also Horst and Sawyer, cited in Jewitt (2009).

33 Wiley and Hilton (2009), Bradwell (2009)
34 Janes (2009), Bradburne (2005)
35 www.TED.com
36 www.khanacademy.org/
37 Wiley and Hilton (2009), Davidson and Goldberg (2009)
38 See also TeachStreet, in Seattle, which offers a similar service (www.teachstreet.com/). As far as I can tell, these services have yet to be evaluated and it would be interesting to see which groups are actually taking up the offer to teach and to learn through these exchanges which are still organized, in many cases, around financial exchange for courses rather than community contribution.
39 Craig *et al.* (2009)
40 Ostrom (1999), Ostrom (2000), Pestoff and Brandsen (2006)
41 Kretzmann and McKnight (1997). See also Edwards (2009).
42 Stephens *et al.* (2008), Elwyn and Edwards (2009)
43 We Want Everything (2009)
44 Vasagar (2010)
45 Barclays University: www.personal.barclays.co.uk/BRC1/jsp/brccontrol?task=articlegraduate&site=pfs&value=6817&menu=4289
46 Homan and Macpherson (2005), Heller (2001)
47 Thompson (2000)
48 Elliot and Woolcock (2008)
49 Richard Sandford reports from Singapore of major pharmaceutical companies partnering with local schools to set up research labs and produce viable commercial products.
50 Davidson and Goldberg (2009)
51 Paul Miller, quoted in Greenhill (2009).
52 See Attwell (2003) and Attwell and Costa (2009) for a discussion of a future of personalized learning environments.
53 Miller (2008: 65)
54 Many children find schools oppressive and violent places. Many children cannot succeed within them. The fantastic NotSchool programme is an example of how digital technologies can be used to build relationships of trust and support around young people to allow them to continue learning outside schools and to build their own personal learning programmes. See www.inclusiontrust.org and www.notschool.org
55 See Levine (2007), Berry and McLaughlin (2007).

2 A new generational contract

1 Ariès (1973), Prout (2005), James and Prout (1990)
2 Lee (2001), Lee (2011)
3 Buckingham (2000)
4 Craft (2010)
5 Selwyn (2003) and Facer *et al.* (2001)
6 Prensky (2001)
7 For a more detailed discussion of these new forms of adulthood and childhood, see Lee (2001) and Beck (1992).

8 Lego, quoted p6 in Jenson (2006).
9 See Jenson (2000), Facer *et al.* (2001).
10 See Harper (2009) and Howse (2009) for summaries of the demographic shifts. Importantly, this is not expected to be only a Western phenomenon. Ageing populations are in evidence internationally, with Asia in particular experiencing a steep decline in fertility as educated women are confronted with starkly divergent prospects depending on whether they choose to have children or not.
11 Leeson (2009)
12 Leeson (2009)
13 Jessel (2009)
14 In 1981 4.3 per cent of employed people in the UK carried out their work mainly at or from home; by 2006, this figure was 11 per cent, 3.2 million workers (Felstead 2009). See also Hogarth and Bosworth (2009) and Round (2009).
15 As Felstead (2009) argues, workers have to devise their own work–life balance in the context of unclear boundaries and competing pressures from managers, colleagues, clients, spouses, children and friends. Workers, therefore, have more discretion over the construction of their daily routines but also need to mobilize high levels of self-direction, self-management and self-motivation.
16 Jewitt (2009)
17 Harper *et al.* (2008), Harper (2009), OECD (2008)
18 Beck (1992)
19 Harper (2009), Macgregor (2003)
20 Today, while around a fifth of professionals may work at home for one day a week, it is only 15 per cent for workers overall. There may be a profound resistance to reshaping the home as a site for paid labour, and an attractiveness to the collegiality and non-domestic interactions in the workplace is frequently undervalued. Different families, therefore, are likely to be differently positioned in their capacity and their desire to merge home and work spaces; although the pressures to colonize family space and time by formal employment are likely to be felt by all of those with work. See Felstead (2009).
21 Mann (2009), Berthoud (2005)
22 Ito *et al.* (2010)
23 Lloyd (2008), United Nations (2003)
24 Ito *et al.* (2010)
25 Ito *et al.* (2010)
26 See also Buckingham (2000) and Craft (2010).
27 Leadbeater (2004: 10)
28 See Fielding (2009) for a critique of student voice activities that construct the child as consumer.
29 Bentley (1998: 80–1)
30 Bauman (2005)
31 Facer and Furlong (2001)
32 Gove (2009)
33 See Biesta (2006: 109).
34 Prout (2008)
35 Sawhill and Monea (2008)
36 Foundation for the Rights of Future Generations: www.intergenerationaljustice.org
37 Willets (2010)
38 Garman (2009) 'This is not youthful rebellion', *Observer*, 8 March 2009.
39 Over the long term, a generation of young people who have grown up living with the consequences of previous generations' decisions are themselves going to be asked to take decisions with potentially profound long-term consequences.

Will we see future generations 'discounted' as they are at the present time, where their demands for clean air, water, food and healthy environments are seen as less important than the needs of today's generations? Or will we see the establishment of new modes of accountability to unborn generations? Some interesting experiments in such forms of governance are emerging as researchers, policy-makers and others begin to struggle with these questions. Researchers in the USA, for example, are beginning to explore how to communicate the potential risks from radiation to future generations who may not speak our languages (Rosenberg and Harding 2005). Others are setting up institutions to specifically represent the future unborn generations and to attempt to speak for them in public debate. Such projects imply the development of intergenerational contracts of care that span multiple generations into the past and long into the future.

40 Sawyer (2009)
41 See Sawyer (2006a, 2006b). See also Chavez and Soep (2005) for an analysis of the 'pedagogy of collegiality' that characterizes successful adult–youth collaboration around digital media production. This approach recognizes the asymmetric relationship between adults and youth, but suggests a more nuanced alternative that allows youth expertise and agency to be recognized and nurtured.
42 The term 'co-conspirator' was coined by Dilan Mahendran and cited by Ito *et al.* (2010).

3 Being human

1 Wertsch (1991), Gibson (1977), Deleuze and Guattari (1987)
2 See the work at Berkeley where they are developing robotic exoskeletons http://berkeley.edu/news/media/releases/2004/03/03_exo.shtml and the work of the biomechatronics group at MIT http://biomech.media.mit.edu/research/research.htm
3 Stanford, Berkeley and Cambridge Universities are all involved in a variety of projects to develop new artificial skin, and the field of biomaterials is seeking to build highly compatible materials for prosthetics. The RSC Chemistry World website provides a good source of insight into the latest developments. For example, www.rsc.org/chemistryworld/News/2010/September/14091001.asp and www.rsc.org/chemistryworld/Issues/2010/July/BiomaterialsRevolution.asp
4 See Kuiken *et al.* (2009). The Society for Neuroscience also provides a good resource for updates in this area. www.sfn.org/index.aspx?pagename=brainBriefings_09_prosthetics
5 Harper *et al.* (2008) see also IBM's digital jewelry project, www.youtube.com/watch?v=NCRBHyjtrt4
6 See the Eyeborg Project http://eyeborgproject.com/about/
7 See Joanna Berzowska's Captain Electric www.captain-electric.net/site/dresses.php and Skorpions projects http://xslabs.net/skorpions/
8 See Cascio (2009).
9 Maher (2008) www.nature.com/news/2008/080409/full/452674a.html
10 Turney (2009)
11 Neuroscience as a field is massively dependent upon developments in computer science and digital technologies, in particular upon the capacity to mobilize massive computing power to enable the sorts of brain imaging techniques that are opening up such new areas of inquiry. Greenfield (2003), Blakemore and Frith (2005), Burnett *et al.* (2009)
12 Torrance and MacLure (2010)

13 Inayatullah (2008a: 120) argues: 'Developments in the new science via meditation and learning experiments are … profound. They suggest that the brain can be altered, new neural pathways created, and old traumas resolved. The brain thus is seen as more malleable than previously thought. IQ can be enhanced via meditation and other soft brain technologies. Will meditation be central to the pedagogy of the university as is currently the state with Gurukul University (www.gurukul.edu) and the TM University (www.tm.org)?'.

14 Cromby (2009), Turney (2009)

15 Sterling (2003: 18)

16 Henderson (2009) www.timesonline.co.uk/tol/news/science/article5786950.ece

17 See discussions in Savalescu and Bostrom (2008).

18 Sterling (2003: 31)

19 Turney (2009)

20 Turney (2009)

21 Lee (2011)

22 Kurzweil (2000)

23 Meyer-Schonberger (2009)

24 Stald (2008: 157)

25 See Microsoft SenseCam: http://research.microsoft.com/en-us/um/cambridge/projects/sensecam/

26 Deane and Sharpe (2009)

27 The Bluefish project was part of a wider city-scale pervasive computing project, www.cityware.org.uk/

28 Nold (2009)

29 Castells (2007)

30 Speck computing involves tiny computers that can be embedded in other materials and which can form networks. See www.specknet.org/

31 For a discussion of Southampton University's slime mould project, see www.newscientist.com/article/dn8718. For a discussion of organic computing see Amos (2006).

32 See Cliff *et al.* (2008). See also the journal *Nanomedicine*, www.futuremedicine.com/loi/nnm

33 See Kurzweil (2000), Moravec (2000) and Martin (2006).

34 The parallel is from Cascio (2009).

35 The rest of Cascio's (2009) article, which maps out a possible 'noocene' era, is well worth a read for a creative exploration of the diverse potential trajectories for enhancing intelligence.

36 See Helliker (2009).

37 Palmer (2007)

38 Carr (2008, 2010)

39 See the American Civil Liberties Union of Texas www.aclutx.org/strategic-campaigns/

40 http://interneteyes.co.uk/

41 Haste (2009)

42 *Star Trek*'s famous alien race where all individuality is subsumed to the collective.

43 Books (2009)

44 This recognition of our interdependence with others is also an account of the individual emerging in a range of other fields. From biology to evolutionary psychology, we are starting to see new narratives emerge which challenge the dominant individualistic competitive account of development. These accounts suggest that we are all, to a greater or lesser extent, symbiotic with other organisms for our survival (consider the millions of bacteria we are dependent upon for the effective functioning of our stomachs); and that groups are more likely to survive if they protect attributes that are beneficial for the group, even if they are detrimental

to the individual. Interdependence and collaboration – with other people, other species and with our cultural and material tools – have always, therefore, played a role in our processes of thinking and flourishing (Saveri *et al.* 2004).

45 One model for this is the 'funds of knowledge' approach developed by Moll and Gonzalez, see Moll *et al.* (1992).

4 Collective, embodied and dangerous knowledge

1 Price *et al.* (2009), O'Malley and Stanton-Fraser (2004). See also the Lifelong Kindergarten Group at MIT, in particular the Object-Based-Media projects www. media.mit.edu/research/groups/object-based-media

2 This shift can be understood as similar to sports teams. The actual players, formations, strategies, managers and kit may change over time, but 'the team' is the same, held together by a history and identity that is bigger than any individual player or event.

3 See Mobile Bristol Projects at www.mobilebristol.com, the 1831 RIOT! project: www.roaring-girl.com/productions/1831-riot/, Igfest: http://igfest.org/, Create-A-Scape: www.createascape.org.uk/

4 Throughout the chapter I distinguish between data, information and knowledge 'with data being raw bits of information, information being organized data in context, and knowledge being the assimilation of the information and understanding of how to use it' (Hess and Ostrom 2007, p. 8).

5 Anderson (2007)

6 Bollier (2007)

7 For a discussion of the various claims of new forms of knowledge production, see Goodings (2009). See also Marien (2007) on a 'world brain'.

8 Anderson (2007)

9 Levy (1997)

10 Benkler (2004)

11 See for example Standage (1999).

12 See Wresch (2007).

13 Levy (1997). Some literary instantiations of these ideas can be found at www. futureofthebook.org

14 Dillon and Bacon (2006)

15 Lessig (1999)

16 Hess and Ostrom (2007)

17 Montgomery (2008)

18 Thornburg (2005)

19 Davidson and Goldberg (2009)

20 Hess and Ostrom (2007)

21 Two UK examples make this point. First, when a new government was elected in the UK in 2010, it closed down Becta, its national agency for strategy on educational technology. As we speak, there is no clearly stated plan for what to do with the massive resource bank of research currently available via the Becta website. Second, when the iPhone first launched in the UK an early app was 'MyRailLite', a free app that allowed users to check live arrivals and departures from UK train stations. After a year and after the concept was successfully proven, National Rail Enquiries decided to withdraw its data from the service and make it available as an expensive paid proprietary application.

22 UK National Archives: www.nationalarchives.gov.uk/about%5Cwho-we-are.htm

23 @biz (2010)

24 The Whuffie Bank: http://thewhuffiebank.org/static/faq

25 A number of researchers, including Charlotte Hess and Elinor Ostrom (2007) and Etienne Wenger *et al.* (2009), are mapping out how we can build sustainable socio-technical commons.

26 New London Group (1997)

27 Jewitt (2009)

28 Price *et al.* (2009), Jewitt (2009)

29 www.live.ac.uk/html/projects_haptic_01.html

30 Price *et al.* (2009) discuss the implications of embodied technologies for new forms of literacy.

31 Cliff *et al.* (2008)

32 http://reprap.org/wiki/Main_Page

33 Some of the new materials in development through nano-engineering are truly astonishing. The capacities of material made from carbon nanotubes, for example, include the capacity to repair itself, strength 30 times greater than Kevlar, electricity producing when a light is shone on it, conductive of electricity in one direction and not the other. Baughman *et al.* (2002).

34 Such processes need not imply massive amounts of waste, as materials used for one prototype can be used to create another, or as old materials can be melted down for use to create new prototypes. Indeed, the capacity to create not only our own prototypes but our own materials may lead to a more conscious attitude to waste similar to the 'cradle to cradle' model of design promoted by Braungart and McDonough (2002).

35 Sterling (2005)

36 For two books that provide interesting takes on possible futures in a world of democratized nano-engineering, see Vernor Vinge's *Rainbow's End* (2006) and Neal Stephenson's *Diamond Age* (1995).

37 For a discussion on the importance of building bridges again between the material and the cognitive, see Sennett (2009). See also Latour (2005) on the relationship between virtuality and 'things'.

38 www.pranavmistry.com/projects/sixthsense/

39 The Ensemble project is exploring how students can be facilitated to build such bottom-up tagging as a basis for shared case-based learning: www.ensemble.ac.uk/about

40 Benkler (2006)

41 Harper *et al.* (2008)

42 Johnson (2001), Cliff *et al.* (2008)

43 Of course, we have always been interdependent with people, resources, our environment and our technologies. The notion of the autonomous individual is profoundly misleading and overlooks the ways in which human agency (the highest aspiration of the myth of the autonomous individual) is built through and with other people and artefacts (Wertsch 1991 and Latour 1992, 2000). The proposed developments, however, promise to make such interdependence and blurring very visible.

44 See Martin (2006: 503) for a list of non-human-like intelligence techniques.

45 Cliff *et al.* (2008)

46 We should observe, of course, that this is a problem with human as well as technical systems. The global financial system, for example, was assumed by many within it to be running just swell, until it crashed, bringing down and seriously damaging economies around the globe.

47 Hoff (2009)

48 OECD (2008)

49 Leeson (2009)

50 See United States Air Force (2009), Sharkey (2009, 2010).

51 Kurzweil and Joy (2005)
52 Rees (2004)
53 Young (2010), Muller and Young (2009)
54 See Adams and Groves (2007) for a discussion about the relationship between knowledge, action and ethics.

5 Mind the gaps

1 When we started work on the Beyond Current Horizons programme, my colleague Richard Sandford suggested to our Expert Advisory Group that we might want to consider profound economic disruptions and meltdown in our scenario development. This was dismissed as too unlikely. What a difference a few years make.
2 Overell (2009)
3 Brabham (2008)
4 See Cowgill (2005).
5 Sawyer (2006b)
6 Bray and Prietula (2007)
7 Sawyer (2006a), Wilson (2009)
8 Brabham (2008)
9 Sites such as YourEncore offer the same model, but exploit changing demographics by targeting retired engineers and scientists, offering them the chance to put their rich expertise to continued good use (www.yourencore.com/). The legal field also offers an example where crowdsourcing is being actively taken up. People seeking to patent their ideas, for example, have to ensure that these ideas are not already in the public domain; this sort of search is time-consuming and very difficult to conduct on an individual basis. Today, websites are set up where the broad outlines of an idea are posted and anyone is invited to find examples of what in the USA is called 'prior art'. Rewards are given to those finding the most relevant examples.
10 Harnessing the knowledge of a massively diverse body of people has also become popular in the field of prediction markets. These markets are predicated upon the concept of the 'wisdom of crowds', which suggests that large numbers of people are better at making judgements than small numbers of experts (Surowiecki 2005). The Hollywood Stock Exchange, for example, is an online game that allows players to buy and sell 'shares' in actors, directors and films. This exchange sells itself on having successfully predicted 32 out of 39 major category Oscar nominees (www.hsx.com). Internal company 'predictions markets' are also emerging, in which employees of companies are able to bet on whether products will be high-quality or poor, whether they will deliver on time or turn up late (Cowgill 2005), predictions that are used to shape management and planning expectations and decisions.
11 Bosworth (2009)
12 Anyone who doubts this should watch the TV series *Mary Portas, Queen of Shops.*
13 Bruce Sterling talks about the shift into the age of the 'gizmo', arguing that we are now expecting to be able to modify and change our products. Superfluous functionality is intentional, as it allows change. See Sterling (2005).
14 See Brabham (2008) for a thorough discussion of these different approaches.
15 Bruns (2008)
16 Such processes are taken to their logical extreme by apps such as the Field Agent, where individuals are paid to check up on retail stores. www.148apps.com/news/field-agent-earn-money-iphone/
17 Brabham (2008)
18 The Mechanical Turk: https://www.mturk.com/mturk/welcome

19 See Virtual Call Centre. www.futuretravelcareers.co.uk
20 Jewitt (2009), Riley (2009)
21 Shirky (2010)
22 See Kücklich (2005), Terranova (2003, 2004).
23 Ross (2009)
24 Felstead (2009), Wilson (2009)
25 Qidi (2006)
26 Hartley and Keane (2006), O'Connor and Xin (2006)
27 For a highly celebratory report see CCID Consulting (2010).
28 Dator and Seo (2004)
29 Wilson (2009), Walker (2000)
30 See Brown and Lauder (2009), Brown *et al.* (2008, 2010), Lauder *et al.* (2009).
31 Brown *et al.* (2008)
32 Keep (2009), Wilson (2009)
33 Florida (2004)
34 Green (2009), Nash (2009)
35 See Anyon (2005), Florida (2004), Green (2009), Nash (2009).
36 Sindic (2009)
37 See Muller and Young (2009), Young (2010), Baker (2008), Appadurai (2006).
38 Cooke and Lawton (2008)
39 Giroux (2009)
40 Young (2010)
41 Bauman (2000a,b)
42 Murray *et al.* (1996)
43 Klein (2008)
44 Giroux (2007: 75)
45 Boseley (2007)
46 See Wilkinson and Pickett (2010). See also Dorling (2010a,b).
47 Aked *et al.* (2009)
48 Reeves (2009), Griffiths and Reeves (2009)
49 Leggett (2005)
50 Simms *et al.* (2010)
51 Sweeney (2010), Bafilemba (2010)
52 Hall and Day (2009), UNICEF (2007), Simms *et al.* (2010)
53 Harvey (2005)
54 Bollier (2007) p 28–29
55 Goodwin and Harris (2001, 2004)
56 The Tellus Institute, based in Boston MA. http://tellus.org/index.php
57 Raskin *et al.* (2002)
58 See, for example, Spratt *et al.* (2009).
59 Wilson (2009), Powdthavee (2009), Layard (2009b)
60 Reeves (2009). See also Layard (2009a,b).
61 Robert Kennedy, quoted in Michaelson *et al.* (2009).
62 Adair Turner, interview with Andrew Simms on BBC Radio 4, *The World Tonight*, 1 January 2010;
63 See, for example, Flow (www.flowidealism.org).
64 Michaelson *et al.* (2009)
65 Sassen (2010)
66 Anyon (2005)
67 Overell (2009)
68 Shirky (2010), Kane (2004), Hagel (2010)
69 Sawyer (2006b)

70 See, for example, the freely distributed Ubuntu Operating System, created by a community of passionate developers and supported by Canonical, a company who provide a range of services and consultancy to support Ubuntu users.
71 Murray *et al.* (2010)
72 Mulgan (2010)
73 Warren and Dubb (2010)
74 See, for example, www.kiva.org. Village Banking is a general term that reflects community ownership of banking services.
75 See Hou (2010), in particular chapters by LaFond, Lawson and Sorensen.
76 Witt (2010), Jacobs (1969)
77 See Kingsnorth and Hine (2009), Raskin *et al.* (2002), Steffen (2009, 2010) and the Transition Town network at www.transitionnetwork
78 See the Sustainable Cities Initiative. http://sustainablecities.dk/en/city-projects/cases/porto-alegre-engaging-citizens-in-city-budgeting
79 Resources to support such activity include David Hicks (2008), Richard Slaughter (2004), Marcus Bussey *et al.* (2008) and Masini (2006).
80 The best estimate at present is that between 66 and 73 per cent of students work before they leave school, with between 15 and 26 per cent working at age 11. See Wilson and Gambin (2009).
81 See Morgan and Sonnino (2008) for a discussion of how school food purchasing, for example, can contribute to sustainable development.

6 Networks, collectives and crowds

1 This is ukedchat, a Twitter weekly 'event' discussion focused on education, supported by a website and in the process of developing other face-to-face events. http://ukedchat.wikispaces.com/
2 boyd (2008)
3 Minton (2009)
4 There are, of course, significant minorities of young people for whom this is not the case and who, detached from home, family and any supportive institutions, find themselves living and working on the streets. For a discussion of the disturbingly high prevalence of detached children in the UK see Smeaton (2009).
5 See Davies (2009), Davies and Merchant (in press), Davies and Merchant (2009) and Carrington and Marsh (2009).
6 Carrington and Marsh (2009), boyd (2008); see also Buckingham (2008a).
7 Heeks (2008)
8 Greenfield (2003), for example, is particularly concerned (amongst other things) about the potentially homogenizing effects of participation in virtual cultures.
9 Bennett (1998)
10 Lawler (2005)
11 Montgomery (2008), Riley (2009)
12 Rheingold (2008)
13 Buckingham (2008b)
14 See Bennett (2008) and the other papers in the MacArthur Foundation Series, in particular boyd (2008), for a further discussion of these issues. See also Ito *et al.* (2010), Reich (2009), Davies (2009), Riley (2009).
15 Rheingold (2008)
16 Rheingold (2008)
17 Rheingold (2008)
18 Newman (2009). See also Jenkins (2009) and Jenkins *et al.* (2007).
19 Dutton (2007)

20 Jenkins (2004: 34–5)
21 Bennett (2008)
22 www.worldmapper.org
23 Michel De Certeau once wrote a beautiful essay called 'Walking in the City' comparing two 'views' of a city. First he talked of the top-down view, the strategic vision of the town planner looking down over the whole city as though from the top of a skyscraper; then he talked of the bottom-up view, the lived experience of the city where routes and places were made by the people who lived in the spaces of the city, where people knew the meaning of these places, but only of the places that were meaningful for them. The development of tools to allow us to map our spaces, and annotate them with our narratives, means that we can begin to combine both the top-down view and the lived experience. See www.cityware.org. uk/ and http://2010.futureeverything.org/conference on the Future City.
24 See Hou (2010).
25 See, for example, Full Fact: www.fullfact.org/aboutfullfact
26 See LoveLewisham and RateMyTeachers.
27 Knight (2010)
28 Shirky (2010)
29 Illich (1971), Freire (1970)
30 See Pledgebank www.pledgebank.com and Kiva www.kiva.org. See also Schonfeld (2009).
31 See THATcamp http://thatcamp.org/about/
32 See New Economics Foundation (2010).
33 Appadurai (2001, 2006)
34 Sources for this discussion include: Office for National Statistics (2009, 2010), Pew Internet Centre (2010) and Delli Carpini (2000).
35 Grant and Selwyn (2009)
36 See also Crook and Harrison (2008), Haste (2009).
37 Morozov (2009)
38 Willett (2008)
39 Castells (2007)
40 The organization Giving What We Can visualizes a comparison of incomes in rich countries with those in poor countries. It then encourages giving a significant percentage of annual salary to charity on an ongoing basis, providing a real test of commitment to make sacrifices (www.givingwhatwecan.org).
41 Steffen (2009)
42 Hargreaves (2008)
43 Castells (2009)
44 See Anyon (2005), in particular Chapter 9, for a discussion of the processes involved in community organizing and social movement building, and Anyon (2009).
45 Haste (2009) provides a more detailed discussion of the implications of digital technologies for citizenship, identity and community.
46 In 2010 the UK's coalition government, for example, launched its website 'Your Freedom' – http://yourfreedom.hmg.gov.uk/, encouraging everyone to 'have their say' on what cuts they wanted. Such a website, divorced from meaningful dialogue in communities and necessarily excluding the millions of people who have limited access to or confidence in using the internet, opens up the possibility of presenting a figleaf of consultation to cover up the exercise of executive power.
47 An extreme form of fast citizenship has been mooted, in which the data generated about individual behaviour are so universally gathered and so systematically analysed that your data comes to act as your proxy in decision-making processes. Your attention to the processes of decision-making and social change is rendered

superfluous, as the system responds adaptively to the ongoing choices and actions of the hundreds of thousands of individuals whose data it is recording. The intelligent system swarms around you, documenting, analysing and building systems around your actions.

48 Castells (2009: 38)

49 I had wondered whether a better image for such slow citizenship might be the augmented street piano. Guy Merchant, for example, has written a brilliant study of the networked publics that formed around a street piano in Sheffield. There is something about music rather than words as a basis for beginning to talk together and build relationships with each other that is potentially very important. The videos that show Luke Jerram's Street Piano projects around the world demonstrate this. The critical issue here, however, is that places that bring people together, but which then connect them with the digital landscape as well as the physical, could act as powerful rallying points for collective and hyperlocal social action (Merchant 2007).

50 Fielding and Moss (2010)

51 Fielding and Moss (2010)

7 A future-building school

1 See Adams and Groves (2007).

2 Small (2009), Anyon (2009)

3 Researchers and practitioners such as David Hicks (2008), Richard Slaughter (2004), Marcus Bussey *et al.* (2008) demonstrate how creating spaces for imagining alternative futures, through foresight activities, through the creative arts, through systematic analysis of contemporary trends, can play a powerful role in equipping individuals and communities to imagine and create strategies for social and educational change; while educational philosophers such as Michael Fielding and Peter Moss (2010) and Gert Biesta (2006) describe how schools can act as resources for reviving democracy and human relationships.

4 Anyon (2005) p 186. There is a long history of research that demonstrates how schools can become powerful resources for and partners in processes of social change. This discussion is inspired, for example, by the work of educators such as Jean Anyon (Anyon 2009) and Jeannie Oakes (Oakes *et al.* 2008), who have demonstrated how schools can act as focal points and resources for urban activism and social change if educators and community organizers are encouraged to work together. Researchers such as Arjun Appadurai (2006) have demonstrated how communities can be supported to research and develop radically new solutions to long-standing problems that allow grassroots interventions in global networks; and Peter Levine (2007, 2008) is beginning to model how educational institutions can play a powerful role in supporting the creation of knowledge commons that are of value to communities in fighting battles for equity. Educators can learn from others such as Luis Moll *et al.* (1992), who have shown how teachers acting as ethnographers in their communities can build upon community knowledge to create inclusive educational settings. The insights of economists such as Roberto Unger (1998) and Jane Jacobs (1969) provide strategies for re-imagining the relationship between education institutions and local economies.

5 Giroux (2007)

8 The future-building school of 2035

1 Thanks to Cathy Burke who told me the story of the museum of uninteresting objects. See also Burke and Dudek (2010).

2 This futures augmented card game is based upon a card game designed by Anna Tsing and Elizabeth Pollman to encourage creative and playful engagement with the different possibilities that the future might hold. See Pollman and Tsing (2005).

9 Making it real

1 See Woods and Woods (2009) for an interesting discussion of a wide range of educational alternatives. See also Gandin and Apple (2002) for discussions of 'citizen schools'.
2 Earthforce: www.earthforce.org/; iEARN: www.iearn.org/; the aProCh website: www.aproch.org/; Riverside school website: www.schoolriverside.com/; talk from school founder: www.ted.com/talks/kiran_bir_sethi_teaches_kids_to_take_charge.html. See also Webster and Johnson (2009) for an overview of sustainable education projects.
3 www.hightechhigh.org/about/design-principles.php
4 See Apple and Beane (2007). The following sites also provide good links to relevant lists of democratic and alternative schools: http://democraticeducation.com/resources/suggested-reading-list-books/; www.educationrevolution.org/lisofdemscho.html
5 See Fielding and Moss (2010).
6 Tasker (2003)
7 See, for example, www.socialenterpriseawards.org.uk/pages/profiles-social-enterprise-in-schools.html#Holbrook%20Centre%20for%20Autism,%20Derbyshire and Room 13.
8 Self-Sufficient Schools Programme: www.teachamantofish.org.uk/selfsufficientschools.php
9 Fielding and Moss (2010) also includes a detailed account of Reggio Emilia practices.
10 Facer (2010). See also www.thersa.org/projects/area-based-curriculum/manchester-curriculum
11 See www.826valencia.org/
12 Oakes *et al.* (2008)
13 Anyon (2005: 158–9)
14 Thomas (2009). See also the Centre for Intergenerational Practice, www.centreforip.org.uk/ for a discussion of a range of projects and activities.
15 Attwell and Costa (2009), Crook and Harrison (2008). See also Saltash Community School.
16 See www.learningscore.org/
17 The School of One, in New York (http://schools.nyc.gov/community/innovation/SchoolofOne/default.htm) is a school structured around highly individualized educational institutions, with each child getting feedback and a revised timetable on a daily basis. Such an approach is unlikely to build the future-building capacities of students, but the tools that they use have the potential, if harnessed to a different educational philosophy, to support new relationships between schools, communities and parents.
18 Gastil and Levine (2005), New Economics Foundation (2010) and the deliberative democracy consortium, www.deliberative-democracy.net/
19 One of the most useful resources for accessing the often unwritten history of community, democratic and informal education is the Infed website run from George Williams College in London by Mark K. Smith. This archive is a powerful resource for enabling rapid access to the rich history that can be drawn on in this area. See www.infed.org.uk/
20 Today there may be a growing constituency of parents and others who want to engage in a deeper debate about educational purpose. The argument that hard

work leading to educational qualifications will pay off with economic return and security is wearing very thin. And it is wearing thin, as Jean Anyon argues, not only for children in communities that have long been economically marginalized, but also for middle-class children whose high-school graduation and degree qualifications might previously have assured reasonable wages and comfortable future. This creates the conditions for a much richer debate about what it will take to create not only educational but economic and social systems that will assure children's future wellbeing.

21 See Cummings *et al.* (2007) for a discussion of the way in which school–community relations are often set up in ways that seek to provide routes out of local communities rather than resources to improve and sustain them.

22 See Department for Children, Schools and Families (2009). See also the Co-operative Schools Network for a discussion of the different ways in which co-operative values can underpin school governance arrangements: http://trusts.beecoop.co.uk/

23 There is a precedent for school-focused assessment in the Mode III assessment approach of the 1980s, which saw schools able to design and set their own examinations (Torrance, 1984, 1986).

24 For discussion see, for example, Elliot (1998) and Alexander (2009). It is also possible to argue that a single national curriculum is necessarily inadequate to a 'futures-literate' education system that recognizes the possibility of multiple futures. An alternative perspective might suggest that rather than seeking for a national educational monoculture, a rich educational ecosystem should be encouraged in which high-quality but diverse educational practices are enacted. This diversity would increase the likelihood of our developing the sorts of prefigurative or pre-adaptive practice that would be useful whatever future emerges. Such a diverse ecosystem would, however, need to be supported by radically improved communication between schools and radically improved sharing of ideas and practice, in order for it to be beneficial on a system-wide scale.

25 Alexander (2009)

26 Luckin (2010a and 2010b) goes a long way towards talking about what this might look like. If combined with other approaches, such as community asset mapping, a very powerful set of tools might emerge.

27 A recent study in the USA showed that education institutions that asked *more* of their parents and their community, rather than less, were most effective in building the social capital within their community that some school leaders see as a prerequisite for their students' success (Small 2009). Over the long run, parents and community groups acting autonomously from the school, able to identify critical community education needs and aspirations, can act as a powerful motor for educational change beyond the school walls (West-Burnham *et al.* 2007). Over the next decade, demographic and employment trends are likely to be such that the demand for lifelong and intergenerational learning will increase (Dex 2009). Changing employment practices could well see an increasing casualization of employment and growing periods of sporadic unemployment. This, combined with an ageing population, means that the number of adults later in life both seeking opportunities to learn themselves and also being able to contribute time to the school should increase. This opens up the possibility of creating a new reciprocal contract between the school and its adult community: when individuals contribute their own resources to the school, so they are able to draw on those resources for their own learning in return. This conception of the school as a platform for intergenerational learning and reciprocal exchange of experience and insight would reconfigure the school as an institution with a wider 'corona' of learners and co-educators, all of whom have a stake in supporting and contributing to the institution.

28 Brennan (2007)
29 Anyon (2005) Chapter 6, *Regional Housing Reform as Education Reform*, describes a number of examples of potential strategies. See also Barnardo's (2010).
30 Such an approach formed the basis for the Byron Review on Child Internet Safety (Byron 2008).
31 The Knowledgeworks Foundation has an interesting and provocative list of potential future roles for professional educators. Knowledgeworks Foundation (2009) www.futureofed.org/about/LearningAgents/
32 If the casualization of employment and the disaggregation of organizations seen in other sectors extends into schools, it is possible that there will be a significant body of 'freelance' educators and researchers affiliated to universities in ways that may make available a significant pool of people for this sort of role. See also the New York 'museum school' as an example of how museums can be seen as educational resources closely integrated with schools. www.nycmuseumschool.net/
33 See The National Coordinating Centre for Public Engagement, www.publicengagement. ac.uk/
34 See Levine (2007), Janes (2009), Appadurai (2001, 2006).
35 Anyon (2005: 199)
36 In other words, we need to take seriously the core democratic and emancipatory claims of the purpose of schooling, while throwing up for debate pretty much everything else. In Nevis *et al.*'s terms, this can be equated to the process of change that goes into the change from caterpillar to butterfly. 'In the world of nature, a caterpillar is transformed into a butterfly; its DNA remains unchanged, but its form and properties are fundamentally different. A butterfly is not a caterpillar with wings strapped on its back' (Nevis *et al.* 1996: 12).

References

@biz/Twitter (2010) Tweet Preservation, Twitter Blog. http://blog.twitter.com/2010/04/tweet-preservation.html

4Chan discussions. http://en.wikipedia.org/wiki/4chan; www.ted.com/talks/christopher_m00t_poole_the_case_for_anonymity_online.html

Adams, B. and Groves, C. (2007) *Future Matters: Action, Knowledge, Ethics.* Leiden/Boston: Brill.

Aked, J., Steuer, N., Lawlor, E. and Spratt, S. (2009) *Backing the Future: Why Investing in Children is Good for Us All.* London: New Economics Foundation.

Aldrich, R. (2008) 'Education for survival: an historical perspective', *History of Education*, 39, 11–14.

Alexander, R. (ed.) (2009) *Children, Their World, Their Education: Final Report and Recommendations of the Cambridge Primary Review.* London: Routledge.

Amazon Mechanical Turk. https://www.mturk.com/mturk/welcome

Amos, M. (2006) *Genesis Machines: The New Science of Biocomputing.* London: Atlantic Books.

Anderson, W. (2007) 'Knowledge in evolution', *Futures*, 39, 915–19.

Anyon, J. (2005) *Radical Possibilities: Public Policy, Urban Education and a New Social Movement.* New York and London: Routledge.

Anyon, J. (2009) 'What is to be Done? Toward a Rationale for Social Movement Building', in H. Svi Shapiro (ed.) *Education and Hope in Troubled Times: Visions of Change for Our Children's World.* London and New York: Routledge, pp. 47–62.

Appadurai, A. (2001) 'Deep democracy: urban governmentality and the horizon of politics', *Environment and Urbanization*, 2001: 13(23).

Appadurai, A. (2006) 'The right to research', *Globalisation, Societies and Education*, 4(2), 167–77.

Apple, M. W. and Beane, J. A. (2007) *Democratic Schools: Lessons in Powerful Education*, 2nd edn. Portsmouth NH: Heinemann.

Ariès, P. (1973) *Centuries of Childhood.* Harmondsworth: Penguin.

Arora, P. (2010) 'Hole-in-the-wall? A digital promise for free learning?' *British Journal of Educational Technology*, 41(5), 689–702.

Attwell, G. (2003) *The Challenge of E-Learning in Small Enterprises: Issues of Policy and Practice in Europe.* Cedefop, Luxembourg: Office for Official Publications of the European Communities.

Attwell, G. and Costa, C. (2009) 'Integrating personal learning and working environments', Review for the Beyond Current Horizons Programme. Bristol: Futurelab. www.beyondcurrenthorizons.org.uk/evidence/work-and-employment/

Bafilemba, F. (2010) *Field Dispatch: Conflict Minerals Windfall for Armed Forces in Eastern Congo*, Enough! Project website, www.enoughproject.org/publications/conflict-minerals-windfall-armed-forces-eastern-congo

Baker, D. (2008) 'Privatization, Mass Higher Education, and the Super Research University: Symbiotic or Zero-sum Trends?' *Die Hochschule* (German journal on higher education).

Baker, D. (2009) 'The schooled society and beyond: the modernizing role of formal education as an institution', Review for the Beyond Current Horizons Programme. Bristol: Futurelab. www.beyondcurrenthorizons.org.uk/evidence/knowledge-creativity-and-communication/

Barbour, M. and Reeves, T. (2009) 'The reality of virtual schools: a review of the literature', *Computers and Education*, 52(2), 402–26.

Barclays University: www.personal.barclays.co.uk/BRC1/jsp/brccontrol?task=article graduate&site=pfs&value=6817&menu=4289

Barnardo's (2010) *Unlocking the Gates: Giving Disadvantaged Children a Fairer Deal in School Admissions*. London: Barnardo's.

Baughman, R., Zakhidov, A. and de Heer, W. (2002) 'Carbon nanotubes – the route towards applications', *Science*, 297(5582), 787–92.

Bauman, Z. (2000a) 'Am I my brother's keeper?', *European Journal of Social Work*, 3(1), 5–11.

Bauman, Z. (2000b) *Liquid Modernity*. Cambridge: Polity.

Bauman, Z. (2005) 'Education in Liquid Modernity', *Review of Education, Pedagogy and Cultural Studies*, 27, 303–17.

Beare, H. and Slaughter, R. (1993) *Education for the Twenty-First Century*. London and New York: Routledge.

Beck, U. (1992) *Risk Society: Towards a new modernity*. London: Sage.

Benkler, Y. (2004) 'Commons based strategies and the problems of patents', *Science*, 20 Vol. 305. no. 5687, 1110–1111.

Benkler, Y. (2006) *The Wealth of Networks: How Social Production Transforms Markets and Freedom*. Yale University Press: New Haven CT. Also available through Wikipedia at www.benkler.org/

Bennett, W. Lance (2008) 'Changing Citizenship in the Digital Age' in W. L. Bennett (ed.), *Civic Life Online: Learning How Digital Media Can Engage Youth*. Cambridge MA: MIT Press.

Bentley, T. (1998) *The Classroom Without Walls*. London: Demos/Routledge.

Berry, R. and McLaughlin, D. (eds) (2007) Localism and the information society: Knowledge Politics:

Berthoud, R. (2005) 'Family formation in multi-cultural Britain: Diversity and change', in G. C. Loury *et al.* (eds), *Ethnicity, Social Mobility and Public Policy: Comparing the US and the UK*. Cambridge: Cambridge University Press, pp. 222–52.

Berzowska, Joanna: Captain Electric www.captain-electric.net/site/dresses.php and Skorpions projects http://xslabs.net/skorpions/

Bhaskar, R. (1975) *A Realist Theory of Science*. London: Verso.

Biesta, G. (2006) *Beyond Learning: Democratic Education for a Human Future*. Boulder/London: Paradigm.

Biesta, G. (2007) 'Why "what works" won't work: evidence-based practice and the democratic deficit in educational research', *Educational Theory*, 57(1), 1–22.

Blakemore, S.-J. and Frith, U. (2005) *The Learning Brain: Lessons for Education*. Malden MA and Oxford: Blackwell.

Bollier, D. (2007) 'The growth of the commons paradigm' in C. Hess and E. Ostrum (eds), *Understanding Knowledge as Commons*. Cambridge MA and London: MIT Press, pp. 3–26.

Books, S. (2009) 'Mechanics of unfairness: how we undercut poor children's educational opportunity', in H. Svi Shapiro (ed.), *Education and Hope in Troubled Times: Visions of Change for Our Children's World*. London and New York: Routledge, pp. 63–75.

Borja, R. R. (2005) 'Cyber school's status', *Education Week*, 24(35), 22–3.

Boseley, S. (2007) 'British children: poorer, at greater risk and more insecure', *The Guardian*, 15/02/07. www.guardian.co.uk/society/2007/feb/14/childrensservices. politics

Bosworth, D. (2009) 'The R&D, knowledge, innovation triangle: education and economic performance', Review for the Beyond Current Horizons Programme. Bristol: Futurelab. www.beyondcurrenthorizons.org.uk/evidence/work-and-employment/

boyd, danah (2008) 'Why youth social network sites: the role of networked publics in teenage social life', in D. Buckingham (ed.), *Youth, Identity, and Digital Media*. Cambridge MA: MIT Press, pp. 119–42.

Brabham, D. (2007) 'Crowdsourcing as a model for problem solving: an introduction and cases', *International Journal of Research into New Media Technologies*, 14(1), 75–90.

Bradburne, J. (2005) 'Laboratory for Change: mak.frankfurt as argument, experiment and example,' first published in French in *Alliage* No 44, automne 2001 and in English in the *International Journal of Arts Management*, 4(1), 2001, 4–12.

Bradwell, P. (2009) *The Edgeless University: Why Higher Education Must Embrace Technology*. London: Demos.

Braungart, M. and McDonough, W. (2002/2009) *Cradle to Cradle: Re-making the Way We Make Things*. London: Vintage.

Bray, D. and Prietula, M. (2007) *Exploration and Exploitation: Managing Knowledge in Turbulent Environments*. International Conference on Information Systems.

Brennan, M. (2007) *The Positive Impacts of Affordable Housing on Education: A Research Summary*. Maryland: Centre for Housing Policy and Enterprise Community Partners.

Brown, A. (2009) 'Developing expertise – moving beyond a focus on workplace competence, assessment and qualifications', Review for the Beyond Current Horizons Programme. Bristol: Futurelab. www.beyondcurrenthorizons.org.uk/evidence/work-and-employment/

Brown, C. and Lauder, H. (2009) 'Social class and education: changes and challenges', Review for the Beyond Current Horizons Programme, Bristol: Futurelab. www.beyondcurrenthorizons.org.uk/evidence/generations-and-lifecourse/

Brown, G. (2010) 'Building Britain's digital future', speech given early 2010, accessed 20 August 2010. www2.labour.org.uk/gordon-browns-speech-on-building-britains-digital-future,2010-03-26

Brown, P., Lauder, H. and Ashton, D. (2008) *Education, Globalisation and the Knowledge Economy: A commentary by the Teaching and Learning Research Programme*. London: ESRC TLRP.

Brown, P., Lauder, H. and Ashton, D. (2010) *The Global Auction: The Broken Promises of Education, Jobs and Rewards*. New York: Oxford University Press.

Bruns, A. (2008) *Blogs, Wikipedia, Second Life, and Beyond: From Production to Produsage*. New York: Peter Lang.

Buckingham, D. (2000) *After the Death of Childhood: Growing Up Digital in an Age of Multimedia*. Policy Press: Cambridge.

Buckingham, D. (2008a) 'Introducing identity', in D. Buckingham (ed.), *Youth, Identity, and Digital Media*. Cambridge MA: MIT Press, pp. 1–24.

Buckingham, D. (2008b) 'Childhood 2025 and beyond', long-list challenge paper for the Beyond Current Horizons Programme. Bristol: Futurelab. www.beyondcurrenthorizons. org.uk/outcomes/other-findings/

Burke, C. and Dudek, M. (2010) 'Experiences of learning within a 20th-century radical experiment in education: Prestolee school, 1919–1952', *Oxford Review of Education*, 36(2), April 2010, 203–18.

Burnett, S., Sebastian, C. and Blakemore, S.-J. (2009) 'Understanding the changing adolescent brain', Review for the Beyond Current Horizons Programme. Bristol: Futurelab. www.beyondcurrenthorizons.org.uk/evidence/generations-and-lifecourse/

Bussey, M., Inayatullah, S. and Milojevic, I. (eds) (2008) *Alternative Educational Futures: Pedagogies for Emergent Worlds*. Rotterdam: Sense Publishers.

Byron, T (2008) Safer Children in a Digital World: The Report of the Byron Review, Nottingham: DCSF, www.dcsf.gov.uk/byronreview/

Carr, N. (2008) 'Is Google making us stupid?', *Atlantic Monthly*. www.theatlantic. com/magazine/archive/2008/07/is-google-making-us-stupid/6868/

Carr, N. (2010) *The Shallows: What the Internet is Doing to Our Brain*. London: W. W. Norton & Co.

Carrington, V. and Marsh, J. (2009) 'Forms of literacy', Review for the Beyond Current Horizons Programme. Bristol: Futurelab. www.beyondcurrenthorizons. org.uk/evidence/knowledge-creativity-and-communication/

Cascio, J. (2009) 'Get smarter', *Atlantic Magazine*, July/August 2009. www. theatlantic.com/doc/200907/intelligence/2

Castells, M. (2007) 'Communication, power and counter-power in the network society', *International Journal of Communication*, 1, 238–66.

Castells, M. (2009) *Communication Power*. Oxford and New York: OUP.

CCID Consulting (2010) 'China's Cultural Creativity Industry Set to Change the Landscape of Urban Industries', 25/2/2010. www.tradingmarkets.com/news/ press-release/urds_ccid-consulting-china-s-cultural-creativity-industry-set-to- change-the-landscape-of-urban-industrie-803656.html

Centre for Intergenerational Practice. www.centreforip.org.uk/

Chavez, V. and Soep, E. (2005) 'Pedagogy of collegiality', *Harvard Educational Review*, Winter 2005.

Chouliaraki, L. and Fairclough, N. (1999) *Discourse in Late Modernity: Rethinking Critical Discourse Analysis*. Edinburgh: Edinburgh University Press.

Claxton, G. (2008) *What's the Point of School? Rediscovering the Heart of Education*. Oxford: Oneworld.

Cliff, D., O'Malley, J. and Taylor, J. (2008) 'Future issues in socio-technical change for UK education', Briefing paper for the Beyond Current Horizons Programme. Bristol: Futurelab. www.beyondcurrenthorizons.org.uk/evidence/other/

Colley, H., Hodkinson, P. and Malcolm, J. (2003) *Informality and Formality in Learning: A Report for the Learning and Skills Research Centre.* Leeds: Learning and Skills Research Centre.

Cooke, G. and Lawton, K. (2008) *Working Out of Poverty: Paper three.* London: Institute of Public Policy Research.

Co-operative College: Schools and Young People. www.co-op.ac.uk/schools-and-young-people/

Cowgill, B. (2005) 'Putting crowd wisdom to work (prediction markets)', Google website, 21/09/2005. http://googleblog.blogspot.com/2005/09/putting-crowd-wisdom-to-work.html

Craft, A. (2010) *Creativity and Education Futures: Learning in a Digital Age.* Nottingham: Trentham.

Craig, J., Horne, M. and Mongan, D. (2009) *The Engagement Ethic: The Potential of Co-Operative and Mutual Governance for Public Services.* London: Innovation Unit.

Cromby, J. (2009) 'Educating persons, imaging brains: the potentials of neuroscience for education', Review for the Beyond Current Horizons Programme. Bristol: Futurelab. www.beyondcurrenthorizons.org.uk/evidence/knowledge-creativity-and-communication/

Crook, C. and Harrison, C. (2008) *Web 2.0 Technologies for Learning at Key Stage 3 and 4, Summary Report.* BECTA: Coventry.

Cummings, C., Todd, L. and Dyson, A. (2007) 'Towards extended schools? how education and other professionals understand community-oriented schooling', *Children and Society*, 21, 189–200.

Daanen, H. and Facer, K. (2007) *2020 and Beyond.* Bristol: Futurelab.

Dator, J. (2008) 'Universities without "Quality" and Quality without "Universities"', in M. Bussey, S. Inayatullah and I. Milojevic (eds), *Alternative Educational Futures: Pedagogies for emergent worlds.* Rotterdam: Sense Publishers, pp. 91–112.

Dator, J. and Seo, Y. (2004) 'Korea as the wave of a future: the emerging Dream Society of icons and aesthetic experience', *Journal of Futures Studies*, 9(1), 31–44.

Davidson, C. and Goldberg, D. (2009) *The Future of Learning Institutions in a Digital Age.* Cambridge MA: MIT Press. http://mitpress.mit.edu/9780262513593

Davies, J. (2009) 'A space for play: crossing boundaries and learning online', in V. Carrington and M. Robinson (eds), *Contentious Technologies: Digital Literacies, Social Learning and Classroom Practices.* London: Sage.

Davies, J. and Merchant, G. (2009) *Web 2.0 for Schools: Learning and Social Participation.* New York: Peter Lang.

Davies, J. and Merchant, G. (in press) 'Negotiating the blogosphere: narratives of the self onscreen', in V. Carrington and M. Robinson (eds), *Contentious Literacies.* London: Routledge Falmer.

Deane, A. and Sharpe, D. (2009) *Big Brother is Watching.* London: Big Brother Watch.

De Certeau, M. (1984) *The Practice of Everyday Life.* Berkeley and Los Angeles CA: University of California Press.

Deleuze, G. and Guattari, F. (1987) *A Thousand Plateaus.* London and New York: Continuum.

Delli Carpini, M. (2000) Gen.com: Youth, Civic Engagement, and the New Information Environment. *Political Communication*, 17, 341–9.

Department for Children, Schools and Families (2009) *Co-operative Schools – Making a Difference*. Nottingham: DCSF. http://publications.education.gov.uk/default.aspx?PageFunction=productdetails&PageMode=publications&ProductId=DCSF-00416-2009&

Department for Children, Schools and Families (2010) *Statistical First Release – Pupil Absence in Schools in England including Pupil Characteristics 2008/2009*. London: DCSF.

Dex, S. (2009) 'Review of future of paid and unpaid work, informal work, homeworking, the place of work in the family (women single parents, workless households), benefits, work attitudes motivation and obligation', Review for the Beyond Current Horizons Programme. Bristol: Futurelab. www.beyondcurrenthorizons.org.uk/evidence/work-and-employment/

Dillon, T. and Bacon, S. (2006) *The Potential of Open Source Approaches for Education*. Bristol: Futurelab.

DiSalvo, B. J., Guzdail, M., Mcklin, T., Meadows, C., Perry, K., Steward, C. and Bruckman, A. (2009) 'Glitch game testers: African American men breaking open the console', paper presented at *New Ground: Innovation in Games, Play, Practice and Theory*. Proceedings of DiGRA 2009.

Dorling, D. (2008) 'Diverse populations', Long-list challenge paper for the Beyond Current Horizons Programme. Bristol: Futurelab. www.beyondcurrenthorizons.org.uk/outcomes/other-findings/

Dorling, D (2010a) *Injustice: Why Social Inequality Persists*. Bristol: Policy Press.

Dorling, D. (2010b) 'Tall tales and ripping yarns', *Adults Learning*, April 2010.

Downes, T. (2002) 'Children and families' use of computers in Australian homes', *Contemporary Issues in Early Childhood*, 3(2), 182–96.

Drotner, K. (2008) 'Leisure is hard work: digital practices and future competencies', in D. Buckingham (ed.), *Youth, Identity, and Digital Media*. Cambridge MA: MIT Press, pp. 167–84.

Dutton, W. (2007) 'Through the network (of networks) – the fifth estate', inaugural lecture, University of Oxford. http://papers.ssrn.com/sol3/papers.cfm?abstract_id=1134502

Earthforce: www.earthforce.org/

Edwards, C. (2009) *Resilient Nation*. London: Demos.

Egan, K. (2009) *The Future of Education: Reimagining Our Schools from the Ground Up*. London and New York: Yale University Press.

Elliott, J. (1998) *The Curriculum Experiment: Meeting the Challenge of Social Change*. Buckingham: Open University Press.

Elliot, F. and Woolcock, N. (2008) 'McDonald's A Level in running a burger bar', *Times Online*, 28 January 2008.

Elwyn, G. and Edwards, A. (2009) *Shared Decision-Making In Health Care: Achieving Evidence-based Patient Choice* (2nd edn). Oxford: Oxford University Press.

Enriquez, J. (2000) *As the Future Catches You*. New York: Random House.

Erstad, O. (2009) 'The learning lives of digital youth: beyond formal and informal literacies', paper given to the closing conference of the ESRC Seminar Series on Adolescence, Education and Digital Technologies, Oxford, June 2009.

Eyeborg project. http://eyeborgproject.com/about/

Facer, K. (2009) *Beyond Current Horizons, Final Report*. Bristol: Futurelab, available in full at www.beyondcurrenthorizons.org.uk/outcomes/reports/final-report-2009/

Facer, K. (2010) *Manchester Curriculum Literature Review: Towards an Area Based Curriculum.* London: RSA. www.thersa.org/projects/area-based-curriculum/manchester-curriculum

Facer, K. and Furlong, J. (2001) 'Beyond the myth of the cyberkid: young people at the margins of the information revolution', *Journal of Youth Studies*, 4(4), 451–69.

Facer, K. and Pykett, J. (2007) *Developing and Accrediting Personal Skills and Competencies.* Bristol: Futurelab.

Facer, K., Sutherland, R., Furlong, R. and Furlong, J. (2001) 'Constructing the child computer user: from public policy to private practice', *British Journal of Sociology of Education*, 4(4).

Facer, K., Furlong, J., Furlong, R. and Sutherland, R. (2003) *ScreenPlay: Children's Use of Computers in the Home.* London: Routledge.

Felstead, A. (2009) 'Detaching work from place: charting the progress of change and its implications for learning', Review for the Beyond Current Horizons Programme. Bristol: Futurelab. www.beyondcurrenthorizons.org.uk/evidence/work-and-employment/

Fielding, M. (2009) 'Interrogating student voice: pre-occupations, purposes and possibilities', in H. Daniels, H. Lauder and J. Porter (eds), *Educational Theories, Cultures and Learning: A Critical Perspective.* London: Routledge, pp. 101–16.

Fielding, M. and Moss, P. (2010) *Radical Education and the Common School: A Democratic Alternative.* London: Routledge.

First College. www.firstcollege.co.uk/

Fisch, K. (2000) *Shift Happens.* http://shifthappens.wikispaces.com/ – original slideshow here: www.youtube.com/watch?v=ljbl-363A2Q. See YouTube for many imitators and critics.

Fisk, N. (1980) *A Rag, a Bone and a Hank of Hair.* Oxford: Oxford Children's Modern Classics.

Florida, R. (2004) Creative class war, how the GOP's anti-elitism could ruin America's economy', *Washington Monthly*, Jan/Feb 2004.

Flow – liberating the entrepreneurial spirit for good. www.flowidealism.org

Foundation for the Rights of Future Generations. www.intergenerationaljustice.org/

Freire, P. (1970) *Pedagogy of the Oppressed.* New York: Herder and Herder.

Fullfact, an online independent fact-checking organization. www.fullfact.org/aboutfullfact

Gandin, L. and Apple, M. (2002) 'Challenging neo-liberalism, building democracy: creating the Citizen School in Porto Alegre, Brazil', *Journal of Education Policy*, 17(2), 259–79.

Garman (2009) 'This is not youthful rebellion', *The Observer*, 8 March 2009.

Gastil, J. and Levine, P. (eds) (2005) *The Deliberative Democracy Handbook: Strategies for Effective Civic Engagement in the Twenty-First Century.* San Francisco CA: JosseyBass/Wiley.

Gates, B. (2005) Keynote speech to the National Education Summit on American Secondary Schools, 26 February 2005.

Gee, J. (2003) *What Videogames Have to Teach Us about Learning and Literacy.* New York: Palgrave Macmillan.

Gibson, J. J. (1977) 'The theory of affordances', in R. Shaw and J. Bransford (eds), *Perceiving, Acting, and Knowing: Toward an Ecological Psychology.* Hillsdale, NJ: Lawrence Erlbaum, pp. 67–82.

Giroux, H. (2004) 'When hope is subversive', *Tikkun*, 19(6).

Giroux, H. (2007) 'Higher education and the politics of hope in the age of authoritarianism: rethinking the pedagogical possibilities of global democracy', *THEOMAI Journal*, primer semestre, number 15, Society and Development Studies.

Giroux, H. (2009) 'Disposable future: dirty democracy and the politics of disposability', in H. Svi Shapiro (ed.), *Education and Hope in Troubled Times: Visions of Change for our Children's World*. London and New York: Routledge, pp. 223–40.

GivingWhatWeCan. www.givingwhatwecan.org

GLBTQ Online High School. www.glbtqonlinehighschool.com/academics.html

Goodings, L. (2009) 'Changes in knowledge construction, participation and networks', Review for the Beyond Current Horizons Programme. Bristol: Futurelab. www.beyondcurrenthorizons.org.uk/evidence/knowledge-creativity-and-communication/

Goodson, I. F. (2006) 'The rise of the life narrative', *Teacher Education Quarterly*, 33(4).

Goodwin, N. and Harris, J. (2001) G-DAE Working Paper No. 01-05: 'Better Principles: New Approaches to Teaching Introductory Economics', paper prepared for 'Alternative Approaches to Economic Education' at the American Economics Association meeting, January 2001.

Goodwin, N. and Harris, J. (eds) (2004) *New Thinking in Macroeconomics: Social, Institutional and Environmental Perspectives*. New York: Edward Elgar.

Gove, M. (2009) 'Failing schools need new leadership', speech to the Conservative Party Conference, Manchester, 7 October 2009. www.conservatives.com/News/Speeches/2009/10/Michael_Gove_Failing_schools_need_new_leadership.aspx

Grant, L. and Selwyn, N. (eds) (2009) 'Learning and social software: researching the realities', *Learning Media and Technology*, 34(2).

Green, A. (2009) 'The importance of place', Review for the Beyond Current Horizons Programme' Bristol: Futurelab. www.beyondcurrenthorizons.org.uk/evidence/work-and-employment/

Greenfield, S. (2003) *Tomorrow's People: How 21st Century Technology is Changing the Way We Think and Feel*. London: Allen Lane.

Greenhill, B. (2009) 'The digital landscape and new education providers', Review for the Beyond Current Horizons Programme. Bristol: Futurelab. www.beyondcurrenthorizons.org.uk/evidence/state-market-third-sector/

Griffiths, S. and Reeves, R. (eds) (2009) *Well-being: How to Lead the Good Life and What Government Should Do to Help*. London: Social Market Foundation.

Grint, K. and Woolgar, S. (1997) *The Machine at Work: Technology, Work and Organisation*. London: Routledge.

Hagel, J. (2010) 'A Labor Day manifesto for a new world', Blogpost, http://edgeperspectives.typepad.com/edge_perspectives/2009/09/a-labor-day-manifesto-for-a-new-world.html

Hall, C. and Day, J. (2009) 'Revisiting the limits to growth after peak oil', *American Scientist*, 97.

Hannam, L. and Razzall, K. (2007) 'Home-schooling on the rise', Channel 4 News, www.channel4.com/news/articles/society/education/homeschooling+on+the+rise/846947.html

Hargreaves, A. (2003) *Teaching in the Knowledge Society: Education in the Age of Insecurity*. Maidenhead: Open University Press.

Hargreaves, A. (2008) 'The coming of post-standardisation: three weddings and a funeral', in C. Sugrue (2008), *The Future of Educational Change: International Perspectives*. Abingdon and New York: Routledge, pp. 15–33.

Harper, R., Rodden, T., Rogers, Y. and Sellen, A. (2008) *Being Human: Human–Computer Interaction in the Year 2020*. Cambridge UK: Microsoft.

Harper, S. (2009) 'Demographic change, generations and the life course', Summative report for the Beyond Current Horizons Programme. Bristol: Futurelab. www.beyondcurrenthorizons.org.uk/evidence/generations-and-lifecourse/

Hartley, J. and Keane, M. (2006) 'Creative industries and innovation in China', *International Journal of Cultural Studies*, 9, 259.

Harvey, D. (2005) *A Brief History of Neoliberalism*. Oxford: OUP.

Haste, H. (2009) 'Identity, communities and citizenship', summative report for the Beyond Current Horizons Programme. Bristol: Futurelab. www.beyondcurrenthorizons.org.uk/evidence/identities-citizenship-communities/

Heeks, R. (2008) 'Current analysis and future research agenda on "gold farming": real-world production in developing countries for the virtual economies of online games', Working Paper no 32, Development Informatics Group, University of Manchester, available to view at: www.sed.manchester.ac.uk/idpm/research/publications/wp/di/index.htm

Heller, N. (2001). 'Changes see corporate universities on rise', *Heller Report on Educational Technology Markets*, v12 i8 p. 1.

Helliker, K. (2009) 'Daring to live your life offline', *Wall Street Journal*, 29/12/2009. http://online.wsj.com/article/SB10001424052748704134104574624343810624208.html

Henderson, M. (2009) 'Genetic code could be used to offer ultimate personal care on NHS', *The Times*, 23 Feb 2009.

Hess, C. and Ostrom, E. (2007) 'Introduction: an overview of the knowledge commons', in C. Hess and E. Ostrom (eds), *Understanding Knowledge as Commons*. Cambridge MA and London: MIT Press, pp. 3–26.

Hicks, D. (2008) 'A futures perspective: lessons from the school room', in M. Bussey, S. Inayatullah and I. Milojevic (eds), *Alternative Educational Futures: Pedagogies for Emergent Worlds*. Rotterdam: Sense Publishers, pp. 75–90.

HM Government (2010) Your Freedom website, consultation on freedom. http://yourfreedom.hmg.gov.uk/

Hoff, A. (2009) 'Families, care and work: changes and challenges', Review for the Beyond Current Horizons Programme. Bristol: Futurelab. www.beyondcurrenthorizons.org.uk/evidence/generations-and-lifecourse/

Hoffman, M. (2007) *'You Won't Remember Me': The Schoolboys of Barbiana Speak to Today*. New York and London: Teachers College Press.

Hogarth, S., Javitt, G. and Melzer, D. (2008) 'The current landscape for direct-to-consumer genetic testing: legal, ethical and policy issues', *Annual Review of Genomics and Human Genetics*, 9, 161–82.

Hogarth, T. and Bosworth, D. (2009) 'Future horizons for work-life balance', Review for the Beyond Current Horizons Programme. Bristol: Futurelab. www.beyondcurrenthorizons.org.uk/evidence/work-and-employment/

Holloway, S. and Valentine, G. (2003) *Cyberkids*. London: Routledge.

Hollywood Stock Exchange. www.hsx.com/

Homan, G and Macpherson, A. (2005) 'E-learning in the corporate university', *Journal of European Industrial Training*, 29(1), 2005, 75–90.

Horst, H. (2009) 'Blurring the boundaries: connectivity, convergence and communication in the new media ecology', Review for the Beyond Current Horizons

Programme. Bristol: Futurelab. www.beyondcurrenthorizons.org.uk/evidence/knowledge-creativity-and-communication/

Hou, J. (2010) *Insurgent Public Space: Guerilla Urbanism and the Remaking of Contemporary Cities*. Abingdon and New York: Routledge.

Howse, K. (2009) 'Review of longevity trends to 2025 and beyond', Review for the Beyond Current Horizons Programme. Bristol: Futurelab. www.beyondcurrenthorizons. org.uk/evidence/generations-and-lifecourse/

Hughes, M. (2009–10) Learning out of School Professorial Fellowship. www. esrcsocietytoday.ac.uk/ESRCInfoCentre/ViewAwardPage.aspx?awardnumber= RES-051-27-0092

Hutchinson, F. (1996) *Educating Beyond Violent Futures*. Abingdon and New York: Routledge.

iEARN. www.iearn.org/

Illich, I. (1971) *Deschooling Society*. Harmondsworth: Penguin Books Ltd.

Inayatullah, S. (2008a) 'Images and trends in tension: the alternative futures of the university', in M. Bussey, S. Inayatullah and I. Milojevic (eds), *Alternative Educational Futures: Pedagogies for Emergent Worlds*. Rotterdam: Sense Publishers, pp. 113–32.

Inayatullah, S. (2008b) 'Mapping educational futures: six foundational concepts and the six pillars approach', in M Bussey, S. Inayatullah and I. Milojevic (eds), *Alternative Educational Futures: Pedagogies for Emergent Worlds*. Rotterdam: Sense Publishers, pp. 13–40.

Institute for the Future of the Book. www.futureofthebook.org/

InterHigh. www.interhigh.net/

Ito, M., Baumer, S., Bittanti, M., boyd, d., Cody, R., Herr-Stephenson, B., Horst, H., Lange, P., Mahendran, D., Martinex, K., Pascoe, C., Perkel, D., Robinson, L., Sims, C. and Tripps, L. (2010) *Hanging Out, Messing Around and Geeking Out: Kids Living and Learning with New Media*. Cambridge, MA: MIT Press.

Ito, M., Horst, H., Bittanti, M., boyd, d., Herr-Stephenson, B., Lange, P., Pascoe, C. and Robinson, L. (2008) *Living and Learning with New Media: Summary of Findings from the Digital Youth Project*. Cambridge MA: MIT Press. http://digitalyouth.ischool.berkeley.edu/report

Jacobs, J. (1969) *The Economy of Cities*. New York: Vintage Books.

James, A. and Prout, A. (1990) *Constructing and Reconstructing Childhood*. Basingstoke: Falmer Press.

Janes, R. (2009) *Museums in a Troubled World: Renewal, Irrelevance or Collapse?* Abingdon and New York: Routledge.

Jenkins, H. (2004) 'The cultural logic of media convergence', *International Journal of Cultural Studies*, 7(1), 33–43.

Jenkins, H. (2009) 'Click click ranger: a transmedia experiment for Korean television', blogpost 6 Nov 2009 on Confessions of an Aca-Fan. http://henryjenkins. org/2009/11/click_click_ranger_a_transmedi.html

Jenkins, H. with Clinton, K., Purushotma, R., Robison, A. and Weigel, M. (2007) 'Confronting the challenges of participatory culture: media education for the twenty-first century', occasional paper on digital media and learning for the John D. and Catherine T. MacArthur Foundation. www.macfound.org

Jenson, J. (2000) 'Canada's shifting citizenship regime: the child as "model citizen"', in M. Keating and T. Salmon (eds), *Decentralisation and Regionalisation: Canada and the United Kingdom Compared*. Montreal: McGill-Queen's University Press.

Jenson, J. (2006) 'Social investment for new social risks: consequences of the LEGO paradigm for children', paper prepared for Jane Lewis (ed.), *Children in Context: Changing Families and Welfare States.* Edward Elgar Publishing, draft 2 accessed via Jane Jenson website.

Jessel, J. (2009) 'Family structures and intergenerational transfers of learning: changes and challenges', Review for the Beyond Current Horizons Programme. Bristol: Futurelab. www.beyondcurrenthorizons.org.uk/evidence/generations-and-lifecourse/

Jewitt, C. (2009) 'Knowledge, creativity and communication', Summative report for the Beyond Current Horizons Programme. Bristol: Futurelab. www.beyondcurrenthorizons. org.uk/evidence/knowledge-creativity-and-communication/

Johnson, S. (2001) *Emergence: The Connected Lives of Ants, Brains, Cities and Software.* London: Penguin.

Joy, B. (2000) 'Why the future doesn't need us', *Wired*, 8.04 , April 2000.

Kane, P. (2004) *The Play Ethic.* London: Macmillan.

Keep, E. (2009) 'Labour market structures and trends, the future of work and the implications for initial education and training', Review for the Beyond Current Horizons Programme. Bristol: Futurelab. www.beyondcurrenthorizons.org.uk/evidence/work-and-employment/

Kelan, E. and Lehnert, M. (2009) 'The millennial generation: generation y and the opportunities for a globalised, networked educational system', Review for the Beyond Current Horizons Programme. Bristol: Futurelab. www.beyondcurrenthorizons.org. uk/evidence/generations-and-lifecourse/

Khajeh-Hosseini, A., Sommerville, I. and Sriram, I. (2010) 'Research challenges for enterprise cloud computing', ACM Symposium on Cloud Computing. http://arxiv.org/abs/1001.3257

Kingsnorth, P. and Hine, D. (2009) Dark Mountain Manifesto. www.dark-mountain.net/about-2/the-manifesto/

Kiva. www.kiva.org/

Klein, N. (2008) *Shock Doctrine.* New York and London: Penguin.

Knight, J. (2010) 'The future of public services online', 5th National Digital Inclusion Conference, London, Wednesday 30 March 2010.

Knowledgeworks Foundation (2008) *2020 Forecast: Creating the Future of Learning.* Palo Alto CA: Knowledgeworks Foundation.

Knowledgeworks Foundation (2009) *Learning Agents for 2020.* www.futureofed.org/about/LearningAgents/

Kretzmann, J. and McKnight, J. (1997) *Building Communities from the Inside Out: A Path Toward Finding and Mobilizing a Community's Assets.* Chicago: Acta Publications.

Kücklich, J. (2005) 'Precarious playbour: modders and the digital games industry', *Fibreculture, The Journal*, issue 5. http://journal.fibreculture.org/issue5/kucklich.html

Kuiken, R., Li, G., Lock, B., Lipschutz, R., Miller, L., Stubblefield, K. and Englehart, K. (2009) 'Targeted muscle reinnervation for real-time myoelectric control of multifunction artificial arms', *JAMA*, 301(6), 619–28.

Kurzweil, R. (2000) *The Age of Spiritual Machines: When Computers Exceed Human Intelligence.* New York and London: Penguin.

Kurzweil, R. and Joy, B. (2005) 'Recipe for destruction', *New York Times*, 17 Oct 2005. www.nytimes.com/2005/10/17/opinion/17kurzweiljoy.html

Latour, B. (1992) 'Where are the missing masses: the sociology of a few mundane artifacts', in W. Bijker and J. Law (eds), *Shaping Technology*. Cambridge MA: MIT Press, pp. 225–58.

Latour, B. (2000) 'When things strike back: a possible contribution of "science studies" to the social sciences', *British Journal of Sociology*, 51(1), 107–23.

Latour, B. (2005) 'From realpolitik to dingpolitik – or how to make things public', introduction to the exhibition 'Making Things Public' at the ZKM (Centre for Art and Media), Karlsruhe, 2005.

Latour, Bruno (1988) *The Pasteurization of France*. Cambridge MA: Harvard University Press.

Lauder, H., Brown, P. and Brown, C. (2009) 'The consequences of global expansion for knowledge, creativity and communication: an analysis and scenario', Review for the Beyond Current Horizons Programme. Bristol: Futurelab. www.beyondcurrenthorizons. org.uk/evidence/knowledge-creativity-and-communication/

Lawes, S., Ledda, M,, McGovern, C., Patterson, S., Perks, D. and Standish, A. (2007) *The Corruption of the Curriculum*. London: Civitas.

Lawler, C. (2005) 'Wikipedia as a learning community: content, conflict, and the "common good"', Proceedings of Wikimania '05, Frankfurt, 4–8 August 2005. Available online at: http://meta.wikimedia.org/wiki/Transwiki:Wikimania05/Paper-CL1

Layard, R. (2009a) *A Good Childhood: Searching for Values in a Competitive Age*. London: The Children's Society/Penguin.

Layard, R. (2009b) 'Afterword: the greatest happiness principle: its time has come', in S. Griffiths and R. Reeves (eds) (2009), *Well-being: How to Lead the Good Life and What Government Should Do to Help*. London: Social Market Foundation.

Leadbeater, C. (2004) *Personalisation Through Participation: A New Script for the Public Services*. London: Demos.

Leadbeater, C. (2008) *We-Think: Mass Innovation Not Mass Production*. London: Profile.

Lee, N. (2001) *Childhood and Society: Growing Up in an Age of Uncertainty*. Buckingham: Open University Press.

Lee, N. M. (2011) *Childhood and Bio-Politics: Climate Change, Bio-science and Human Futures*. London: Palgrave Macmillan.

Lee, N. M. and Motzkau, J. F. (2011) 'Navigating the Bio-Politics of Childhood', *Childhood: A Global Journal of Child Research*, 18(1).

Lee, N. (2008) 'Childhood 2025 and beyond', long-list challenge paper for the Beyond Current Horizons Programme. Bristol: Futurelab. www.beyondcurrenthorizons. org.uk/outcomes/other-findings/

Lee, N. (2009) 'Childhood and education: changes and challenges', Review for the Beyond Current Horizons Programme. Bristol: Futurelab. www. beyondcurrenthorizons.org.uk/evidence/generations-and-lifecourse/

Leeson, G. (2009) 'Later life and education: changes and challenges', Review for the Beyond Current Horizons Programme. Bristol: Futurelab. www.beyondcurrenthorizons. org.uk/evidence/generations-and-lifecourse/

Leggett, J. (2005) *Half Gone: Oil, Gas, Hot Air and the Global Energy Crisis*. London: Portobello.

Lessig, L. (1999) 'Code and the commons', keynote given at a conference on Media Convergence, Fordham Law School, New York, 9 February 1999.

Levine, P. (2007) 'Collective action, civic engagement and the knowledge commons', in C. Hess and E. Ostrum (eds), *Understanding Knowledge as Commons*. Cambridge MA and London: MIT Press, pp. 247–76.

Levine, P. (2008) 'A public voice for youth: the audience problem in digital media and civic education', in W. L. Bennett (ed.), *Civic Life Online: Learning How Digital Media Can Engage Youth*. Cambridge MA: MIT Press, pp. 119–38.

Levy, P. (1997) *Collective Intelligence: Mankind's Emerging World in Cyberspace*. Cambridge MA: Perseus.

Lifelong Kindergarten Group, MIT. www.media.mit.edu/research/groups/lifelong-kindergarten

Lloyd, J. (2008) *The State of Intergenerational Relations Today*. London: International Longevity Centre.

Loi, D. and Dillon, P. (2006) 'Adaptive educational environments as creative spaces', *Cambridge Journal of Education*, 36(3), 363–81.

Love Lewisham website. www.lovelewisham.org/

Luckin, R. (2010a) *Re-designing Learning Contexts*. London and New York: Routledge.

Luckin, R. (2010b) 'The ecology of resources model of context: a unifying representation for the development of learning-oriented technologies', International Conference on Mobile, Hybrid, and On-line Learning.

Macgregor, D. (2003) 'Psychology, meaning and the challenges of longevity', *Futures*, 35, 575–88.

Maher, B. (2008) 'Look who's doping', *Nature*, 452, 674–5.

Mann, R. (2009) 'Evolving family structures, roles and relationships in light of ethnic and social change', Review for the Beyond Current Horizons Programme. Bristol: Futurelab. www.beyondcurrenthorizons.org.uk/evidence/generations-and-lifecourse/

Marien, M. (2007) 'The future of human benefit knowledge: notes on a World Brain for the 21st century', *Futures*, 39, 955–62.

Martin, J. (2006) *The Meaning of the 21st Century: A Vital Blueprint for Ensuring Our Future*. London: Transworld.

Masini, E. (2006) 'Rethinking futures studies', *Futures*, 38, 1158–68.

McNeill, J. and McNeill, W. (2003) *The Human Web: A Bird's-eye View of World History*. New York and London: W. W. Norton & Co.

Merchant, G. (2007) 'Mind the gaps: discourses and discontinuity in digital literacies', *E-Learning*, 4(3).

Meyer-Schonberger, V. (2009) *Delete – The Virtue of Forgetting in the Digital Age*. Princeton: Princeton University Press.

Michaelson, J., Abdallah, S., Steuer, N., Thompson, S. and Marks, N. (2009) *National Accounts of Well-being: Bringing Real Wealth onto the Balance Sheet*. London: New Economics Foundation.

Miller, P. quoted in Greenhill, B. (2009) 'The digital landscape and new education providers', Review for the Beyond Current Horizons Programme. Bristol: Futurelab. www.beyondcurrenthorizons.org.uk/evidence/state-market-third-sector/

Miller, R. *et al.* (2008) *School's Over: Learning Spaces in Europe in 2020: An Imagining Exercise on the Future of Learning*. Luxembourg: Office for Official Publications of the European Communities.

Milojevic, I. (2005) *Educational Futures: Dominant and Contesting Visions*. Abingdon and New York: Routledge.

Minton, A. (2009) *Ground Control: Fear and Happiness in the Twenty-First Century City*. London: Penguin.

MIT (2010) *Handbook of Collective Intelligence*. MIT Center for Collective Intelligence, wikisite reviewed July 2010.

Moll, L., Amanti, C., Neff, D. and Gonzalez, N. (1992) 'Funds of knowledge for teaching: using a qualitative approach to connect homes and classrooms', *Theory into Practice*, 31(2), *Qualitative Issues in Educational Research*, pp. 132–41.

Montgomery, K. (2008) 'Youth and digital democracy: intersections of practice, policy, and the marketplace', in W. L. Bennett (ed.), *Civic Life Online: Learning How Digital Media Can Engage Youth*. Cambridge MA: MIT Press, 2008, pp. 25–50.

Moravec, H. (2000) *Mere Machine to Transcendent Mind*. Oxford: Oxford University Press.

Morgan, K. and Sonnino, R. (2008) *The School Food Revolution: Public Food and the Challenge of Sustainable Development*. London: Earthscan.

Morozov, E. (2009) 'How dictators watch us on the web', *Prospect Magazine*, 18/11/2009. www.prospectmagazine.co.uk/2009/11/how-dictators-watch-us-on-the-web/

Morrow, V. (2009) 'The global financial crisis and children's happiness: a time for revisioning', *Childhood*, 16, 293.

Mulgan, G. (1998) *Connexity: How to Live in a Connected World*. Boston MA: Harvard Business School Press.

Mulgan, G. (ed.) (2010) *Making Good Society: Final Report of the Commission of Inquiry into the Future of Civil Society in the UK and Ireland*. Dunfermline and London: Carnegie UK Trust. www.futuresforcivilsociety.org

Muller, J. and Young, M. (2009) 'Three scenarios for the future – lessons from the sociology of knowledge', Review for the Beyond Current Horizons Programme. Bristol: Futurelab. www.beyondcurrenthorizons.org.uk/evidence/knowledge-creativity-and-communication/

Murray, C., Lister, R., Field, F., Brown, J., Walker, A., Deakin, N., Alcock, P., David, M., Phillips, M. and Slipman, S. (1996) *Charles Murray and the Underclass: The Developing Debate*. London: IEA Health and Welfare Unit.

Murray, R., Caulier-Grice, J. and Mulgan, G. (2010) *The Open Book of Social Innovation*. London: NESTA/Young Foundation.

Nash, N. (2009) 'Future issues in socio-technical change for UK citizenship: the importance of "place"', Review for the Beyond Current Horizons Programme. Bristol: Futurelab. www.beyondcurrenthorizons.org.uk/evidence/identities-citizenship-communities/

National Archives. www.nationalarchives.gov.uk/about%5Cwho-we-are.htm

National Center for Educational Statistics (2009) *Digest of Education Statistics*. http://nces.ed.gov/programs/digest/d09/tables/dt09_038.asp

Nevis, E., Lancourt, J. and Vassallo, H. (1996) *Intentional Revolutions: A Seven-Point Strategy for Transforming Organizations*. New York: Jossey-Bass Inc Pub.

New Economics Foundation (2010) *CrowdWise: Turning Differences into Effective Decisions*. London: New Economics Foundation.

New London Group (1997) 'Pedagogy of multi-literacies', *Harvard Educational Review*, 66(1).

Newman, N. (2009) 'The rise of social media and its impact on mainstream journalism', Reuters Institute for the Study of Journalism Working Paper. Oxford: University of Oxford.

Nold, C. (2009) *Emotional Cartography: Technologies of the Self.* www.emotionalcartography. net

Notschool. www.notschool.net

Oakes, J., Renee, M., Rogers, J. and Lipton, M. (2008) 'Research and community organising as tools for democratising educational policymaking', in C. Sugrue (2008), *The Future of Educational Change: International Perspectives.* Abingdon and New York: Routledge, pp. 136–54.

Obama, B. (2010) Education speech archived on Education Futures website 07/01/10. www.educationfutures.com/2010/01/07/obama-education-is-national-security-issue/

O'Connor, J. and Xin, G. (2006) 'A new modernity? The arrival of "creative industries" in China', *International Journal of Cultural Studies,* 9, 271.

OECD (2008) *The Future of the Family to 2030: A Scoping Report.* Paris: OECD.

Office for National Statistics (2009) *Internet Statistical Bulletin 2009.* www.statistics. gov.uk/StatBase/Product.asp?vlnk=5672

Office for National Statistics (2010) *Pupil Absence in Schools in England (2008/09).*

Office for National Statistics (2010) 'Internet access: 60% of adults access Internet every day in 2010'. www.statistics.gov.uk/cci/nugget.asp?id=8

O'Hara, M. (2007) 'Strangers in a strange land: knowing, learning and education for the global knowledge society', *Futures,* 39, 930–41.

O'Malley, C. and Stanton-Fraser, D. (2004) *Learning with Tangible Technologies.* Bristol: Futurelab.

Ostrom, E. (1999) 'Crossing the great divide. Coproduction, synergy and development, polycentric governance and development', Reading from M. D. McGinnes (ed.), *Workshop in Political Theory and Policy Analysis.* Ann Arbor MI: University of Michigan Press.

Ostrom, E. (2000) 'Crowding out citizenship', *Scandinavian Political Studies,* 23(1), 1–16.

Overell, S. (2009) 'The meaning of work', Review for Beyond Current Horizons Programme. Futurelab: Bristol. www.beyondcurrenthorizons.org.uk/evidence/work-and-employment/

Palmer, S. (2007) *Toxic Childhood.* London: Orion.

Papert, S. (1993) *The Children's Machine: Rethinking the School in the Age of the Computer* (new edition). New York: Basic Books.

Pestoff, V. and Brandsen, T. (2006) Public management review: a special issue on co-production, Co-Production. *The Third Sector and the Delivery of Public Services,* 8(4).

Pew Internet Centre (2010) *Report: Internet, Broadband, and Cell Phone Statistics.* www.pewinternet.org/Reports/2010/Internet-broadband-and-cell-phone-statistics/Report.aspx

Pledgebank. www.pledgebank.com/

Plowman, L., McPake, J. and Stephens, C. (2008) 'Just picking it up? Young children learning with technology at home', *Cambridge Journal of Education,* 38(3), 303–19.

Pollman, E. and Tsing, A. (2005) 'Global futures: the game', in D. Rosenberg and S. Harding (eds), *Histories of the Future.* Duke University Press, pp. 105–22.

Powdthavee, N. (2009) 'Happiness and well-being', Review for the Beyond Current Horizons Programme. Bristol: Futurelab. www.beyondcurrenthorizons.org.uk/evidence/work-and-employment/

Prensky, M. (2001) *Digital Game-based Learning.* New York: McGraw-Hill.

Price, S., Roussos, G., Falcao, T. and Sheridan, J. (2009) 'Technology and embodiment: relationships and implications for knowledge, creativity and communication', Review for the Beyond Current Horizons Programme. Bristol: Futurelab. www. beyondcurrenthorizons.org.uk/evidence/knowledge-creativity-and-communication/

Prout, A. (2005) *The Future of Childhood*. Abingdon, Oxford and New York: Routledge Falmer.

Prout, A. (2008) 'Childhood 2025 and beyond', long-list challenge paper for the Beyond Current Horizons Programme. Bristol: Futurelab. www.beyondcurrenthorizons.org. uk/outcomes/other-findings/

Qidi, W. (2006) 'Creative industries and innovation in China', *International Journal of Cultural Studies*, 9, 263.

Quest to Learn school website. http://q2l.org/node/13

Raskin, P., Banuri, T., Gallopin, G., Gutman, P., Hammond, A., Kates, R. and Swart, R. (2002) *The Great Transition: The Promise and Lure of the Times Ahead*. Boston MA: Stockholm Environment Institute/Tellus Institute.

Rate My Teachers. www.ratemyteachers.com/

Rees, M. (2004) *Our Final Hour: A Scientist's Warning*. New York: Basic Books.

Reeves, R. (2009) 'The new utilitarianism', in S. Griffiths and R. Reeves (eds) (2009), *Well-being: How to Lead the Good Life and What Government Should Do to Help*. London: Social Market Foundation.

Reich, J. (2009) 'Reworking the web, reworking the world: how web 2.0 is changing our society', Review for the Beyond Current Horizons Programme. Futurelab: Bristol. www.beyondcurrenthorizons.org.uk/evidence/identities-citizenship-communities/

RepRap. http://reprap.org/wiki/Main_Page

Rheingold, H. (2008) 'Using participatory media and public voice to encourage civic engagement', in W. L. Bennett (ed.), *Civic Life Online: Learning How Digital Media Can Engage Youth*. Cambridge MA: MIT Press, 2008, pp. 97–118.

Riley, S. (2009) 'Identity, community and selfhood: understanding the self in relation to contemporary youth cultures', Review for the Beyond Current Horizons Programme. Bristol: Futurelab. www.beyondcurrenthorizons.org.uk/evidence/identities-citizenship-communities/

Riverside school. www.schoolriverside.com/

Rogoff, B. (2003) *The Cultural Nature of Human Development*. Oxford and New York: Oxford University Press.

Rose, N. (2001) 'The politics of life itself', *Theory, Culture and Society*, 18(6), 1–30.

Rosenberg, D. and Harding, S. (2005) *Histories of the Future*. Durham and London: Duke University Press.

Ross, A. (2009) 'On the digital labor question', paper given at the Vera List Center for Art and Politics at the New School. https://lists.thing.net/pipermail/idc/2009-November/004039.html

Round, A. (2009) 'The boundaries between informal and formal work', Review for the Beyond Current Horizons Programme. Bristol: Futurelab. www. beyondcurrenthorizons.org.uk/evidence/work-and-employment/

Saltash Community School. www.saltash.net/main/index.php

Sandford, R. and Beetham, H. (2009) 'Beyond current horizons scenarios', in K. Facer (ed.), *Beyond Current Horizons Final Report*. Bristol: Futurelab, pp. 209–30. www.beyondcurrenthorizons.org.uk/outcomes/reports/final-report-2009/

Sassen, S. (2010) 'When places have deep economic histories', in S. Goldsmith and L. Elizabeth (eds), *What We See: Advancing the Observations of Jane Jacobs*. Oakland CA: New Village Press.

Savalescu, J. and Bostrom, N. (2008) *Human Enhancement*. Oxford: Oxford University Press.

Saveri, A., Rheingold, H., Soojung-Kim Pang, A. and Vian, K. (2004) *Towards a New Literacy of Cooperation in Business: Managing Dilemmas in the 21st Century*. Menlo Park CA: Institute for the Future.

Sawhill, I. and Monea, E. (2008) 'Old news', *Democracy: A Journal of Ideas*, Summer (9).

Sawyer, K. (2006a) 'The new science of learning', in K. Sawyer (ed.), *Cambridge Handbook of the Learning Sciences*. New York: Cambridge University Press, pp. 1–16.

Sawyer, K. (2006b) 'Educating for innovation', *Thinking Skills and Creativity*. 1(1), 41–8.

Sawyer, K. (2009) 'The future of learning in the age of innovation', Review for the Beyond Current Horizons Programme. Bristol: Futurelab. www.beyondcurrenthorizons.org.uk/evidence/knowledge-creativity-and-communication/

Sayer, A. (2000) *Realism and Social Science*. London: Sage.

Schonfeld, E. (2009) 'Four years after founding, Kiva hits $100 million in microloans', *TechCrunch*, 1/1/2009. http://techcrunch.com/2009/11/01/four-years-after-founding-kiva-hits-100-million-in-microloans/

Seedcamp. http://seedcamp.com/pages/about_seedcamp

Sefton-Green, J. (1998) *Digital Diversions*. London: Routledge.

Sefton-Green, J. (2009) 'Location, location, location: rethinking space and place as sites and contexts for learning', Review for the Beyond Current Horizons Programme. Bristol: Futurelab. www.beyondcurrenthorizons.org.uk/evidence/knowledge-creativity-and-communication/

Sefton-Green, J. and Buckingham, D. (1998) 'Digital visions: children's "creative" uses of multi-media technologies', in J. Sefton-Green (ed.), *Digital Diversions: Youth Culture in the Age of Multi-media*. London: UCL.

Self-Sufficient Schools Programme. www.teachamantofish.org.uk/selfsufficientschools.php

Selwyn, N. (2003) 'Doing IT for the kids: re-examining children, computers and the information society', *Media, Culture and Society*, 25, 351–78.

Selwyn, N. (2011) *Education and Technology*. London: Continuum.

Sennett, R. (2009) *The Craftsman*. London: Penguin.

SenseCam. http://research.microsoft.com/en-us/um/cambridge/projects/sensecam/

Sharkey, N. (2009) 'The robot arm of the law grows longer', *IEEE Computer*, August 2009. www.computer.org/portal/web/computer/home

Sharkey, N. (2010) *2084: Big Robot is Watching You: The Future of Robots for Policing, Surveillance and Security*. University of Sheffield. www.dcs.shef.ac.uk/~noel/

Shirky, C. (2010) *Cognitive Surplus: Creativity and Generosity in a Connected Age*. New York: Allen Lane.

Sidorkin, A. (2009) *Labor of Learning: Market and the Next Generation of Educational Reform*. Rotterdam and Taipei: Sense Publishers.

Silverstone, R. and Hirsch, E. (eds) (1992) *Consuming Technologies: Media and Information in Domestic Spaces*. London: Routledge.

Simms, A., Johnson, V. and Chowla, P. (2010) *Growth isn't Possible: Why We Need a New Economic Direction*. London: New Economics Foundation.

Sindic, D. (2009) 'National identities: are they declining?', Review for the Beyond Current Horizons Programme. Bristol: Futurelab. www.beyondcurrenthorizons.org.uk/evidence/identities-citizenship-communities/

SixthSense. www.ted.com/index.php/talks/pattie_maes_demos_the_sixth_sense.html

Slaughter, R. (2004) *Futures Beyond Distopia: Creating Social Foresight*. London and New York: Routledge Falmer.

Small, M. (2009) *Unanticipated Gains: Origins of Network Inequality in Everyday Life*. New York: Oxford University Press.

Smeaton, E. (2009) *Off the Radar: Children and Young People on the Streets in the UK*. Railway Children, Sandbach. www.railwaychildren.org.uk/article.asp?id=873&highlight=off the radar

Spratt, S., Simms, A., Neitzert, E. and Ryan-Collins, J. (2009) *The Great Transition*. London: New Economics Foundation.

Stald, G. (2008) 'Mobile identity: youth, identity, and mobile communication media', in D. Buckingham (ed.), *Youth, Identity, and Digital Media*. Cambridge MA: MIT Press, pp. 143–64.

Standage, T. (1999) *The Victorian Internet*. Phoenix.

Steffen, A. (ed.) (2008) *Worldchanging: A User's Guide for the 21st Century*. New York: Harry N. Abrams.

Steffen, A. (2009) 'Transition towns or bright green cities?', Worldchanging website, 27 October 2009. www.worldchanging.com/archives/010672.html

Steffen, A. (2010) 'Putting the future back in the room', Worldchanging website, 26 April 2010. www.worldchanging.com/archives/011102.html

Stephen, C., McPake, J., Plowman, L. and Berch-Heyman, S. (2008) 'Learning from the children: exploring preschool children's encounters with ICT at home', *Journal of Early Childhood Research*, 2008, 6, 99.

Stephens, L., Ryan-Collins, J. and Boyle, D. (2008) *Co-production: A Manifesto for Growing the Core Economy*. London: New Economics Foundation.

Stephenson, N. (1995) *The Diamond Age, or a Young Lady's Illustrated Primer*. London: Penguin.

Sterling, B. (2003) *Tomorrow Now: Envisioning the Next 50 Years*. New York: Random House.

Sterling, B. (2005) *Shaping Things*. Cambridge MA: MIT Press.

Suicide Machine. www.suicidemachine.org/

Surowiecki, J (2005) *The Wisdom of Crowds*. New York: Anchor Books.

Sustainable Cities. http://sustainablecities.dk/en/city-projects/cases/porto-alegre-engaging-citizens-in-city-budgeting

Sweeney, E. (2010) 'Mines' harsh human toll is no deep, dark secret', *Boston Globe*, 15 March 2010. www.boston.com/business/technology/articles/2010/03/15/congolese_mines_are_ransacked_for_minerals_used_in_high_tech_devices/?page=2

Tasker, M. (2003) *Smaller Structures in Secondary Education: A Research Digest*. Human Scale Education. www.hse.org.uk/publications.php

TeachStreet. www.teachstreet.com/

Terranova, T. (2003) 'Free labor: producing culture for the digital economy', electronic book review, 20-06-2003. www.electronicbookreview.com/thread/technocapitalism/voluntary (reviewed August 2010)

Terranova, T. (2004) *Network Culture: Politics for the Information Age*. London and Ann Arbor MI: Pluto Press.

THATCamp. http://thatcamp.org/about/

Thomas, M. (2009) *Think Community: An Exploration of the Links between Intergenerational Practice and Informal Adult Learning*. NIACE. http://shop.niace.org.uk/thinkcommunity.html

Thompson, G. (2000) 'Unfulfilled prophecy: the evolution of corporate colleges', *Journal of Higher Education*, 71(3), 322–41.

Thornburg, N. (2005) Inside the Chinese Hack Attack, *Time*, 25 August 2005.

Torrance, H. (1984) 'School-based examining: a mechanism for school-based professional development and accountability', *British Educational Research Journal*, 10(1), 1984, 71–81.

Torrance, H. (1986) 'Expanding school-based assessment: issues, problems and future possibilities', *Research Papers in Education*, 1(1), 1986, 48–59.

Torrance, H. and MacLure, M. (2010) *The Social Brain and the Curriculum: An Interpretive Report*. London: RSA. www.thersa.org/projects/education-seminars-2010

Transition towns. http://transitionculture.org/shop/the-transition-handbook/

Turney, J. (2009) 'Biofutures – a selective review of biological discovery prospects and education to 2025', Briefing paper for the Beyond Current Horizons Programme. Bristol: Futurelab. .

ukedchat. http://ukedchat.wikispaces.com/

Unger, R. (1998) *Democracy Realized: The Progressive Alternative*. London and New York: Verso.

UNICEF (2007) *Our Climate, Our Children, Our Responsibility: The Implications of Climate Change for the World's Children*. London: UNICEF. www.mtnforum.org/rs/ol/browse.cfm?tp=vd&docID=4087

United Nations (2003) *Intergenerational Relations in Young People in a Globalising World, World Youth Report*. New York: United Nations.

United States Air Force (2009) *Unmanned Aircraft Systems Flight Plan 2009–2047*. USAF: Washington DC, available at: www.scribd.com/doc/17312080/United-States-Air-Force-Unmanned-Aircraft-Systems-Flight-Plan-20092047-Unclassified

Vasagar, J. (2010) 'School leavers choosing graduate employers over university', *The Guardian*, 13/08/10. www.guardian.co.uk/education/2010/aug/13/school-leavers-apply-to-graduate-employers

Vinge, V. (2006) *Rainbow's End*. New York: Tor.

Virtual call centre. www.futuretravelcareers.co.uk/

Walker, T. (2000) 'The "lump-of-labor" case against work-sharing: populist fallacy or marginalist throwback?', in L. Golden and D. Figart (eds), *Working Time: International Trends, Theory and Policy Perspectives*. London: Routledge.

Warren, D. and Dubb, S. (2010) *Growing a Green Economy for All: From Green Jobs to Green Ownership*. College Park MD: Democracy Collaborative at the University of Maryland.

We Want Everything (2009) *Communiqué from an Absent Future*. http://wewanteverything.wordpress.com/2009/09/24/communique-from-an-absent-future/

Webster, K. and Johnson, C. (2009) *Sense and Sustainability: Educating for a Low Carbon World*. www.senseandsustainability.com

Wenger, E., White, N. and Smith, J. (2009) *Digital Habitats: Stewarding Technology for Communities*. Portland OR: Cpsquare.

Wertsch, J. (1991) *Voices of the Mind*. Cambridge: Harvard University Press.

West-Burnham, J., Farrar, M. and Otero, G. (2007) *Schools and Communities: Working Together to Transform Children's Lives*. London: Network Continuum Education.

Whuffie Bank. www.thewhuffiebank.org/static/faq

Wiley, D. and Hilton, J. (2009) 'Openness, dynamic specialisation and the disaggregated future of higher education', *International Review of Research in Open and Distance Learning*, 10(5).

Wilkinson, R. and Pickett, K. (2010) *Spirit Level: Why More Equal Societies Almost Always Do Better*. London: Allen Lane.

Willets, D. (2010) *The Pinch: How the Baby Boomers Took Their Children's Future – And How They Can Give It Back*. London: Atlantic Books.

Willett, R. (2008) 'Consumer citizens online: structure, agency, and gender in online participation', in D. Buckingham (ed.), *Youth, Identity, and Digital Media*. Cambridge MA: MIT Press, 2008, pp. 49–70.

Williams, R. (2006) 'Compressed foresight and narrative bias: pitfalls in assessing high technology futures', *Science as Culture*, 15(4), 327–48.

Wilson, R. (2009) 'The future of work and implications for education', Summative report for the Beyond Current Horizons Programme. Bristol: Futurelab. www.beyondcurrenthorizons.org.uk/evidence/work-and-employment/

Wilson, R. and Gambin, L. (2009) 'Work and employment challenge quick reviews', for the Beyond Current Horizons Programme. Bristol: Futurelab. www.beyondcurrenthorizons.org.uk/evidence/work-and-employment/

Witt, S. (2010) 'The grace of import replacement', in S. A. Goldsmith and L. Elizabeth (eds), *What We See: Advancing the Observations of Jane Jacobs*. Oakland CA: New Village Press.

Woods, P. and Woods, G. (2009) *Alternative Education for the 21st Century: Philosophies, Approaches, Visions*. New York: Palgrave Macmillan.

Woods, P., Ashley, R. and Woods, G. (2005) *Steiner Schools in England* (Research Report RR645). Nottingham: DFES Publications.

Woolgar, S. (ed.) (2002) *Virtual Society? Technology, Cyberbole, Reality*. Oxford: Oxford University Press.

Wresch, M. (2007) 'The Machine is Us/ing Us (Final Version)'. www.youtube.com/watch?v=NLlGopyXT_g

Wright, E. O. (2009) *Envisioning Real Utopias*. Verso. www.ssc.wisc.edu/~wright/ERU.htm

Young, M. (1998) *The Curriculum of the Future: From the 'New Sociology of Education' to a Critical Theory of Learning*. London: Routledge Falmer.

Young, M. (2010) 'Educational policies for a knowledge society: reflections from a sociology of knowledge perspective', keynote lecture, 29 June 2010, GOETE Kick off Meeting, Tübigen.

YourEncore network. www.yourencore.com/

Index